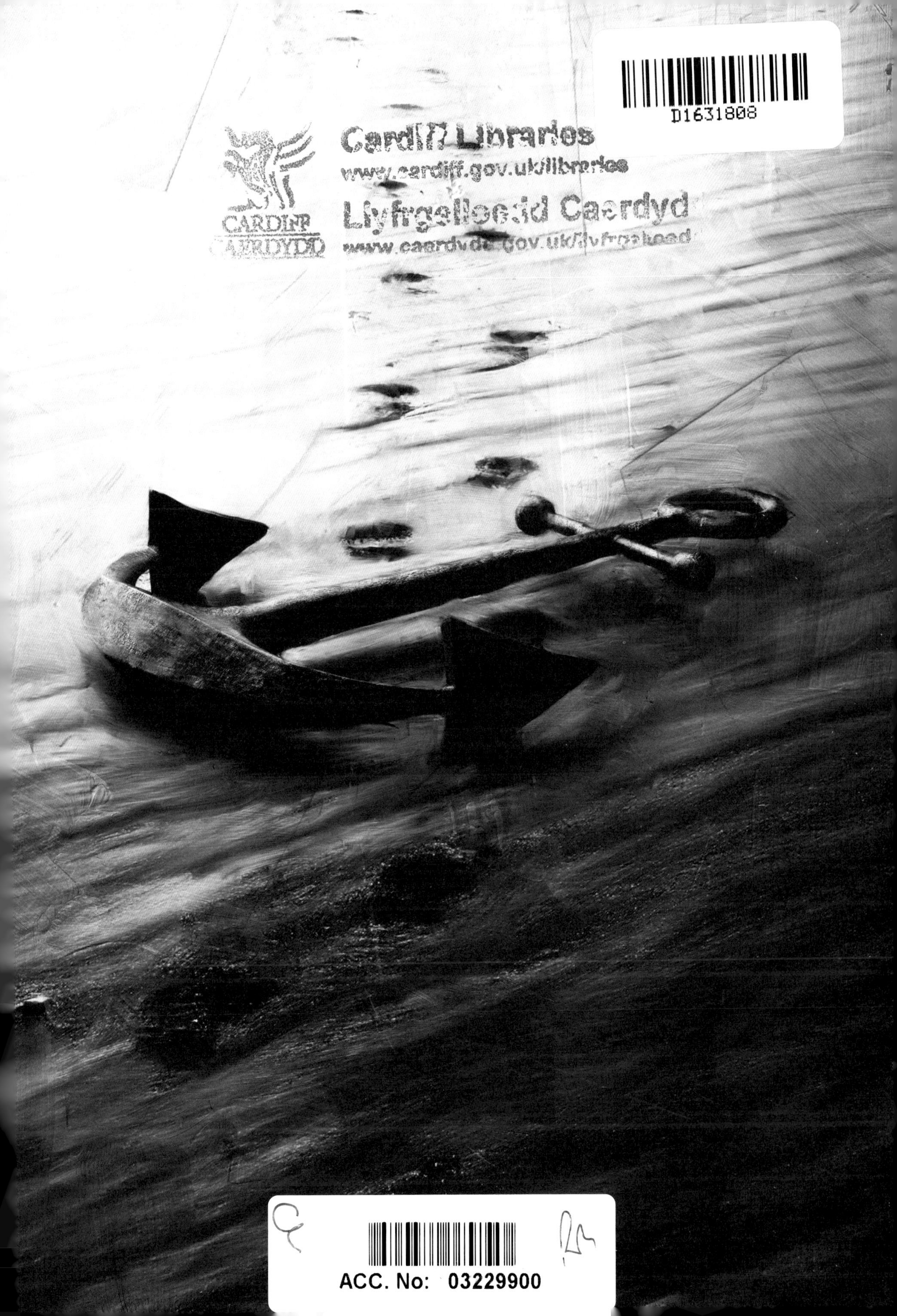

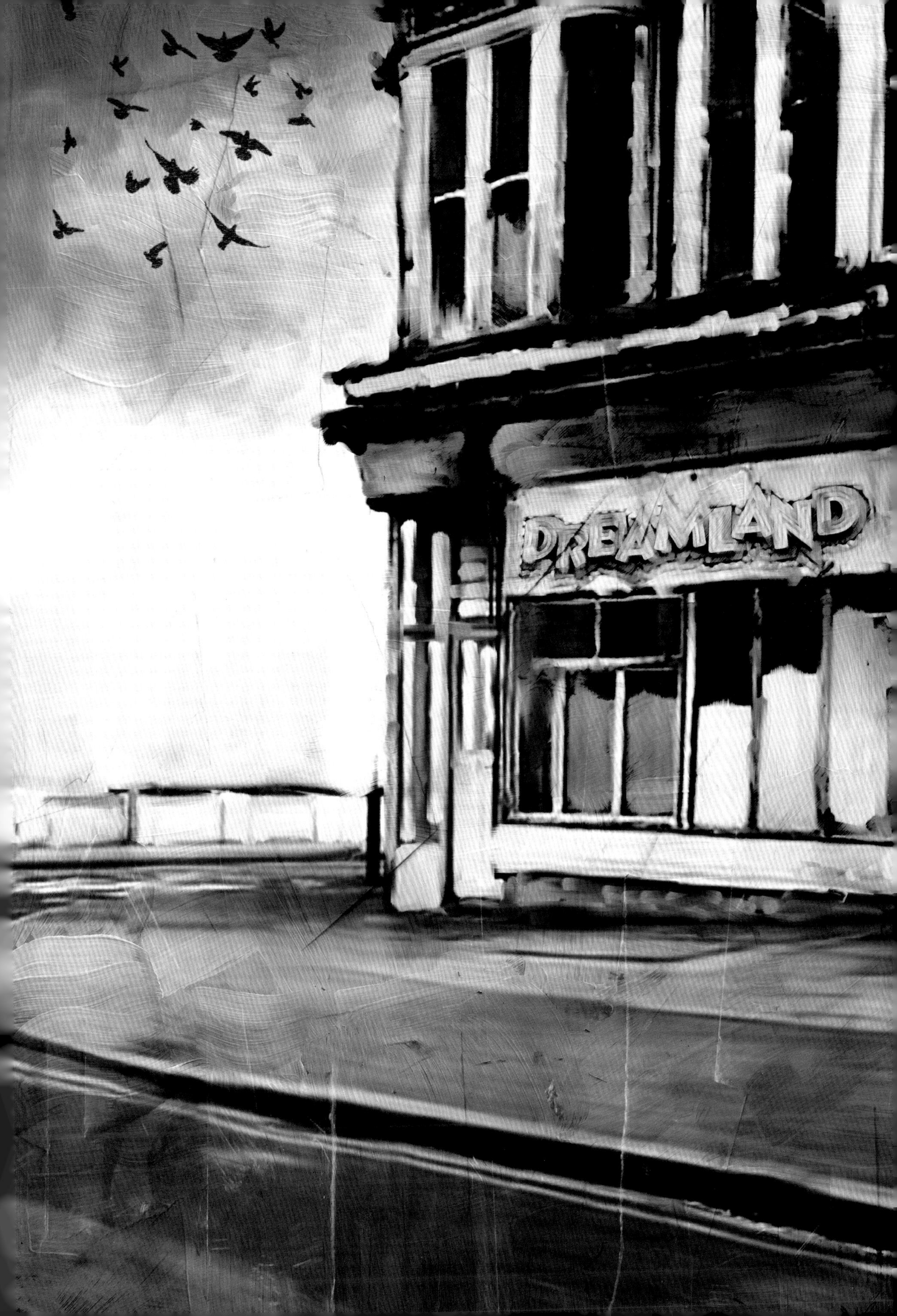
DREAMLAND

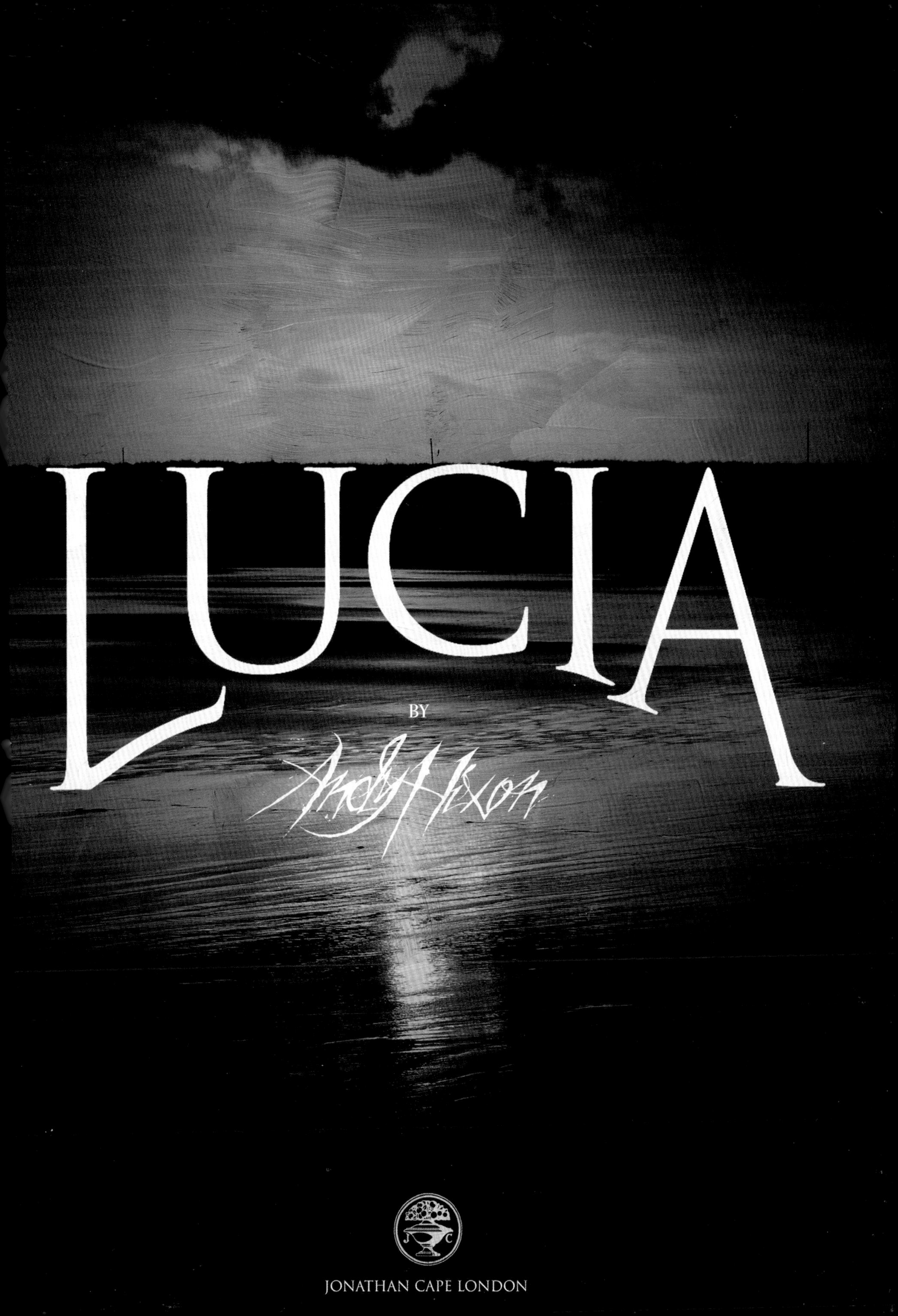

LUCIA

BY

Andy Hixon

JONATHAN CAPE LONDON

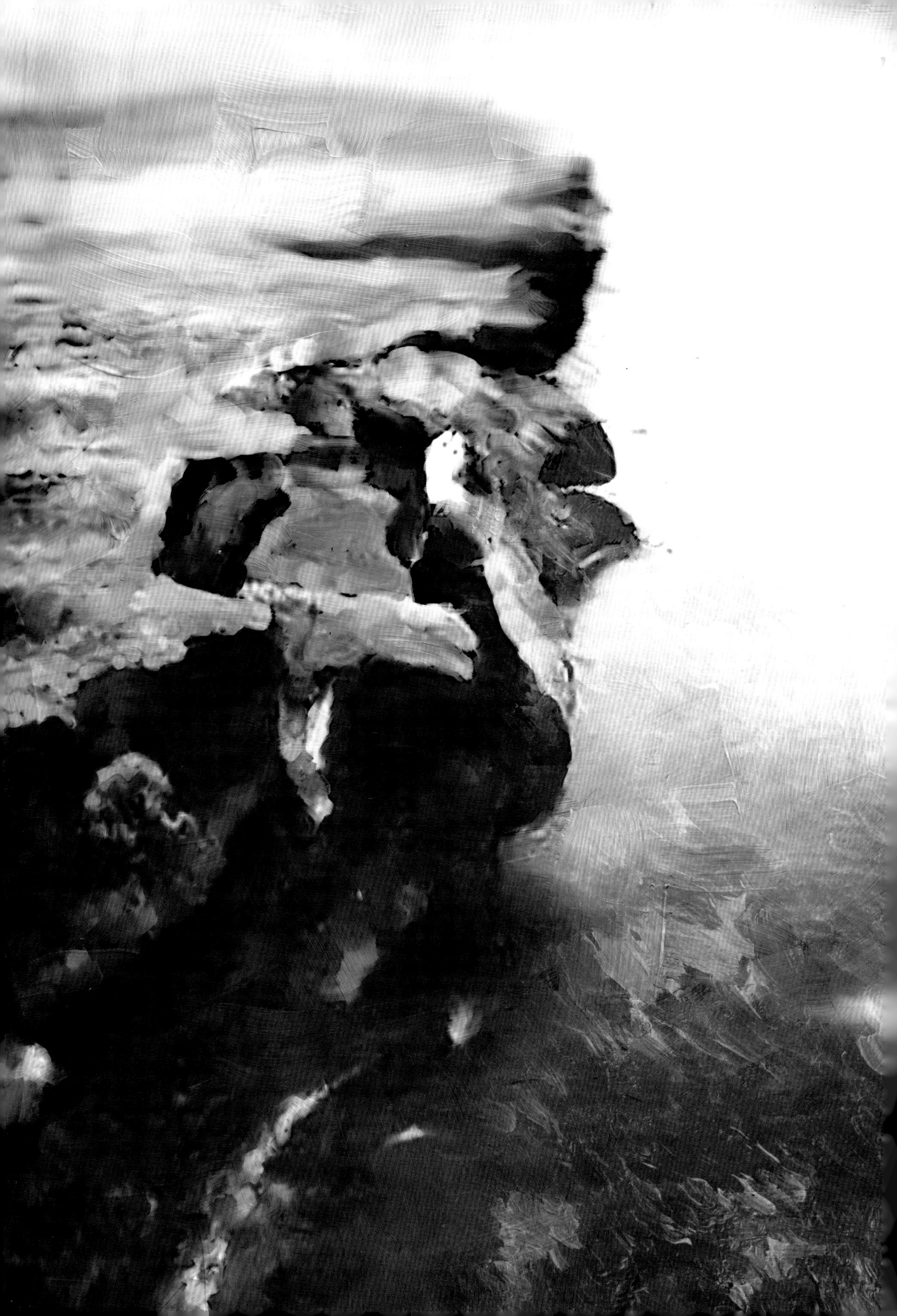

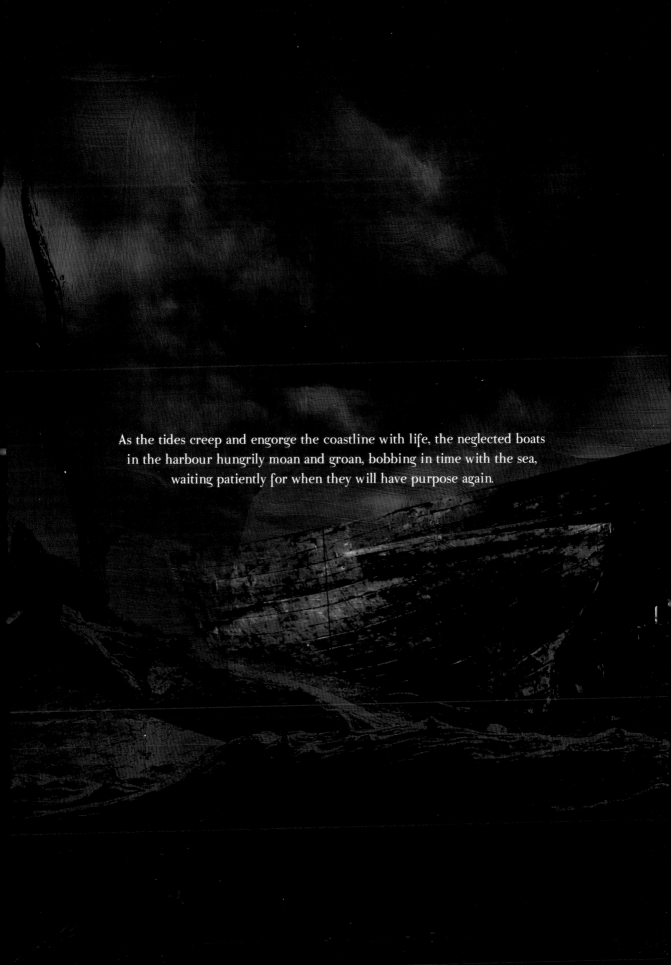

As the tides creep and engorge the coastline with life, the neglected boats in the harbour hungrily moan and groan, bobbing in time with the sea, waiting patiently for when they will have purpose again.

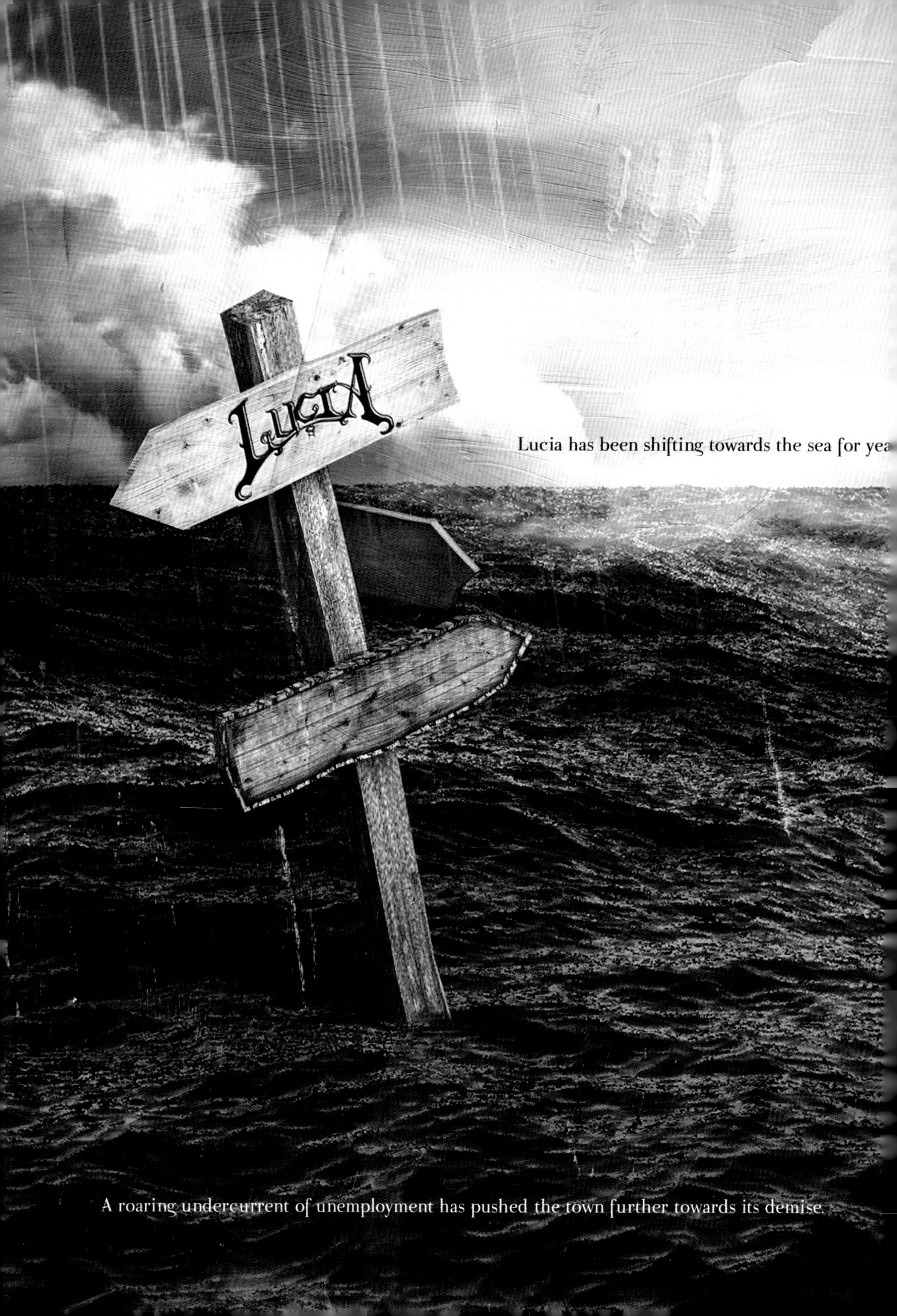
LUCIA

Lucia has been shifting towards the sea for yea

A roaring undercurrent of unemployment has pushed the town further towards its demise.

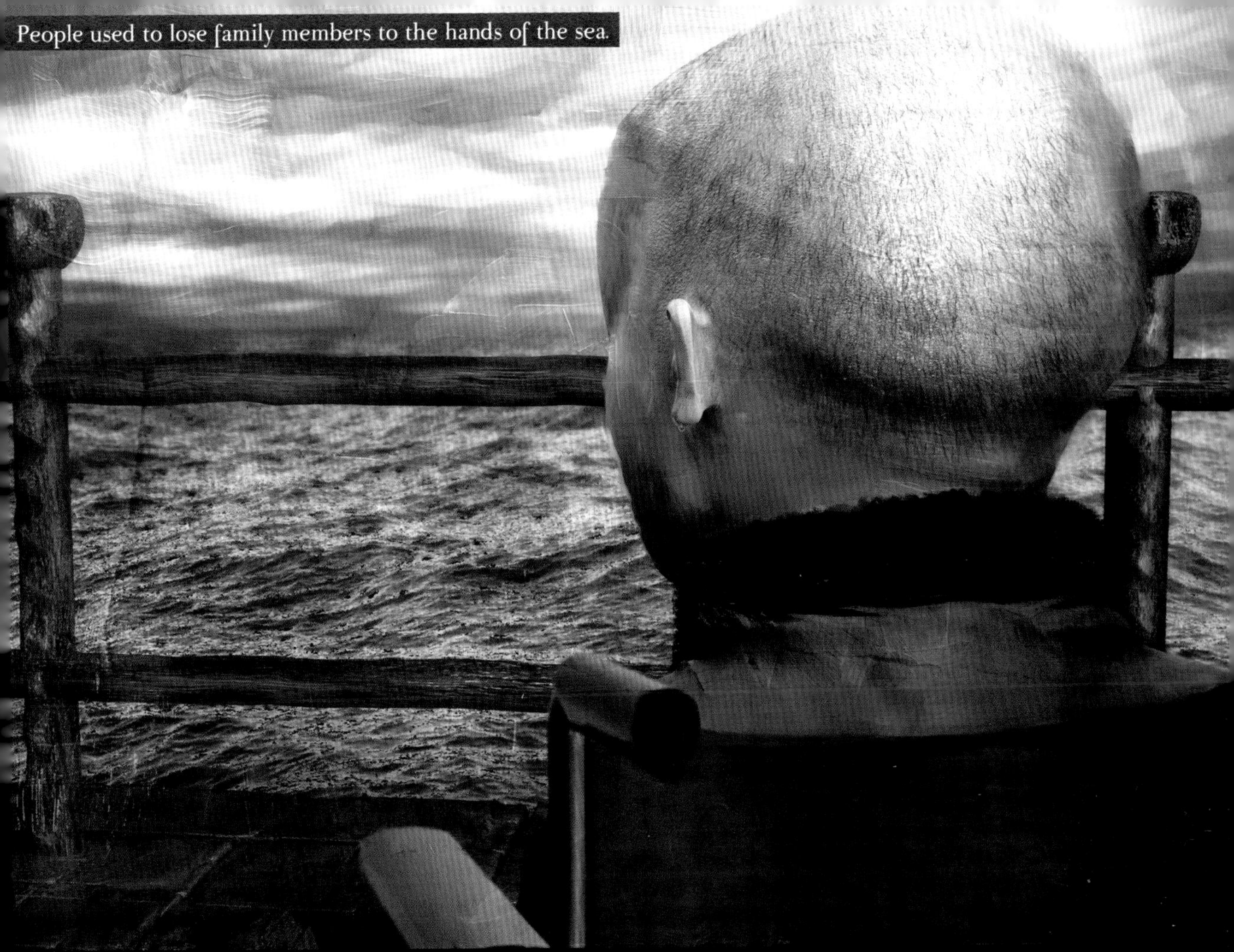
People used to lose family members to the hands of the sea.

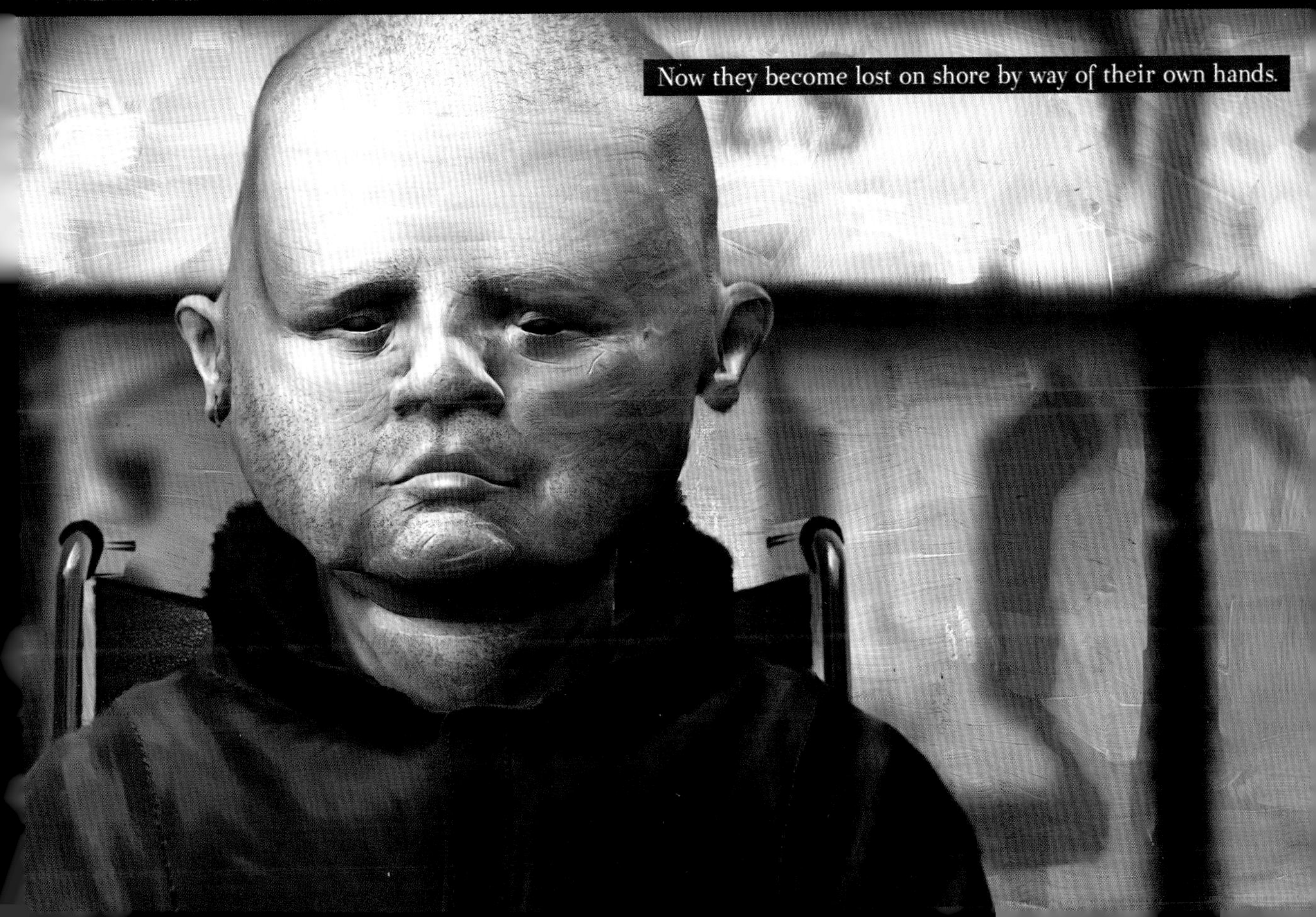
Now they become lost on shore by way of their own hands.

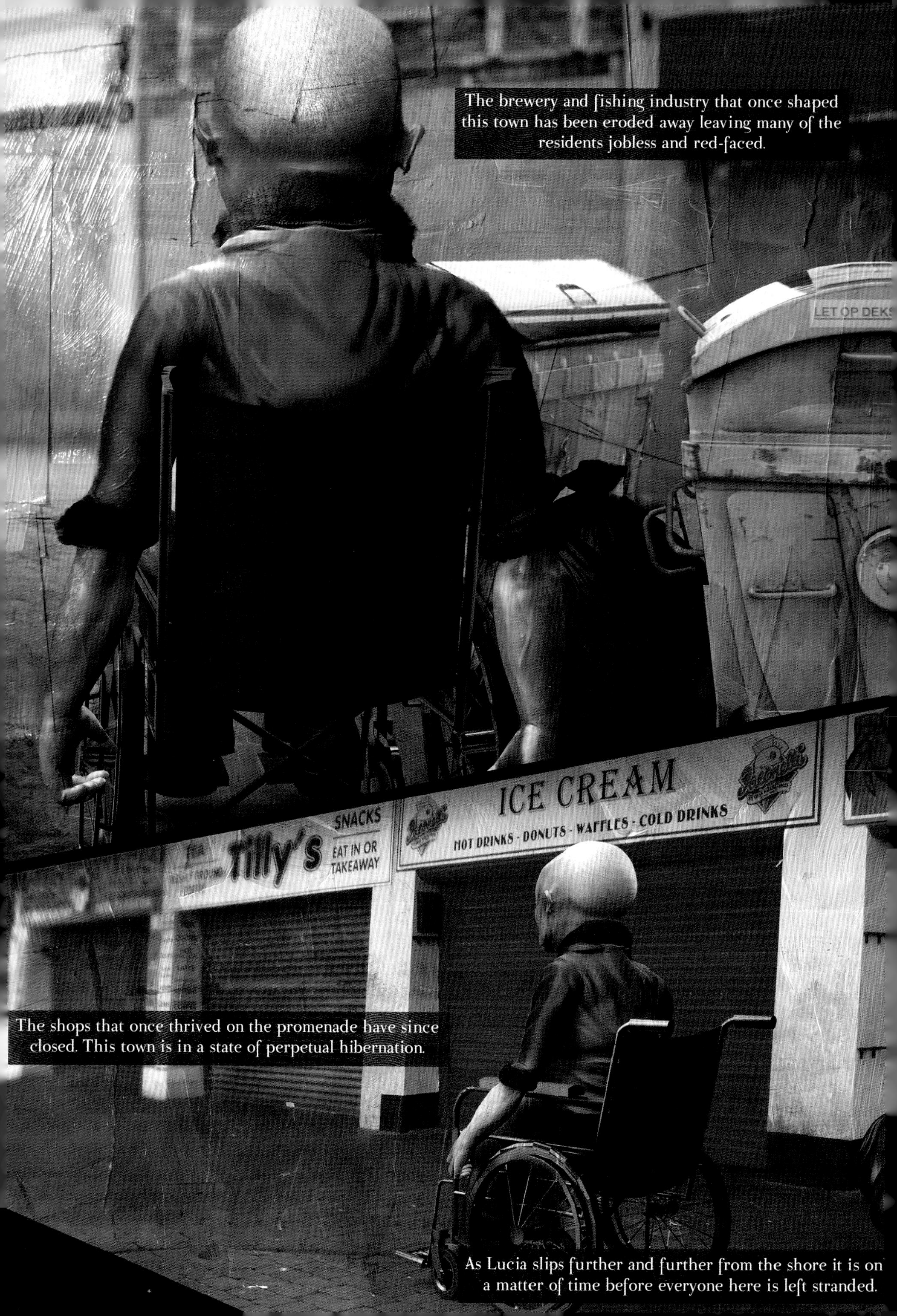
The brewery and fishing industry that once shaped this town has been eroded away leaving many of the residents jobless and red-faced.
ICE CREAM
HOT DRINKS - DONUTS - WAFFLES - COLD DRINKS
SNACKS
Tilly's
EAT IN OR TAKEAWAY
The shops that once thrived on the promenade have since closed. This town is in a state of perpetual hibernation.
As Lucia slips further and further from the shore it is on a matter of time before everyone here is left stranded.

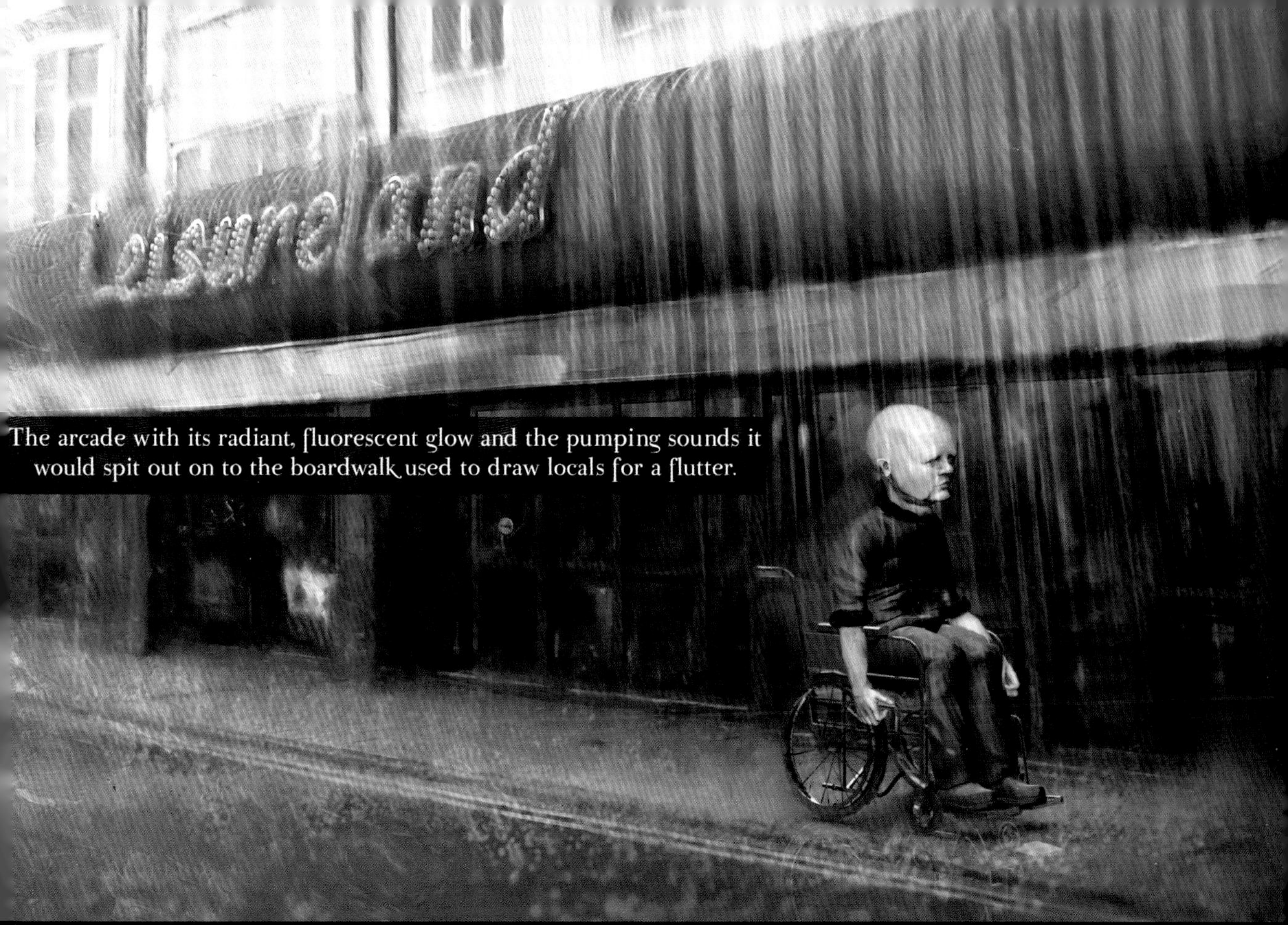
The arcade with its radiant, fluorescent glow and the pumping sounds it would spit out on to the boardwalk used to draw locals for a flutter.

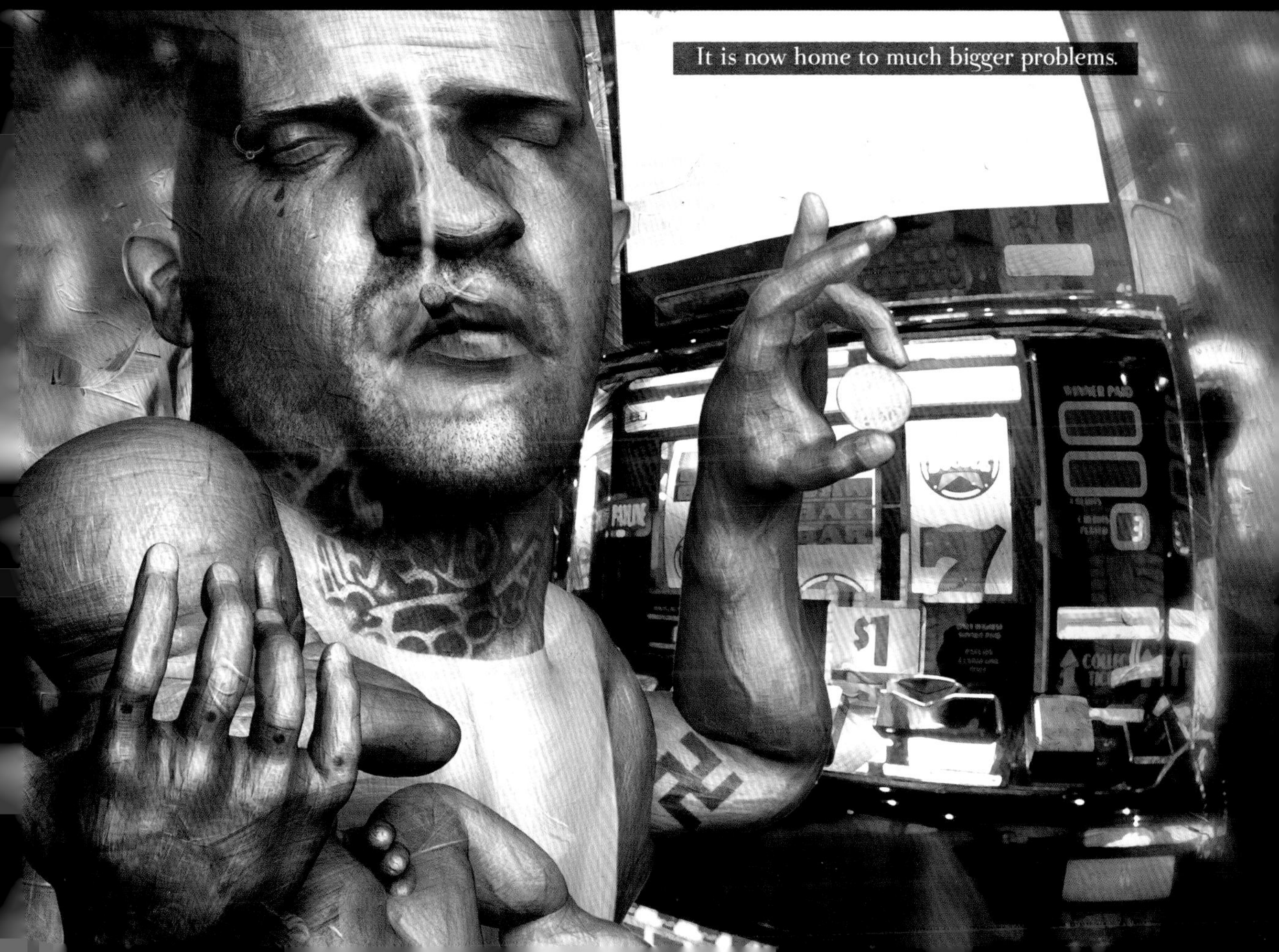
It is now home to much bigger problems.
$1

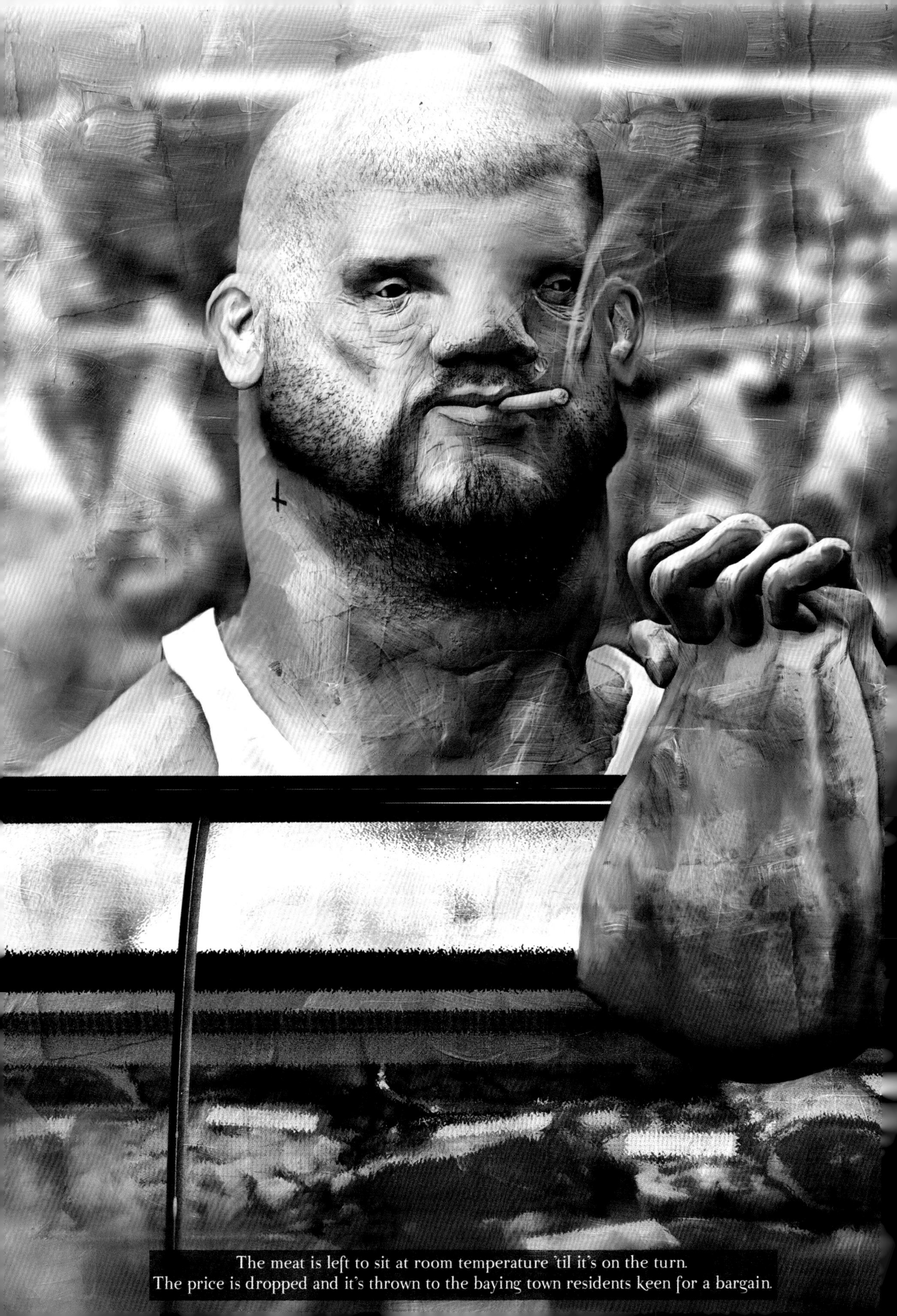

The meat is left to sit at room temperature 'til it's on the turn.
The price is dropped and it's thrown to the baying town residents keen for a bargain.

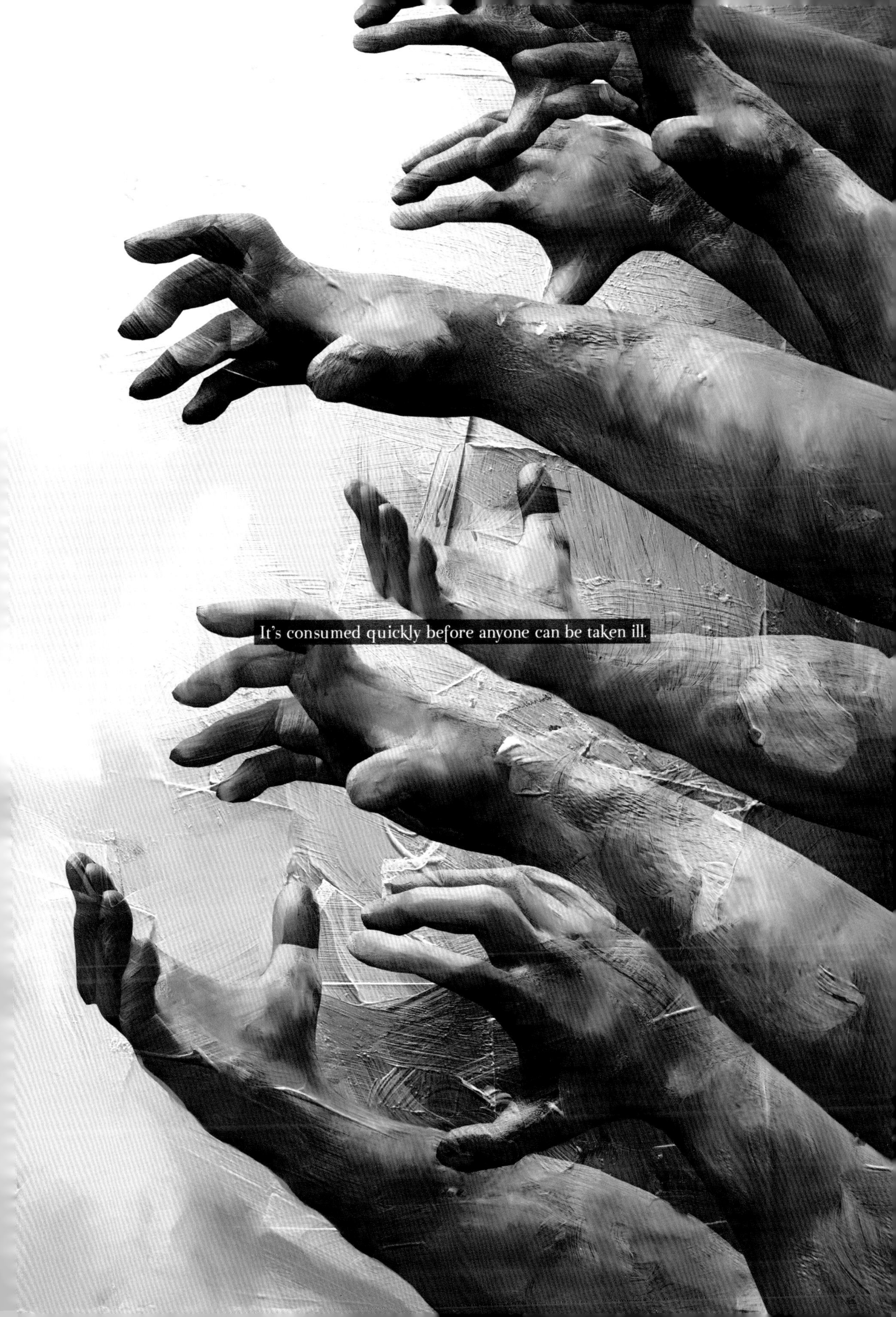
It's consumed quickly before anyone can be taken ill.

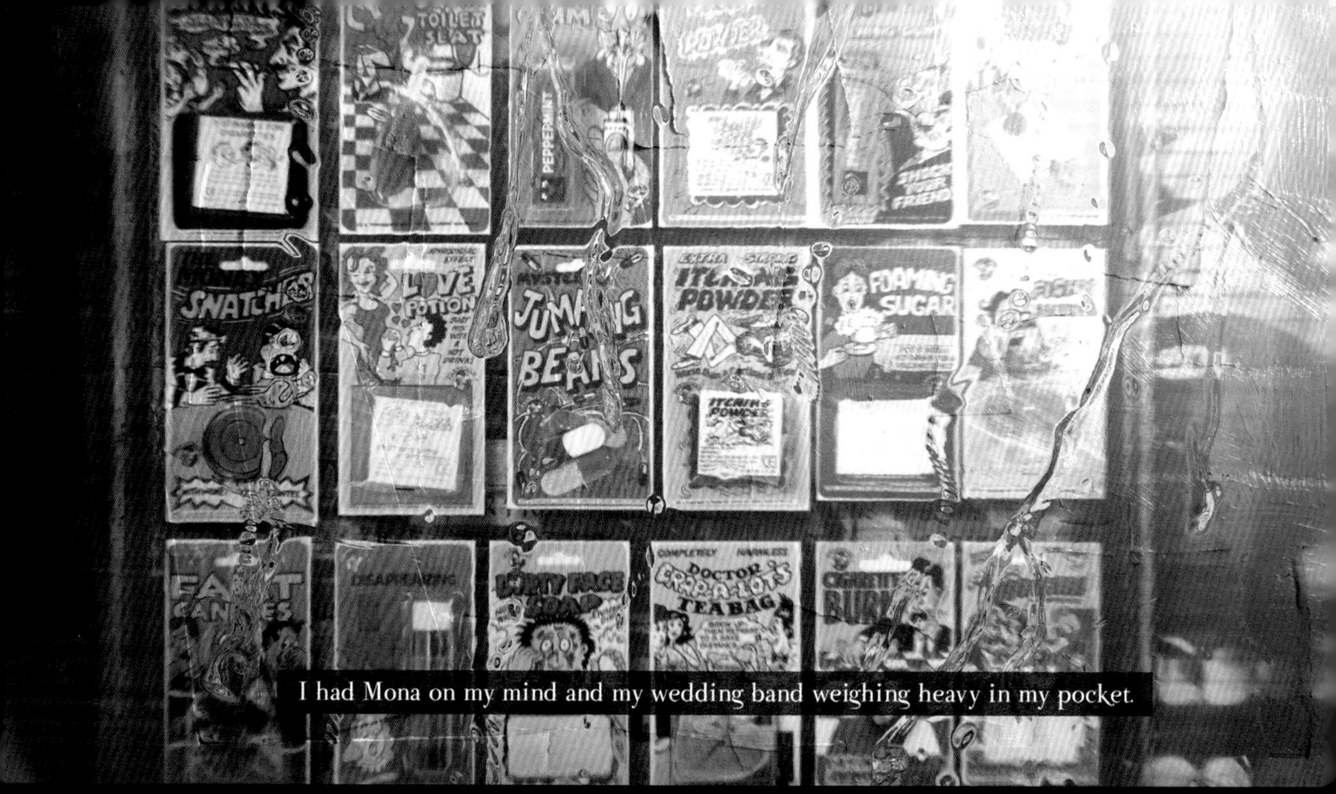
FOAMING SUGAR
PEPPERMINT
TEA BAG
I had Mona on my mind and my wedding band weighing heavy in my pocket.

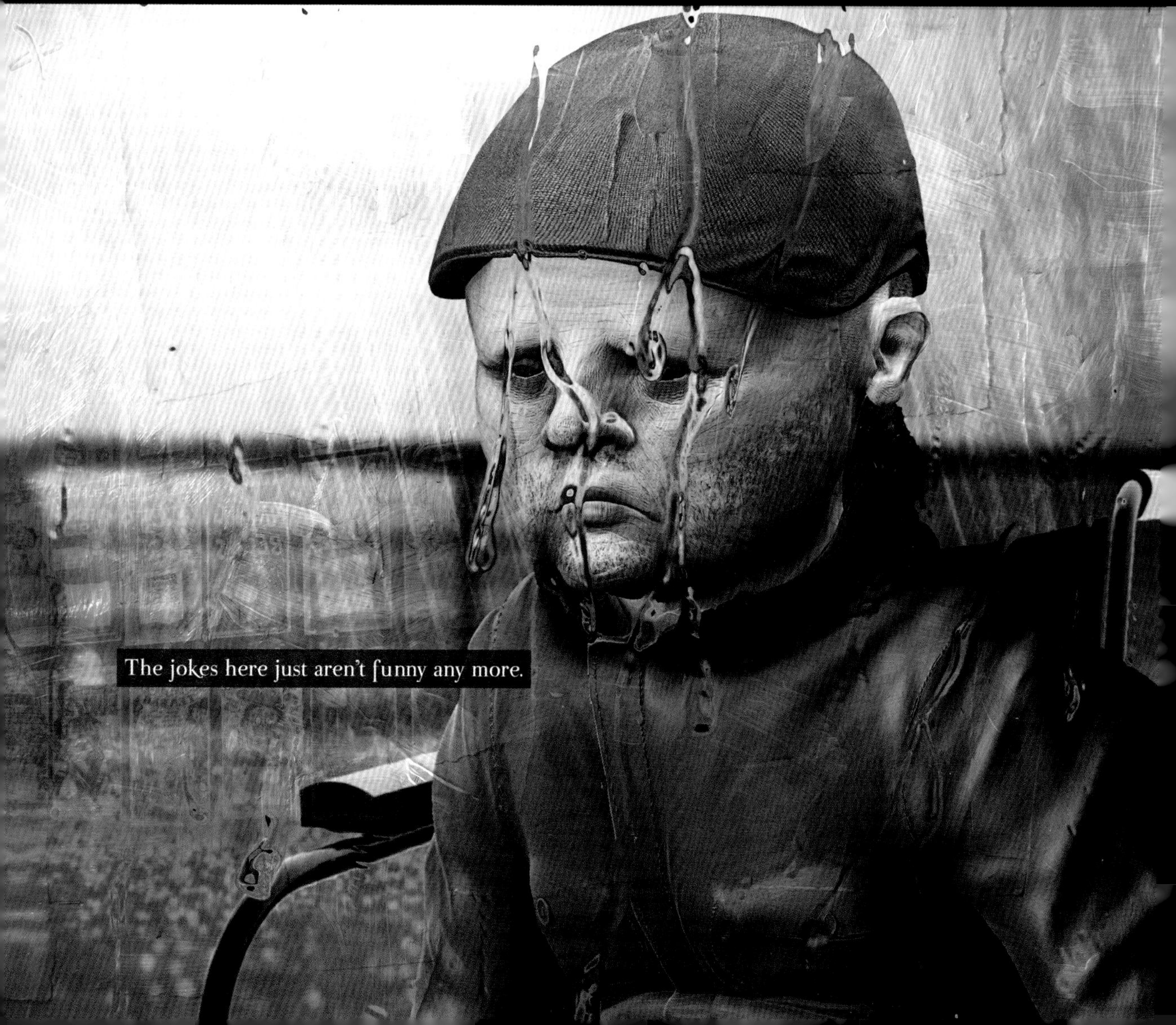
The jokes here just aren't funny any more.

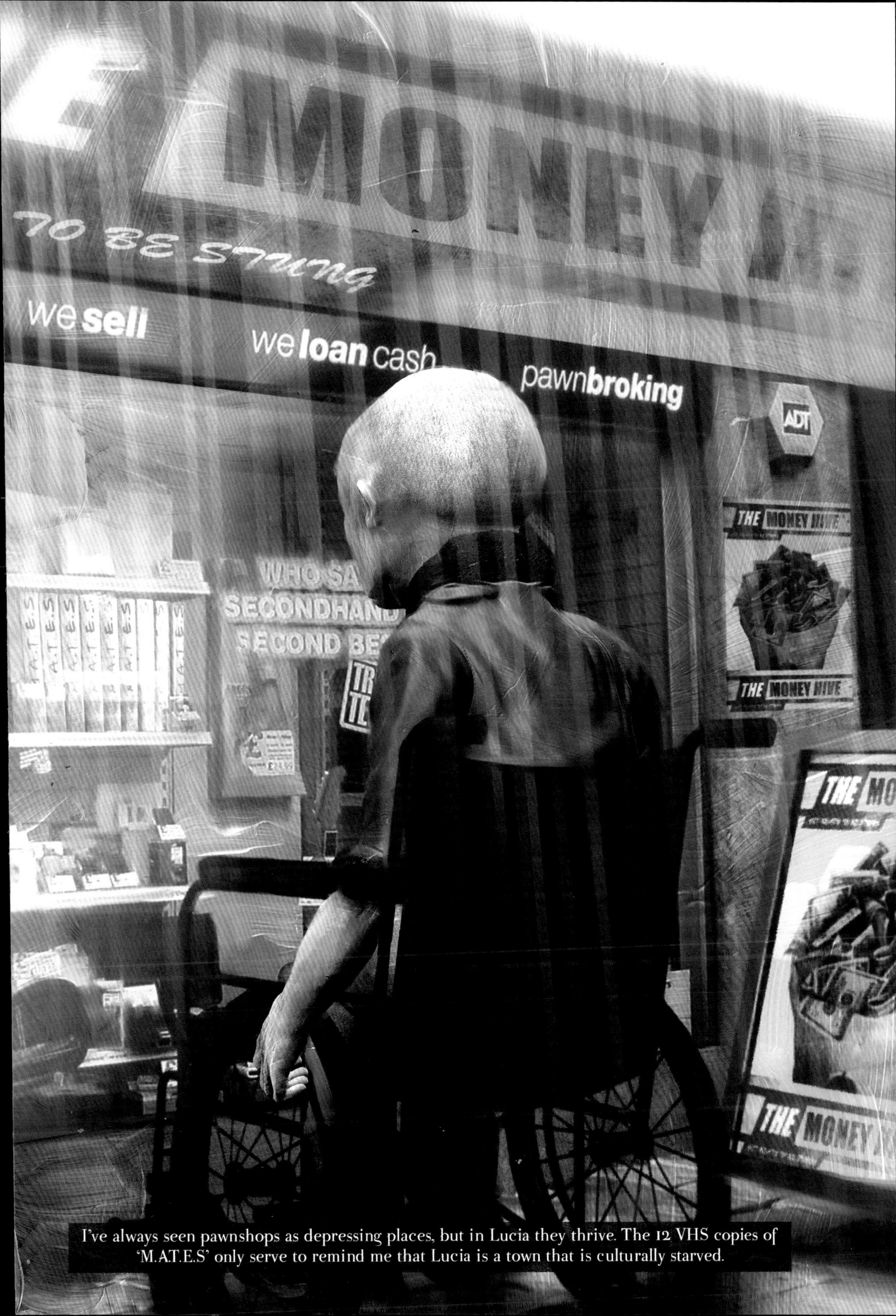
MONEY
we sell
we loan cash
pawnbroking
ADT
THE MONEY HIVE
SECONDHAND
THE MONEY HIVE

I've always seen pawnshops as depressing places, but in Lucia they thrive. The 12 VHS copies of 'M.A.T.E.S' only serve to remind me that Lucia is a town that is culturally starved.

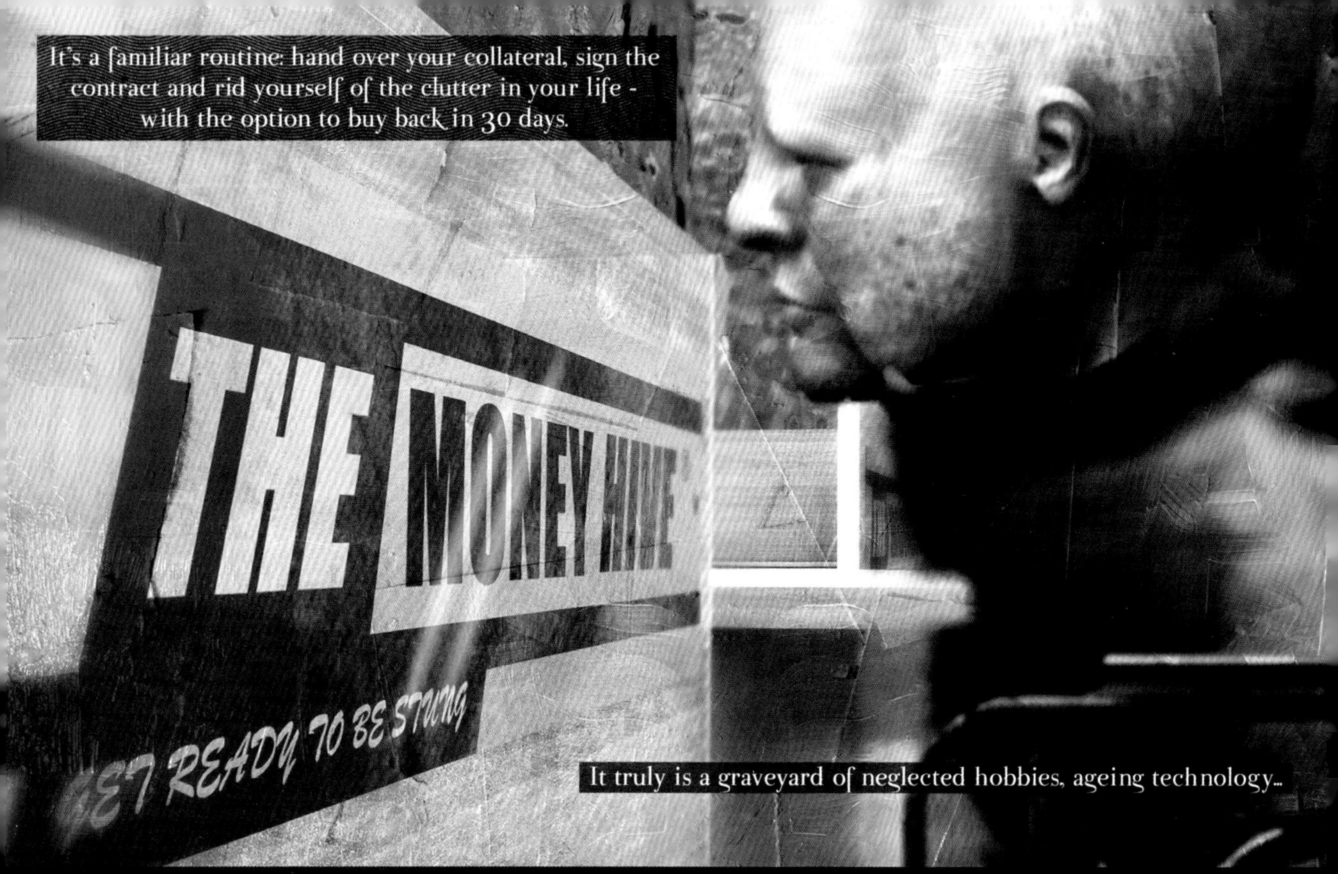
It's a familiar routine: hand over your collateral, sign the contract and rid yourself of the clutter in your life - with the option to buy back in 30 days.
THE MONEY
READY TO BE STUNG
It truly is a graveyard of neglected hobbies, ageing technology...

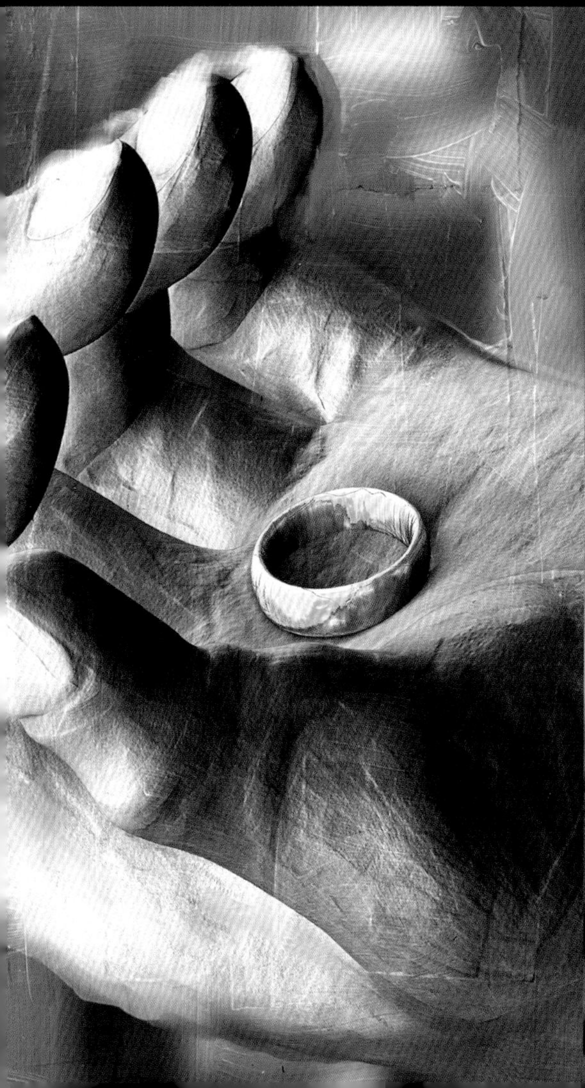

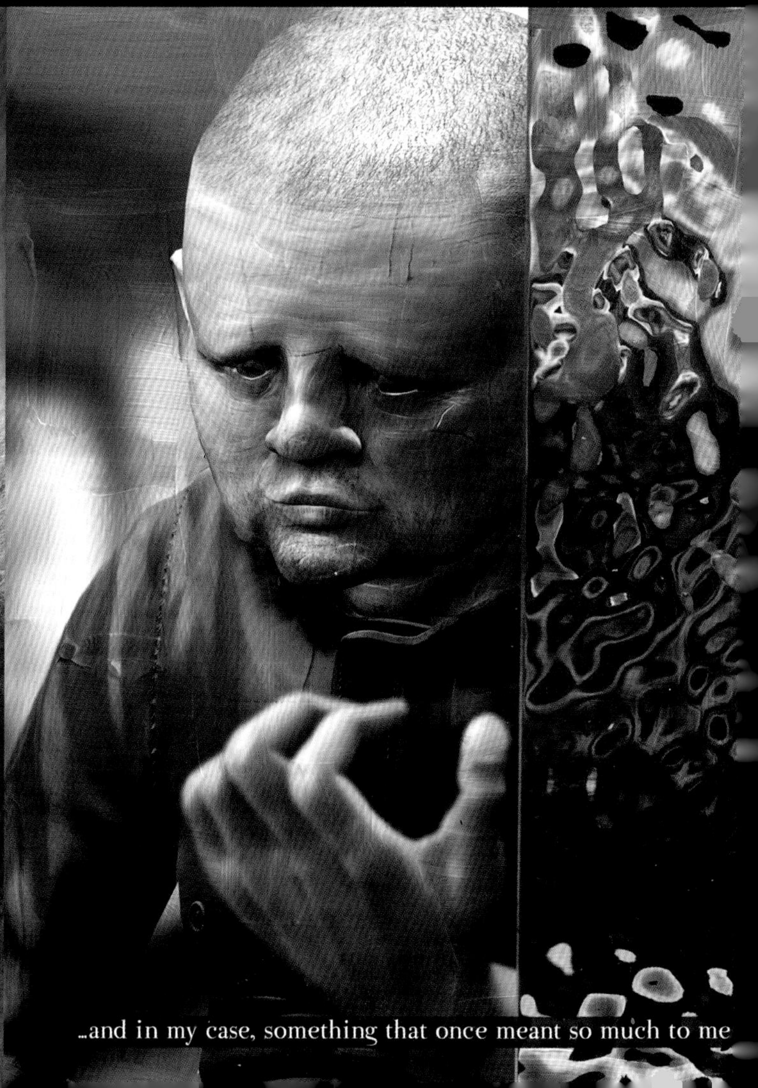
...and in my case, something that once meant so much to me

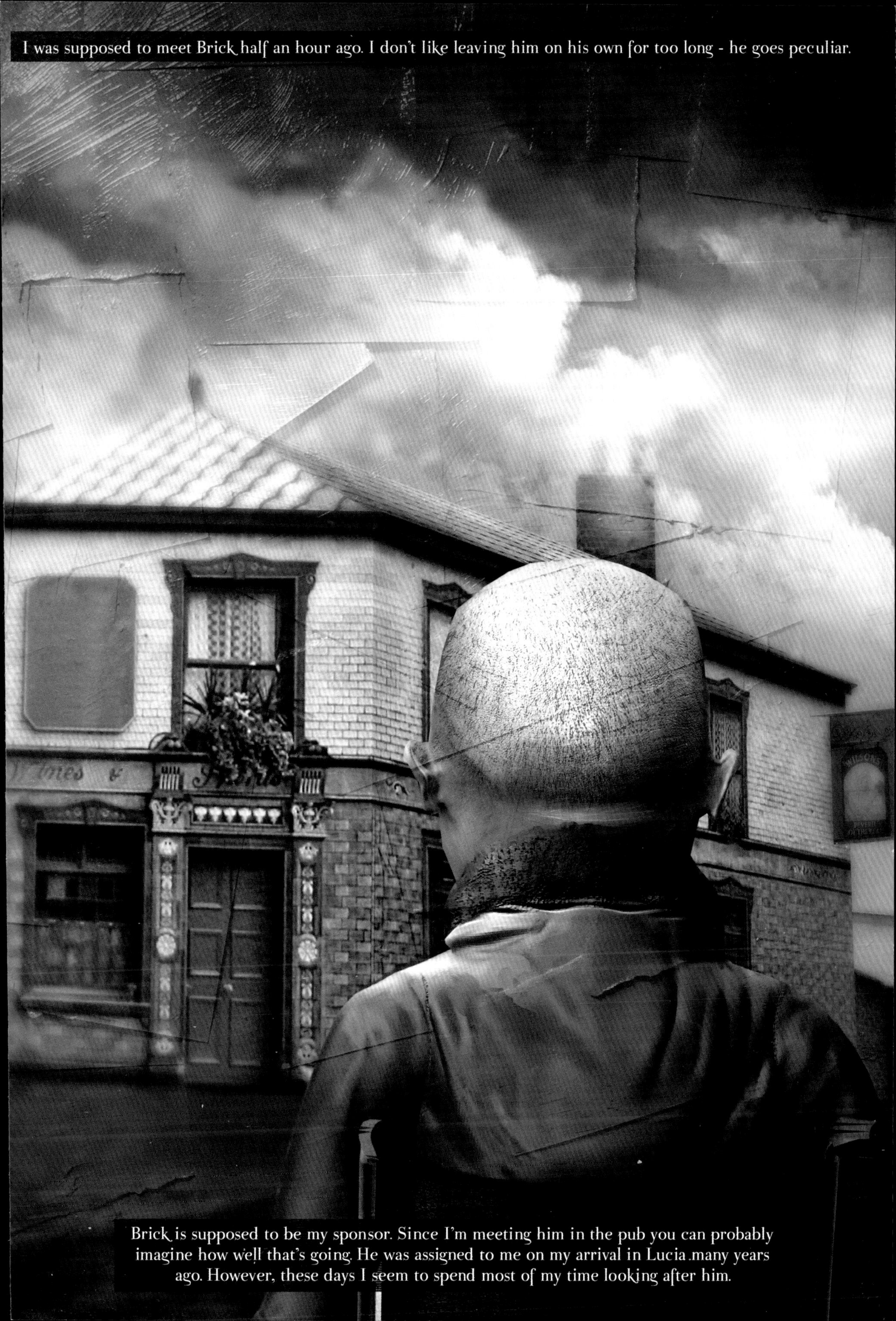
I was supposed to meet Brick half an hour ago. I don't like leaving him on his own for too long - he goes peculiar.
Brick is supposed to be my sponsor. Since I'm meeting him in the pub you can probably imagine how well that's going. He was assigned to me on my arrival in Lucia many years ago. However, these days I seem to spend most of my time looking after him.

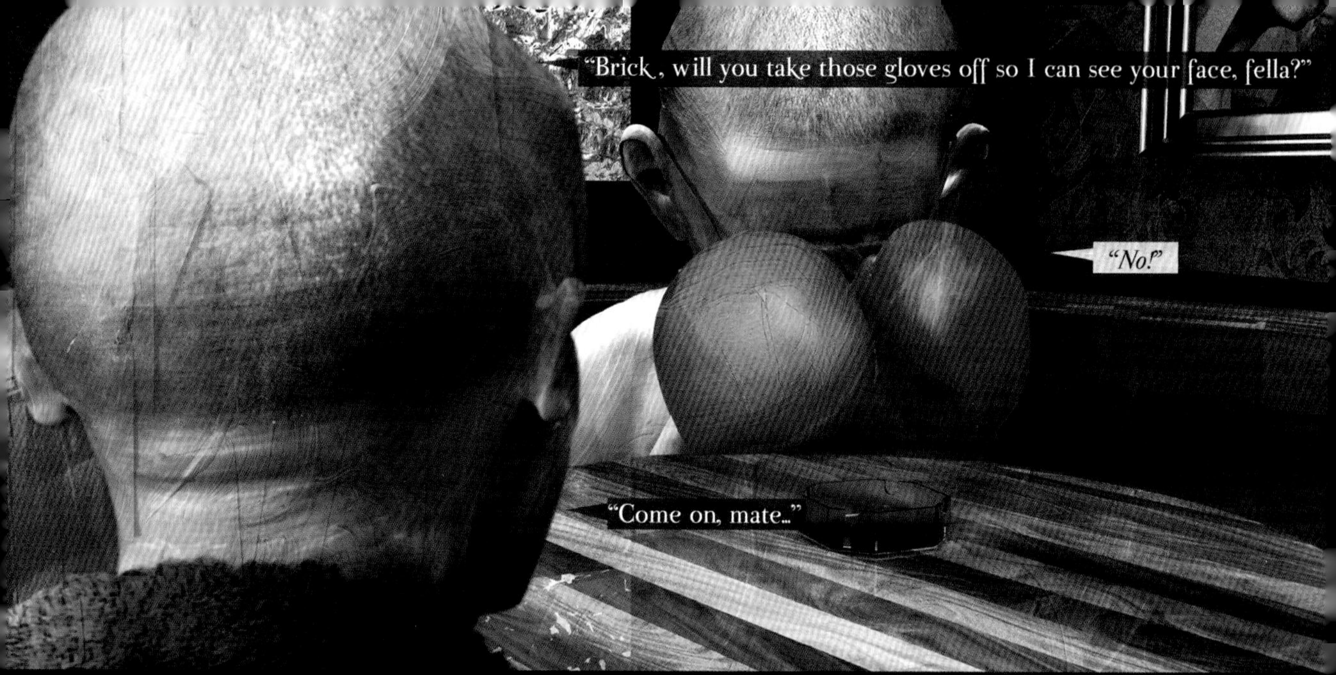
"Brick, will you take those gloves off so I can see your face, fella?"
"No!"
"Come on, mate..."
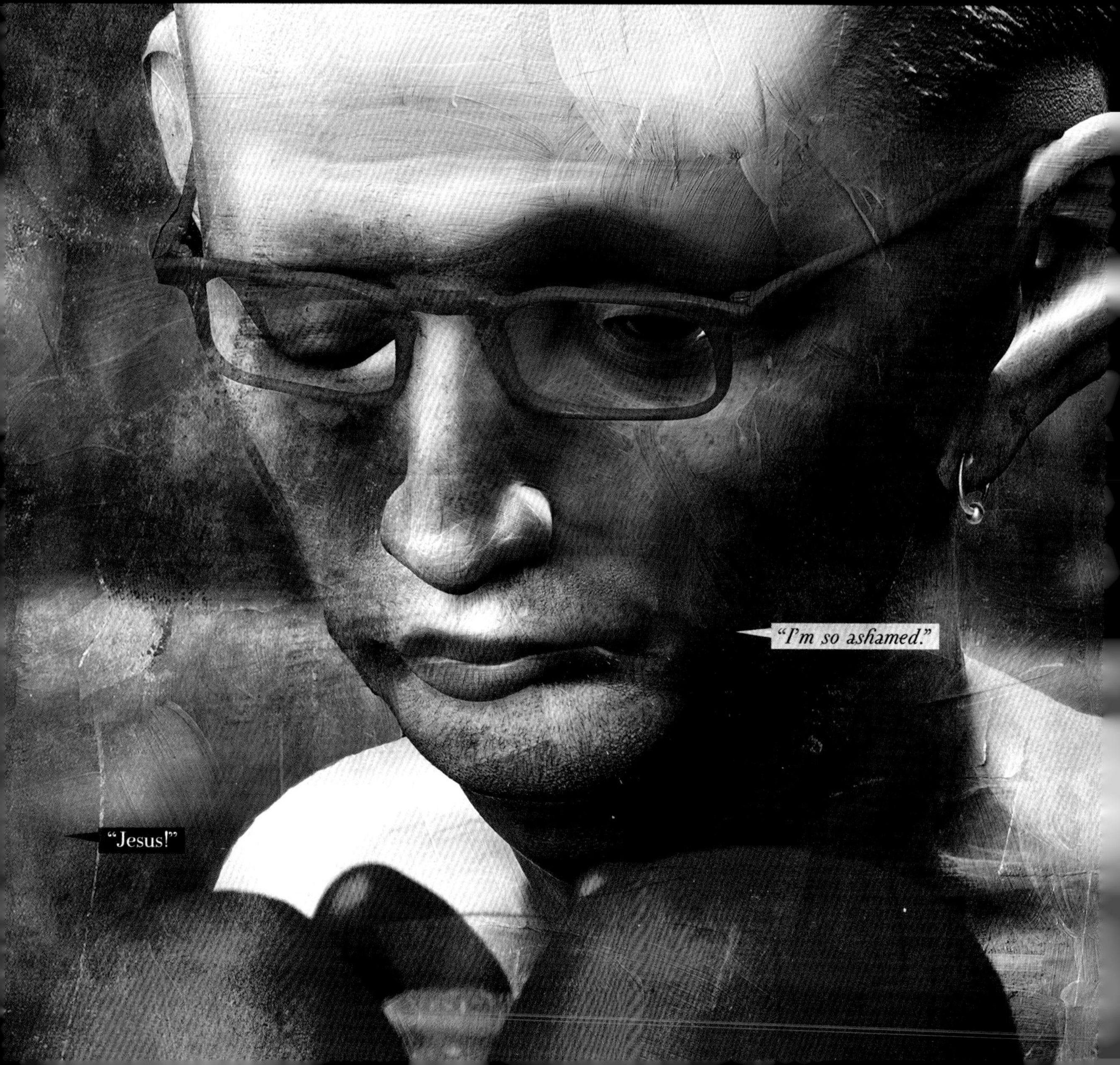
"I'm so ashamed."
"Jesus!"

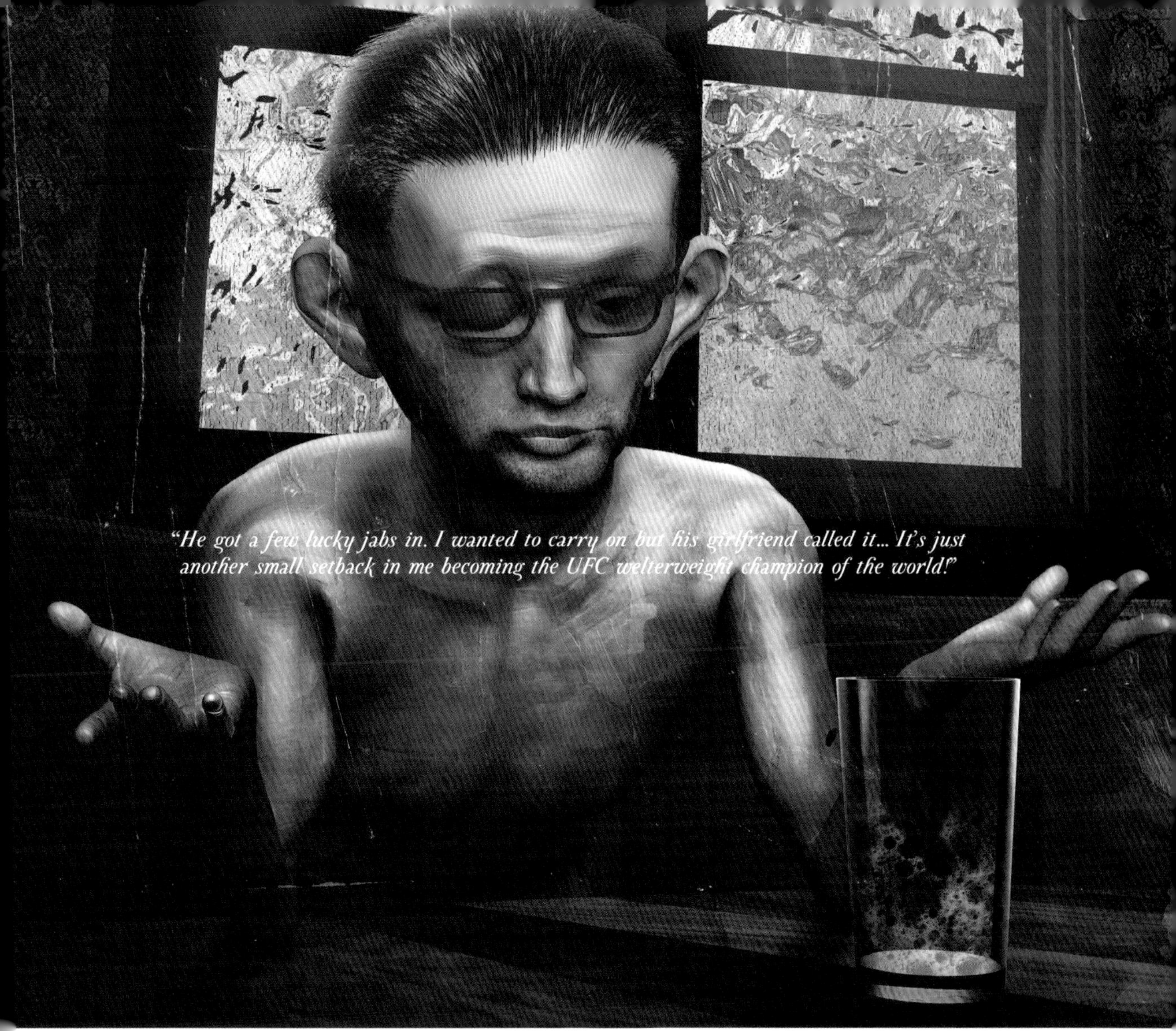
"He got a few lucky jabs in. I wanted to carry on but his girlfriend called it... It's just another small setback in me becoming the UFC welterweight champion of the world!"

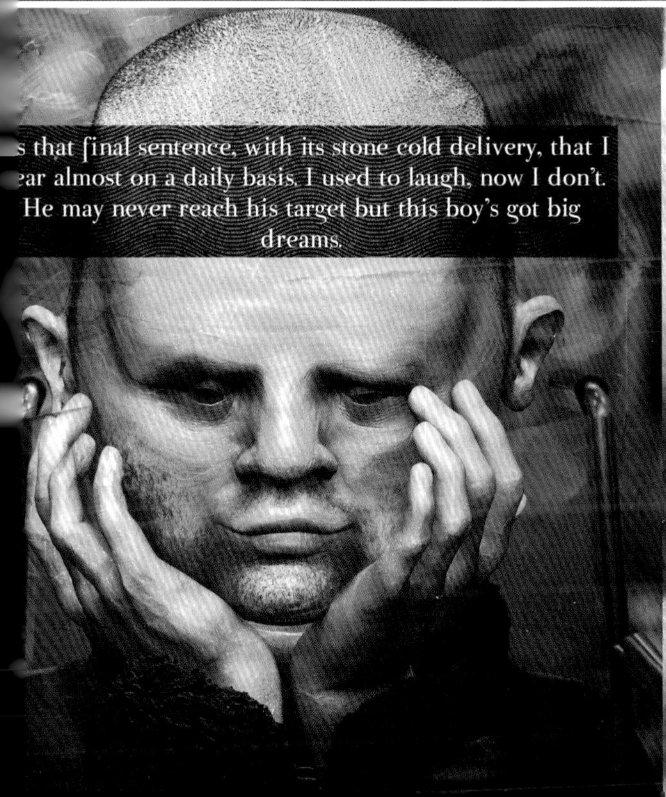
s that final sentence, with its stone cold delivery, that I
ear almost on a daily basis. I used to laugh, now I don't.
He may never reach his target but this boy's got big
dreams.

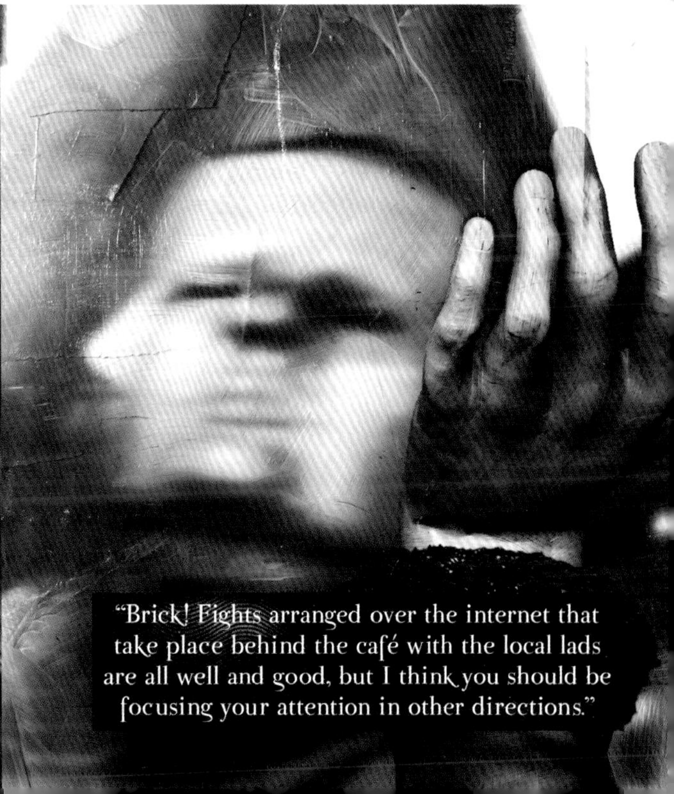
"Brick! Fights arranged over the internet that take place behind the café with the local lads are all well and good, but I think you should be focusing your attention in other directions."

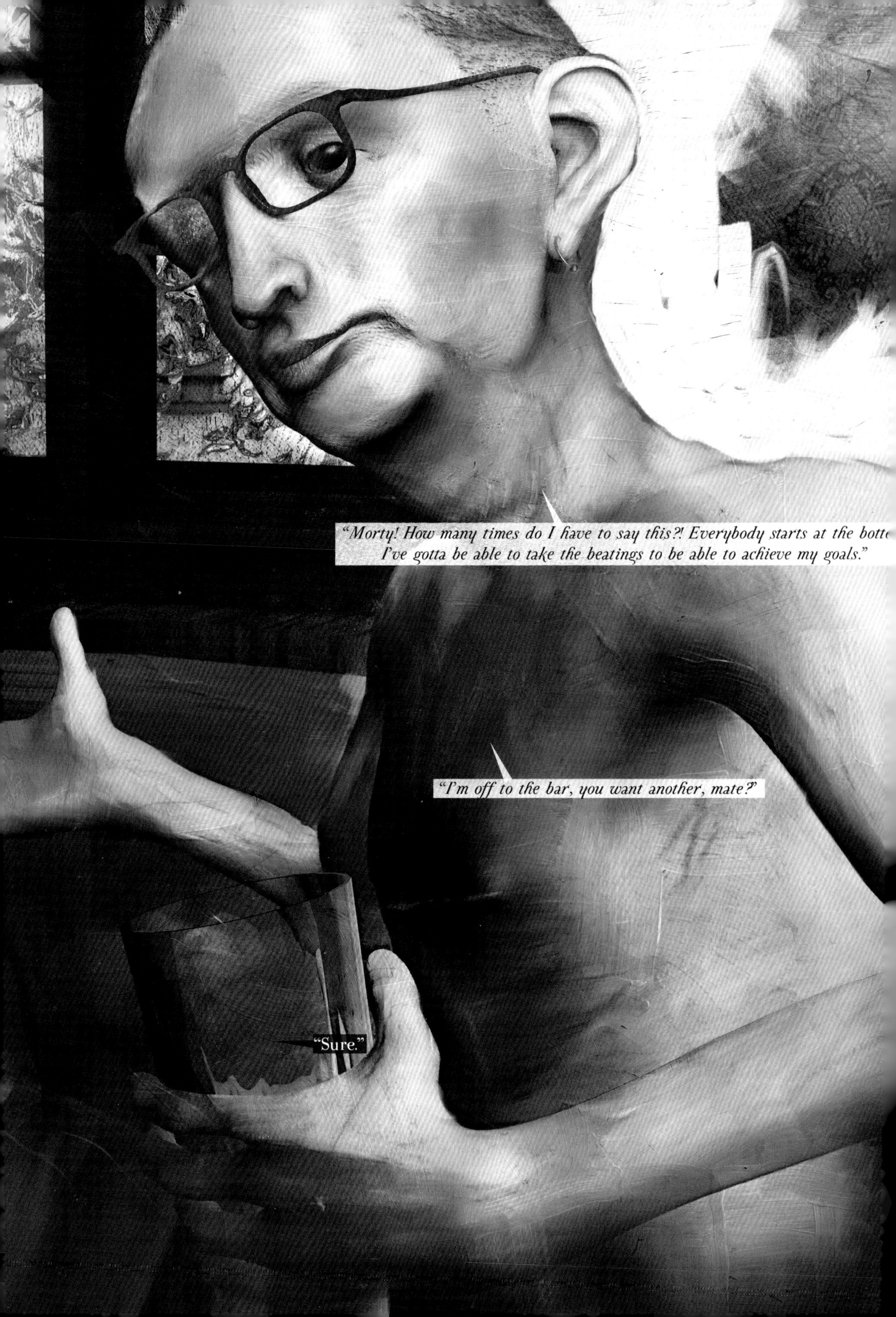

"Morty! How many times do I have to say this?! Everybody starts at the bott
I've gotta be able to take the beatings to be able to achieve my goals."
"I'm off to the bar, you want another, mate?"
"Sure."

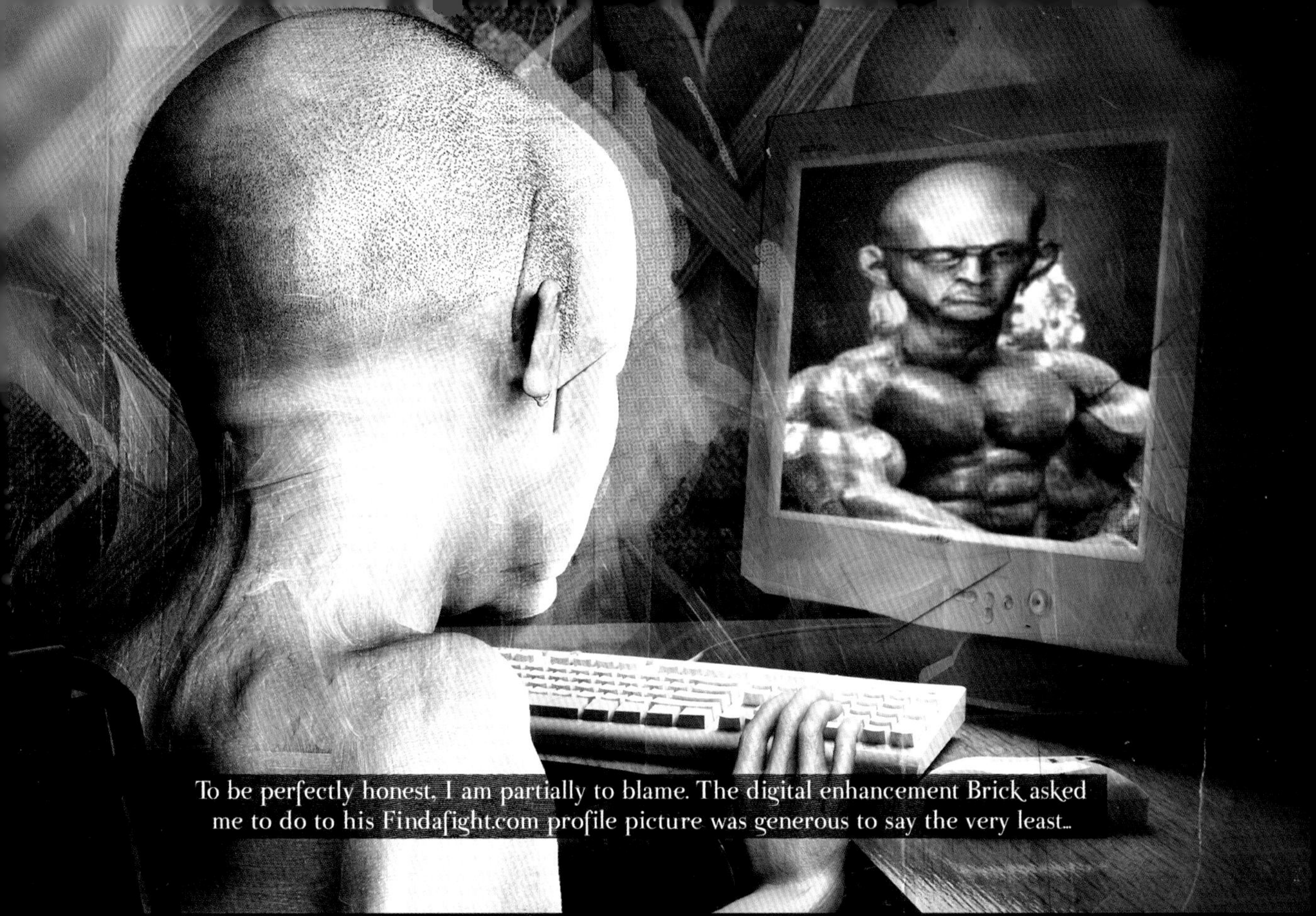
To be perfectly honest, I am partially to blame. The digital enhancement Brick asked me to do to his Findafight.com profile picture was generous to say the very least...

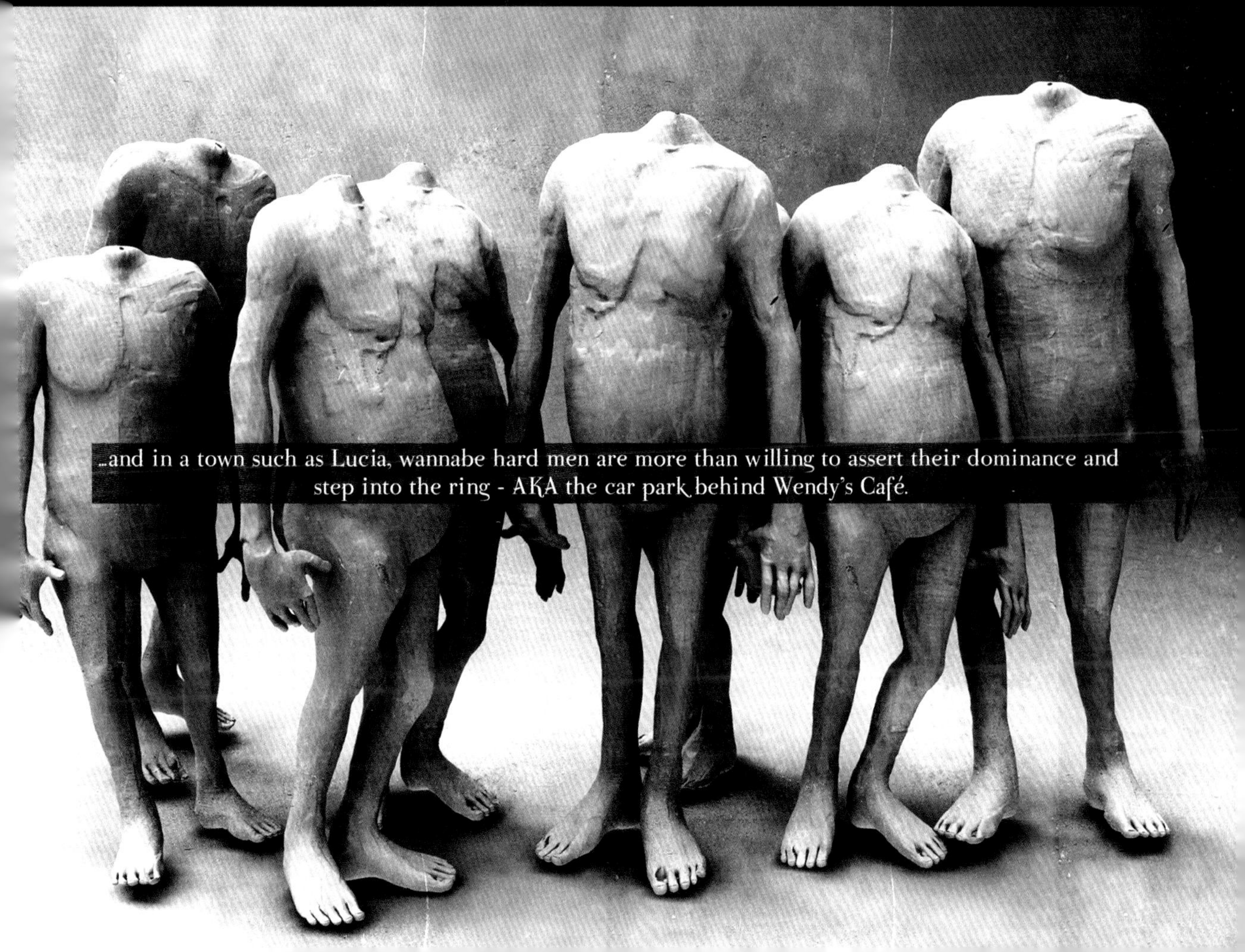
...and in a town such as Lucia, wannabe hard men are more than willing to assert their dominance and step into the ring - AKA the car park behind Wendy's Café.

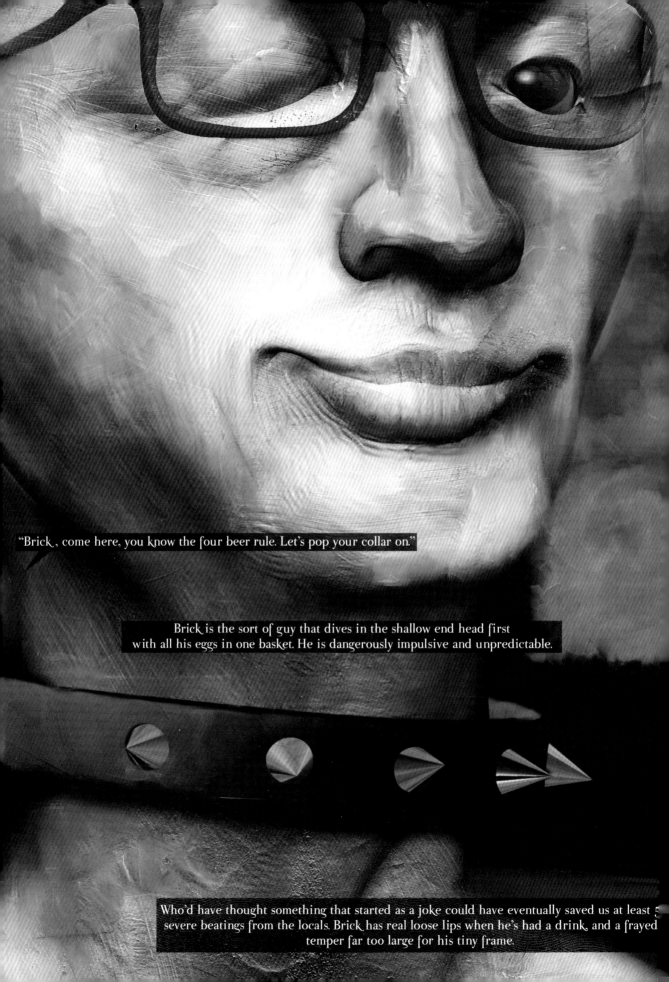

"Brick, come here, you know the four beer rule. Let's pop your collar on."

Brick is the sort of guy that dives in the shallow end head first
with all his eggs in one basket. He is dangerously impulsive and unpredictable.

Who'd have thought something that started as a joke could have eventually saved us at least 5
severe beatings from the locals. Brick has real loose lips when he's had a drink, and a frayed
temper far too large for his tiny frame.

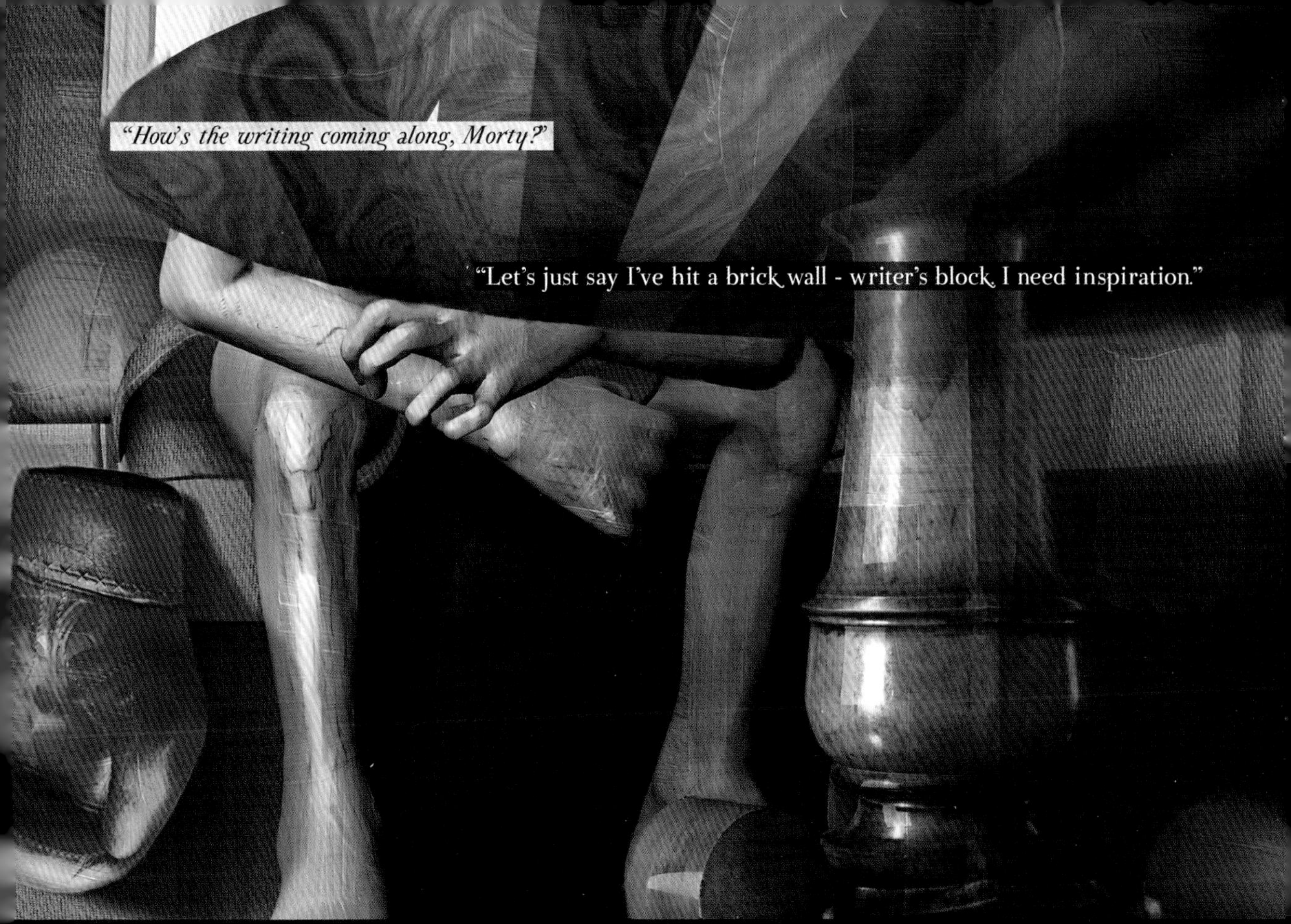
"How's the writing coming along, Morty?"
"Let's just say I've hit a brick wall - writer's block. I need inspiration."

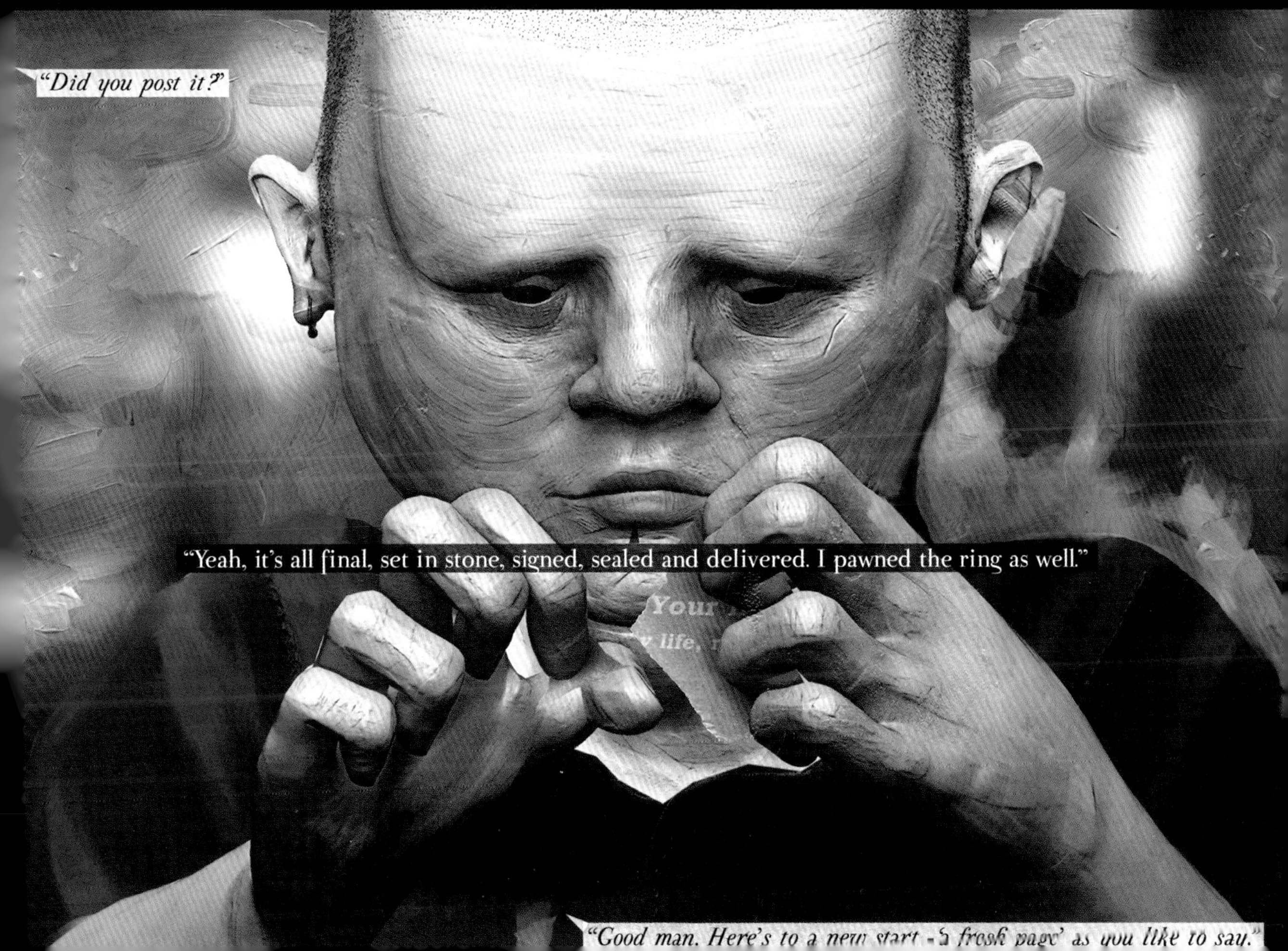
"Did you post it?"
"Yeah, it's all final, set in stone, signed, sealed and delivered. I pawned the ring as well."
"Good man. Here's to a new start - 'a fresh page' as you like to say."

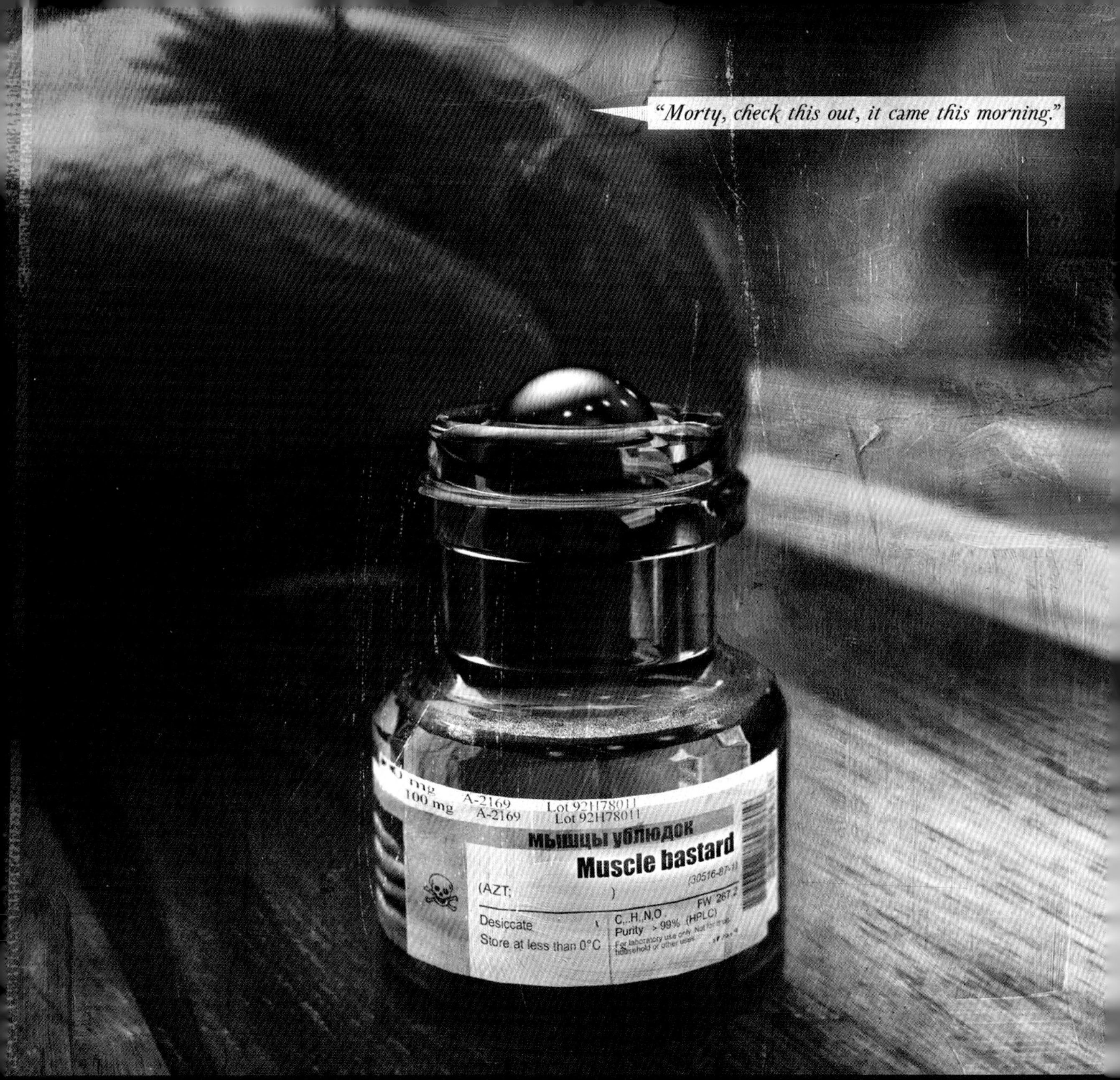
"Morty, check this out, it came this morning."
100 mg A-2169 Lot 92H78011
Мышщы ублюдок
Muscle bastard
(AZT;)
Desiccate
Store at less than 0°C
Purity >99% (HPLC)

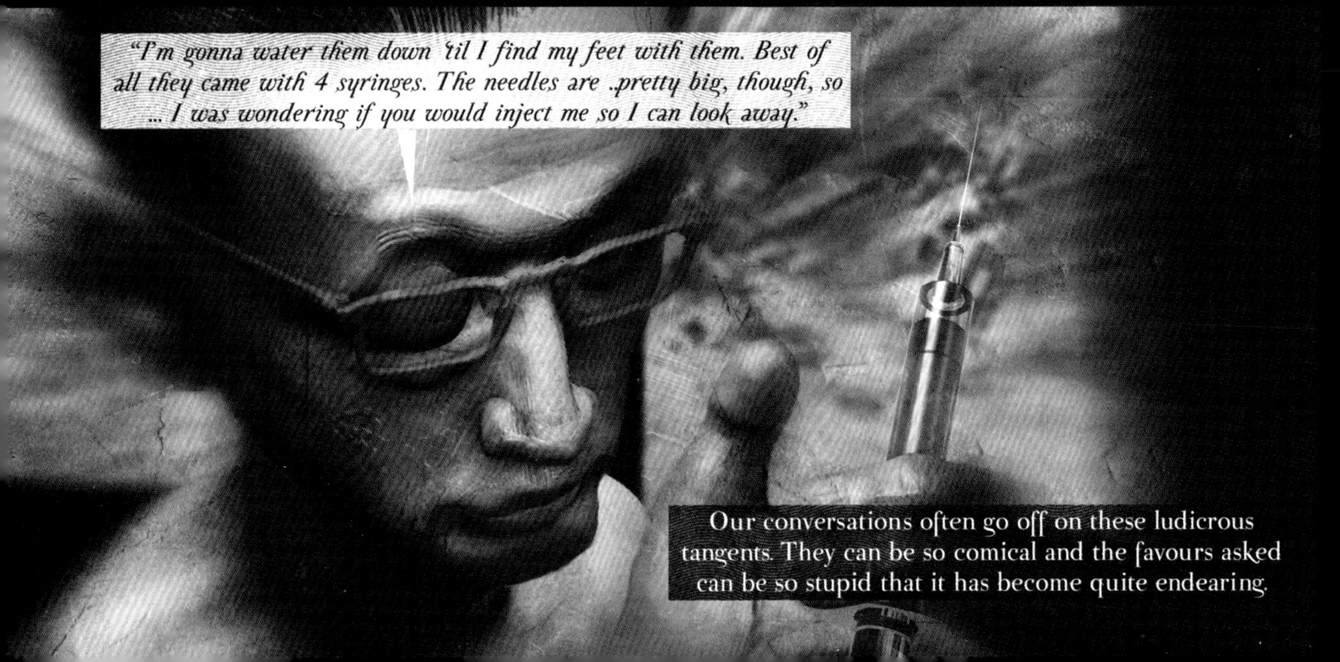
"I'm gonna water them down 'til I find my feet with them. Best of all they came with 4 syringes. The needles are ..pretty big, though, so ... I was wondering if you would inject me so I can look away."
Our conversations often go off on these ludicrous tangents. They can be so comical and the favours asked can be so stupid that it has become quite endearing.

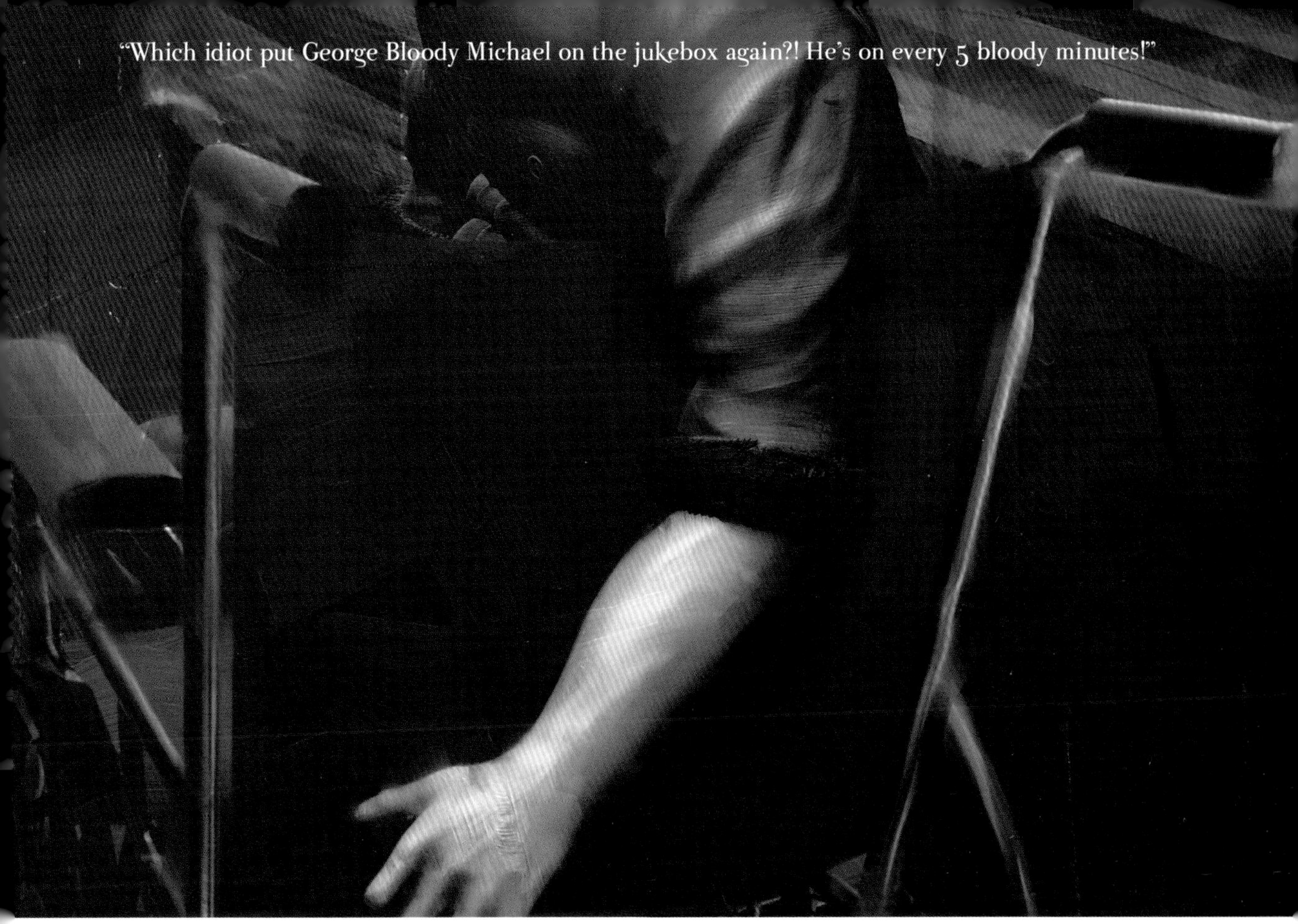
"Which idiot put George Bloody Michael on the jukebox again?! He's on every 5 bloody minutes!"

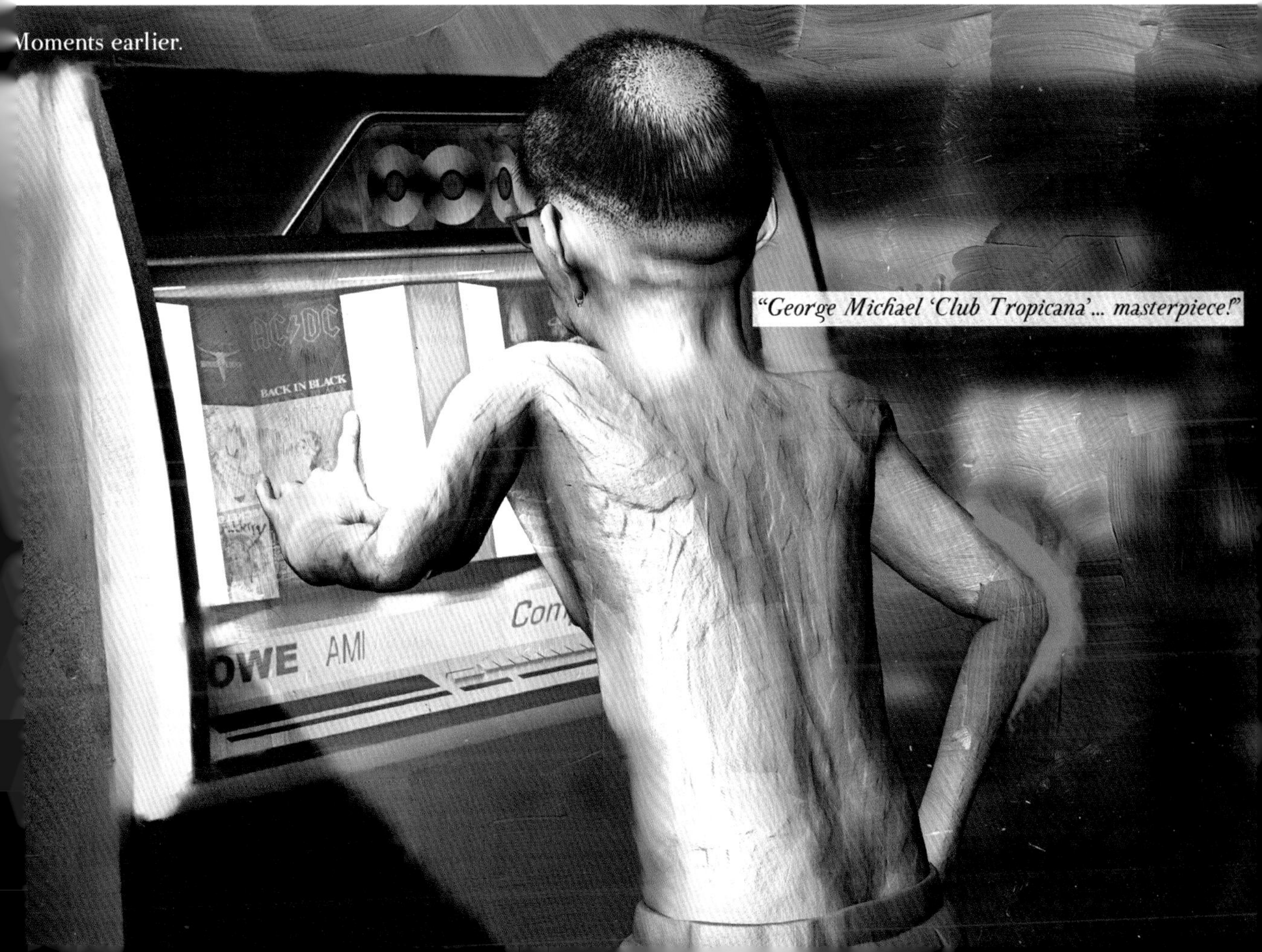
Moments earlier.
AC/DC
BACK IN BLACK
AMI
"George Michael 'Club Tropicana'... masterpiece!"

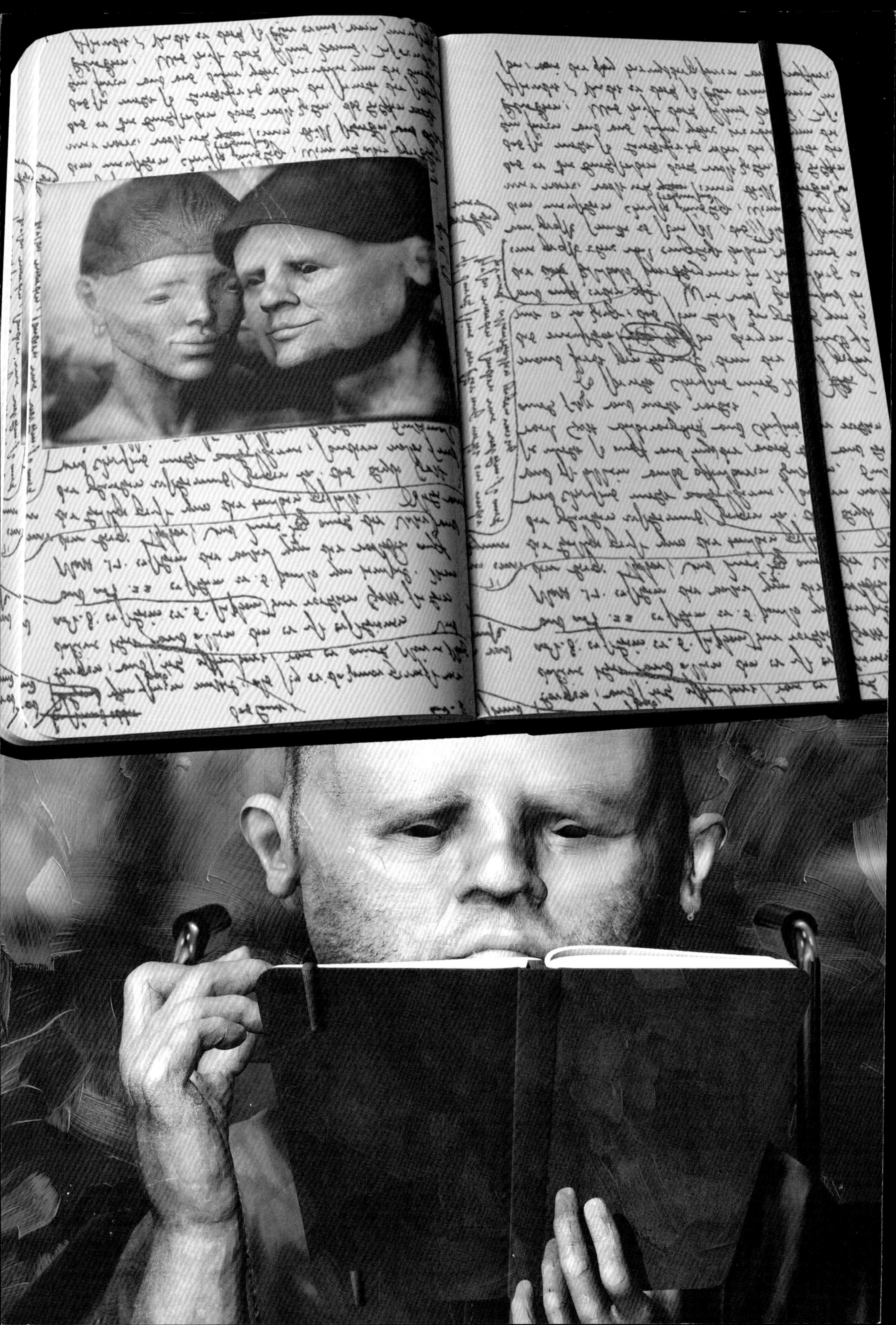

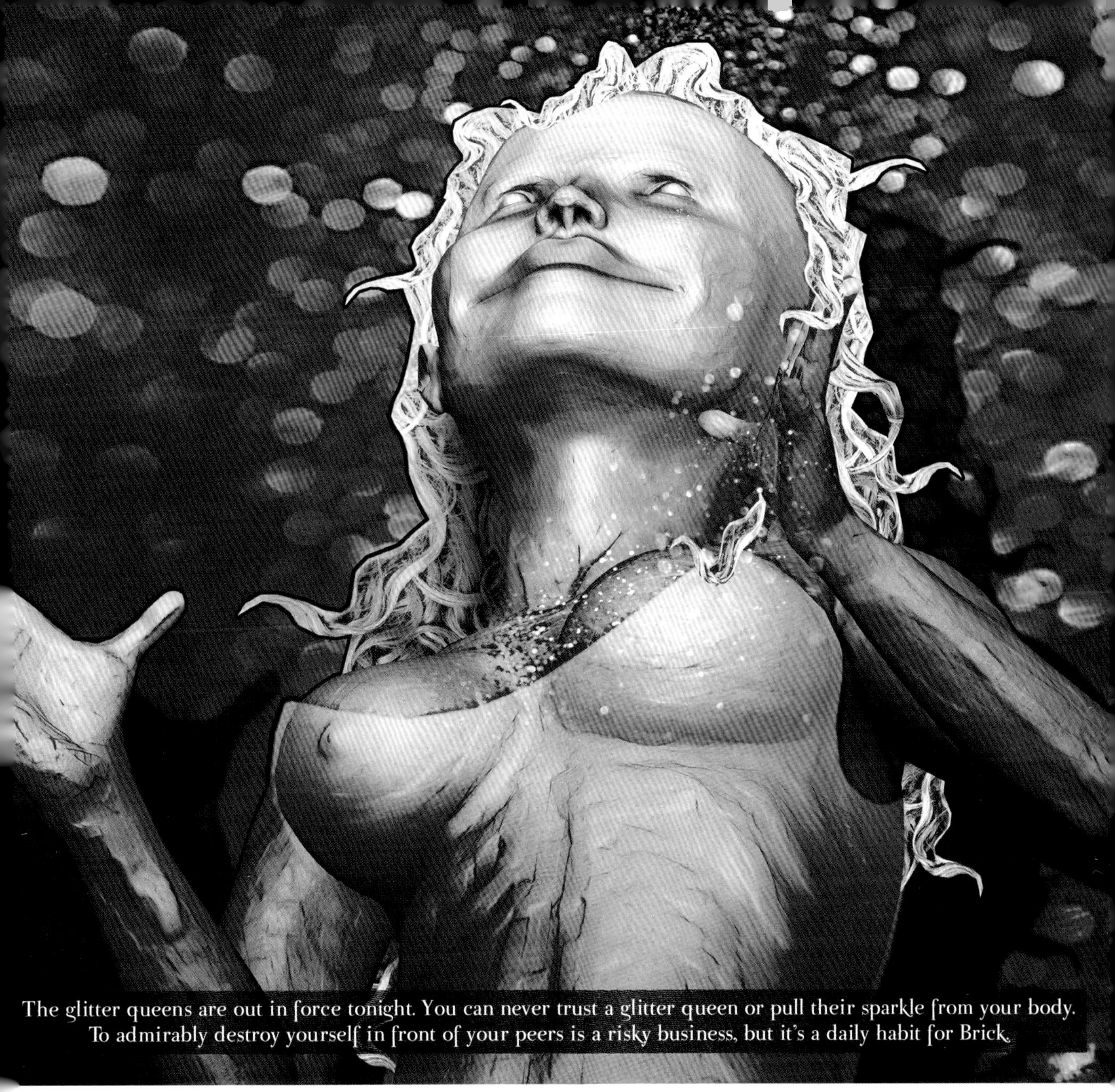
The glitter queens are out in force tonight. You can never trust a glitter queen or pull their sparkle from your body.
To admirably destroy yourself in front of your peers is a risky business, but it's a daily habit for Brick.

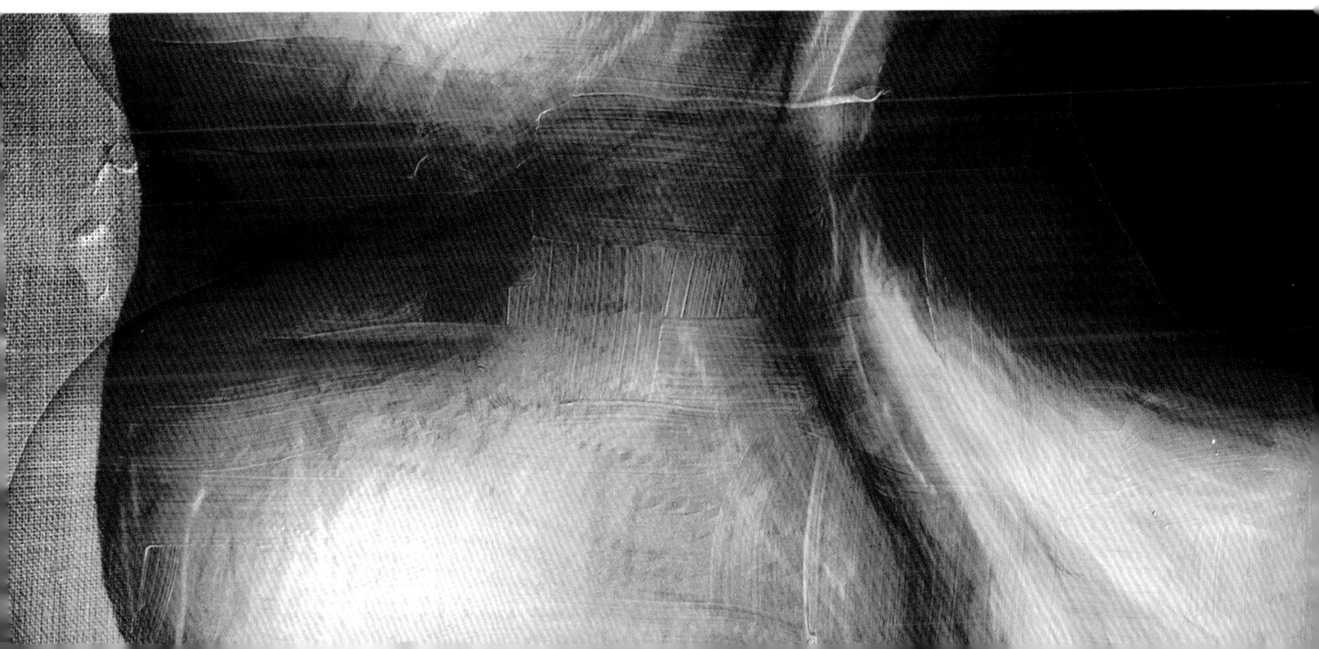

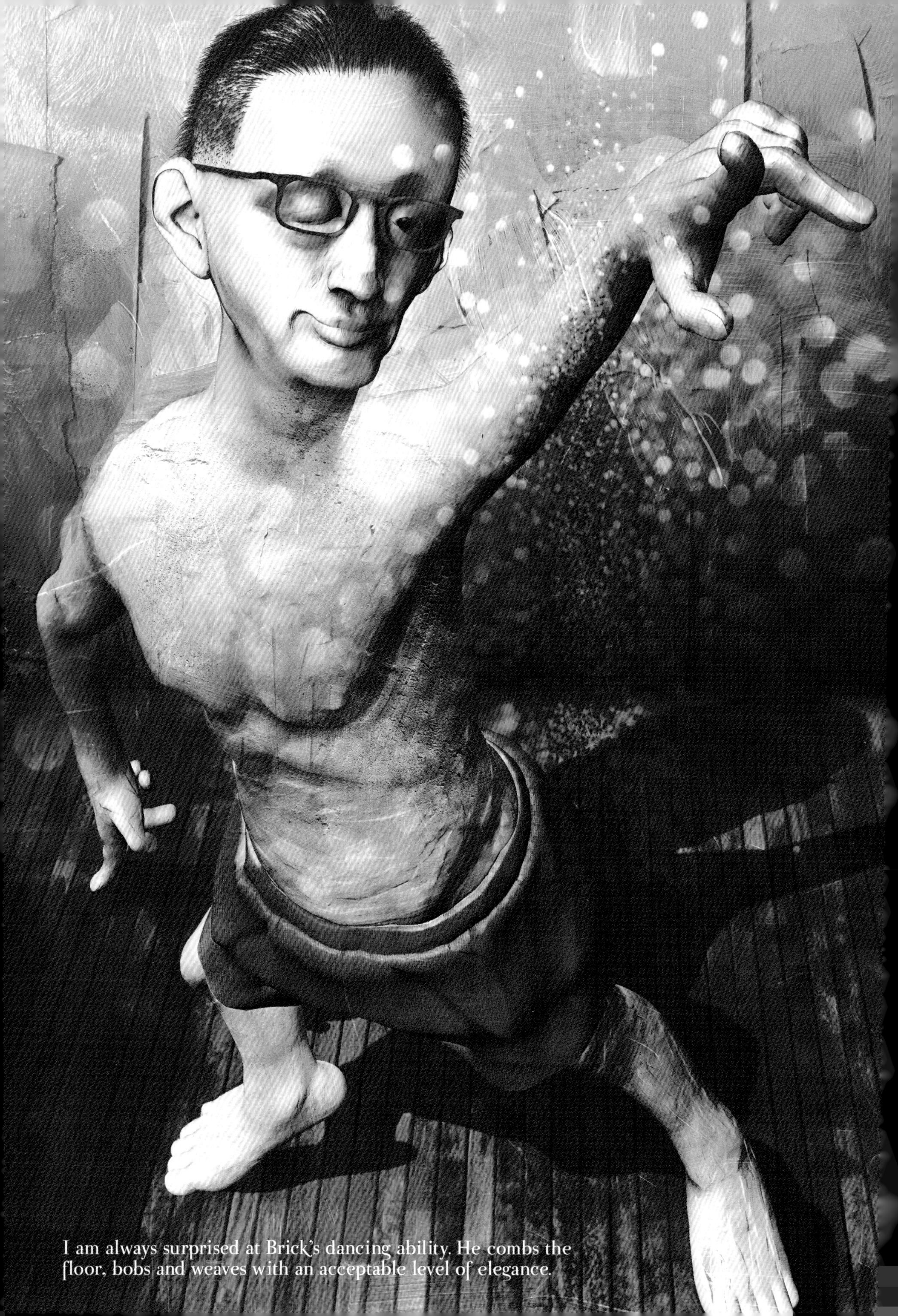

I am always surprised at Brick's dancing ability. He combs the floor, bobs and weaves with an acceptable level of elegance.

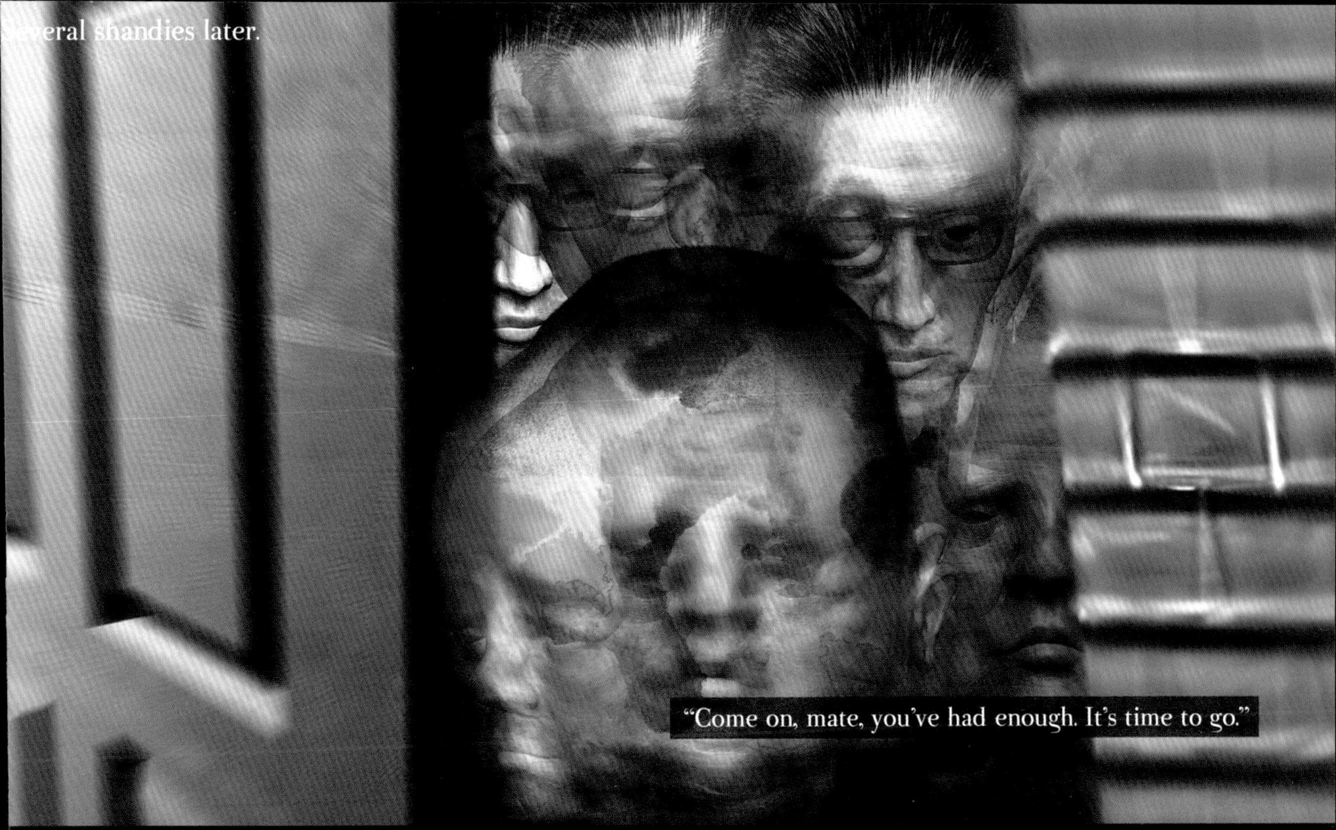
Several shandies later.
"Come on, mate, you've had enough. It's time to go."

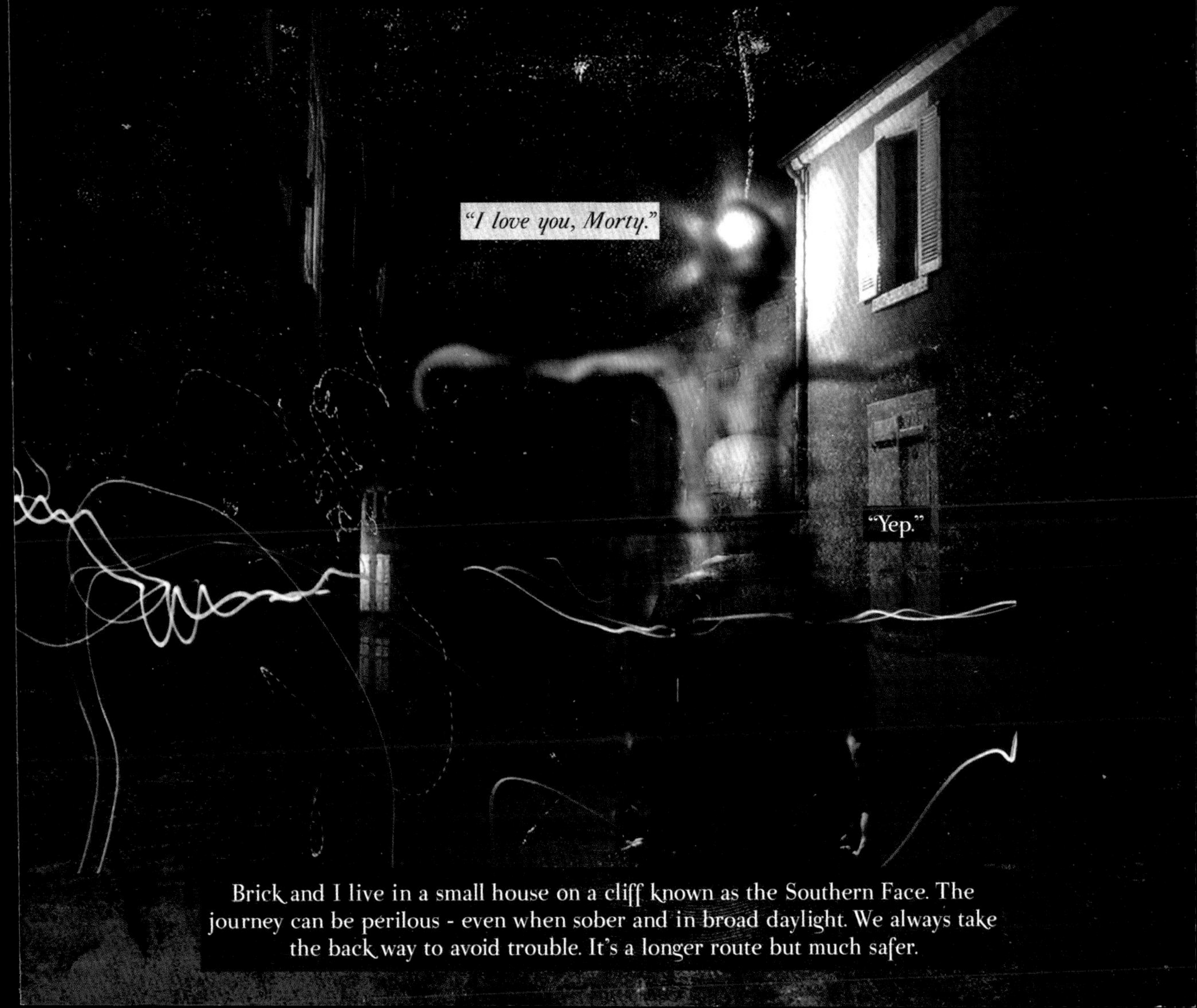
"I love you, Morty."
"Yep."
Brick and I live in a small house on a cliff known as the Southern Face. The journey can be perilous - even when sober and in broad daylight. We always take the back way to avoid trouble. It's a longer route but much safer.

After my separation from Mona, my first idea was to find a place for Brick and I to live. Brick was homeless at the time and living in the closed Gents toilets by the breakwater. He only had one boxing glove, was swearing at the sea and chasing the tide out a lot at the time.

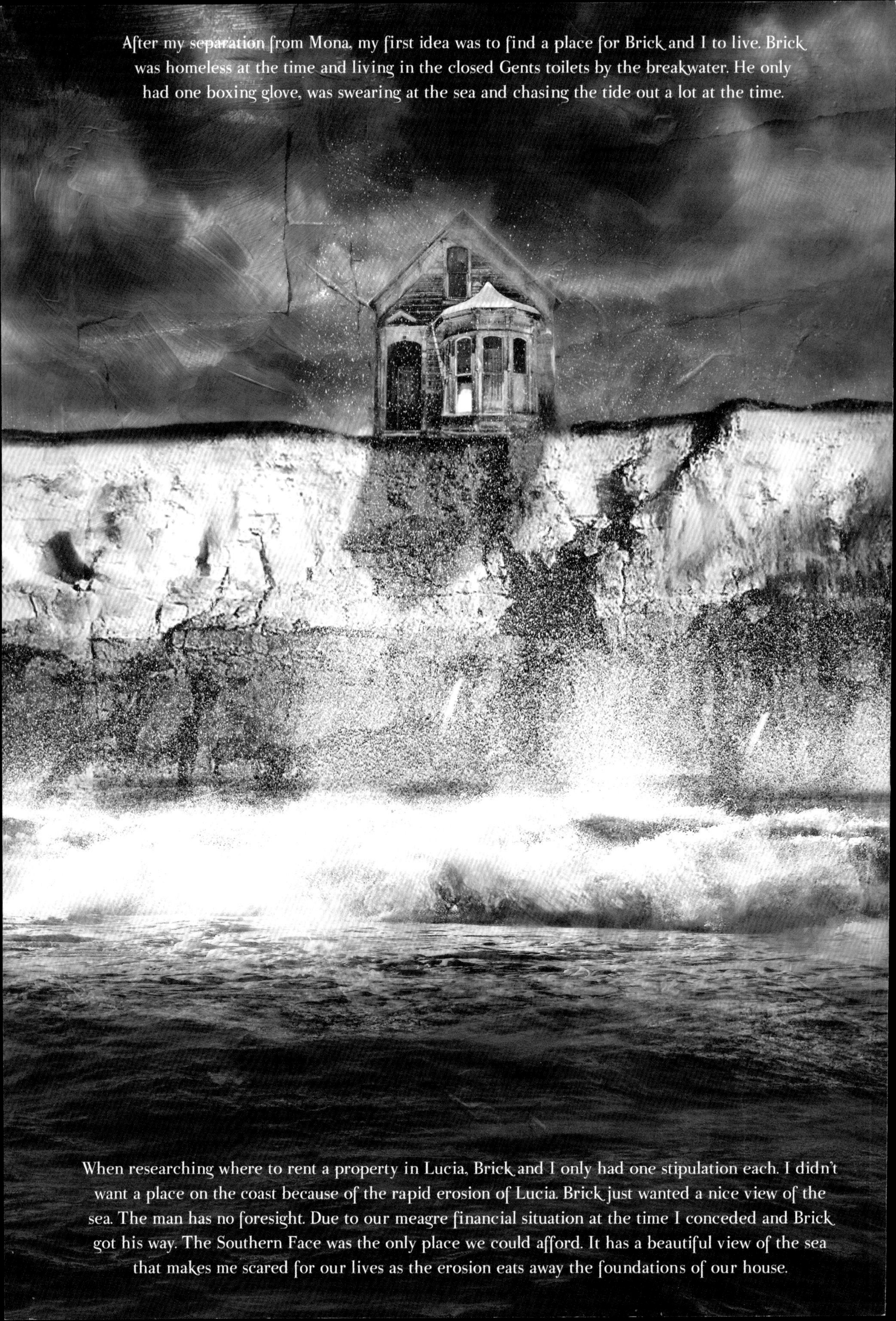

When researching where to rent a property in Lucia, Brick and I only had one stipulation each. I didn't want a place on the coast because of the rapid erosion of Lucia. Brick just wanted a nice view of the sea. The man has no foresight. Due to our meagre financial situation at the time I conceded and Brick got his way. The Southern Face was the only place we could afford. It has a beautiful view of the sea that makes me scared for our lives as the erosion eats away the foundations of our house.

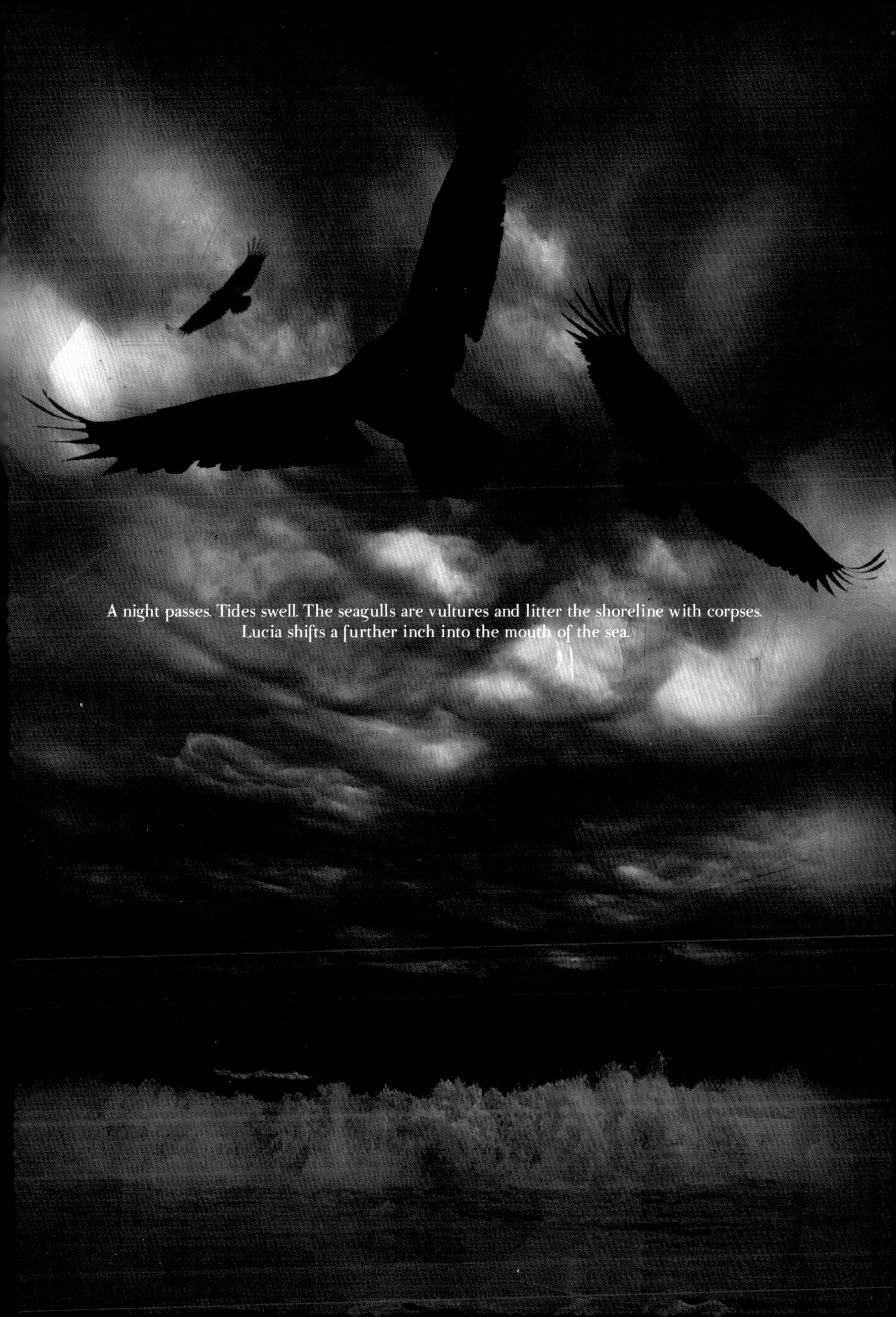

A night passes. Tides swell. The seagulls are vultures and litter the shoreline with corpses.
Lucia shifts a further inch into the mouth of the sea.

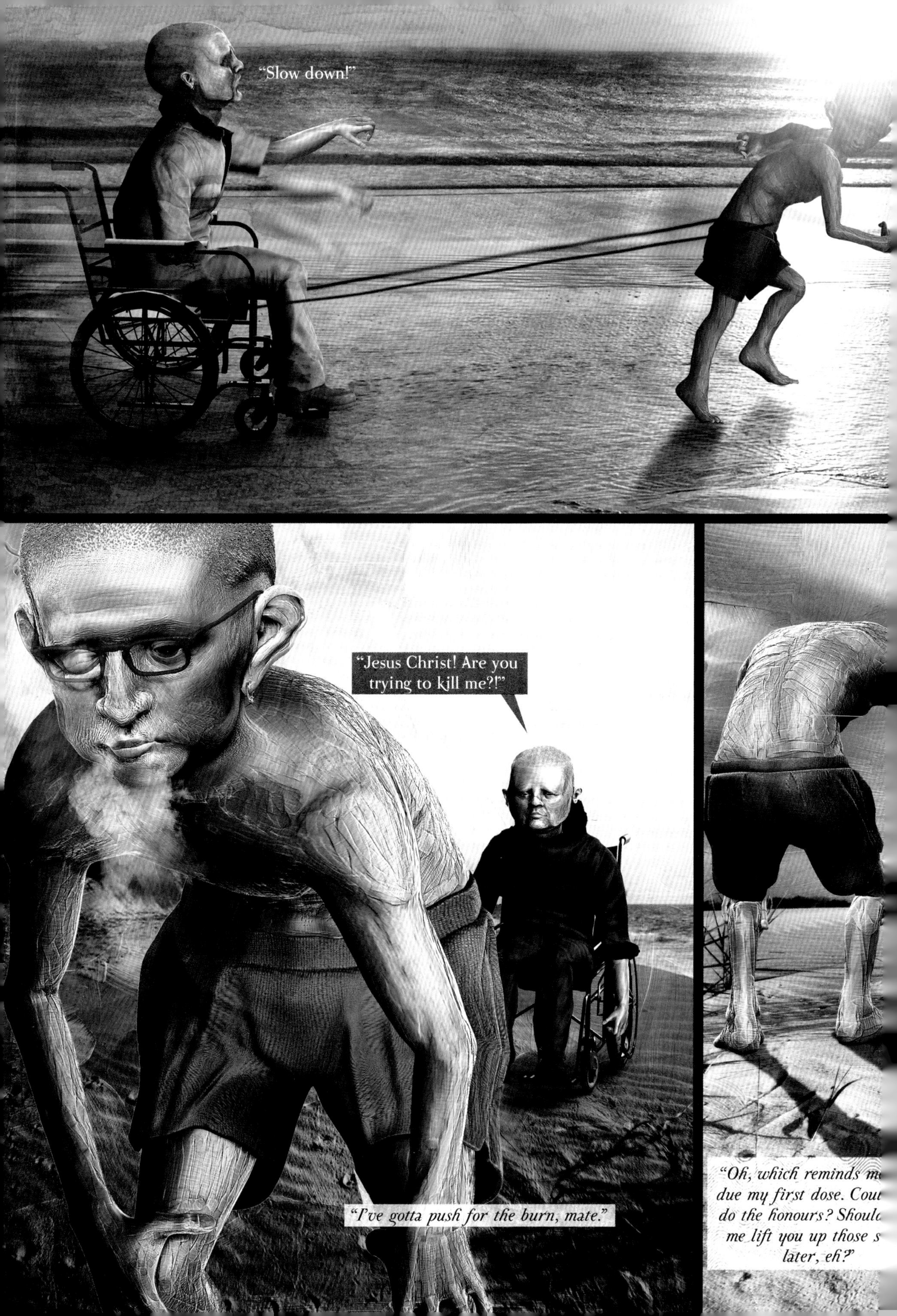
"Slow down!"
"Jesus Christ! Are you trying to kill me?!"
"I've gotta push for the burn, mate."
"Oh, which reminds m
due my first dose. Cou
do the honours? Should
me lift you up those s
later, eh?"

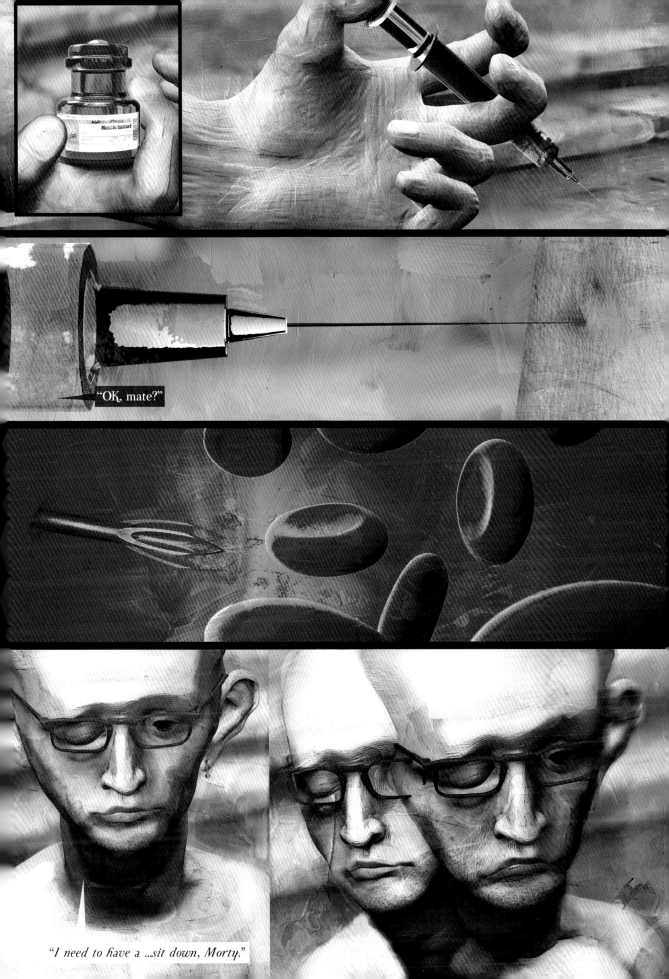

"OK, mate?"

"I need to have a ...sit down, Morty."

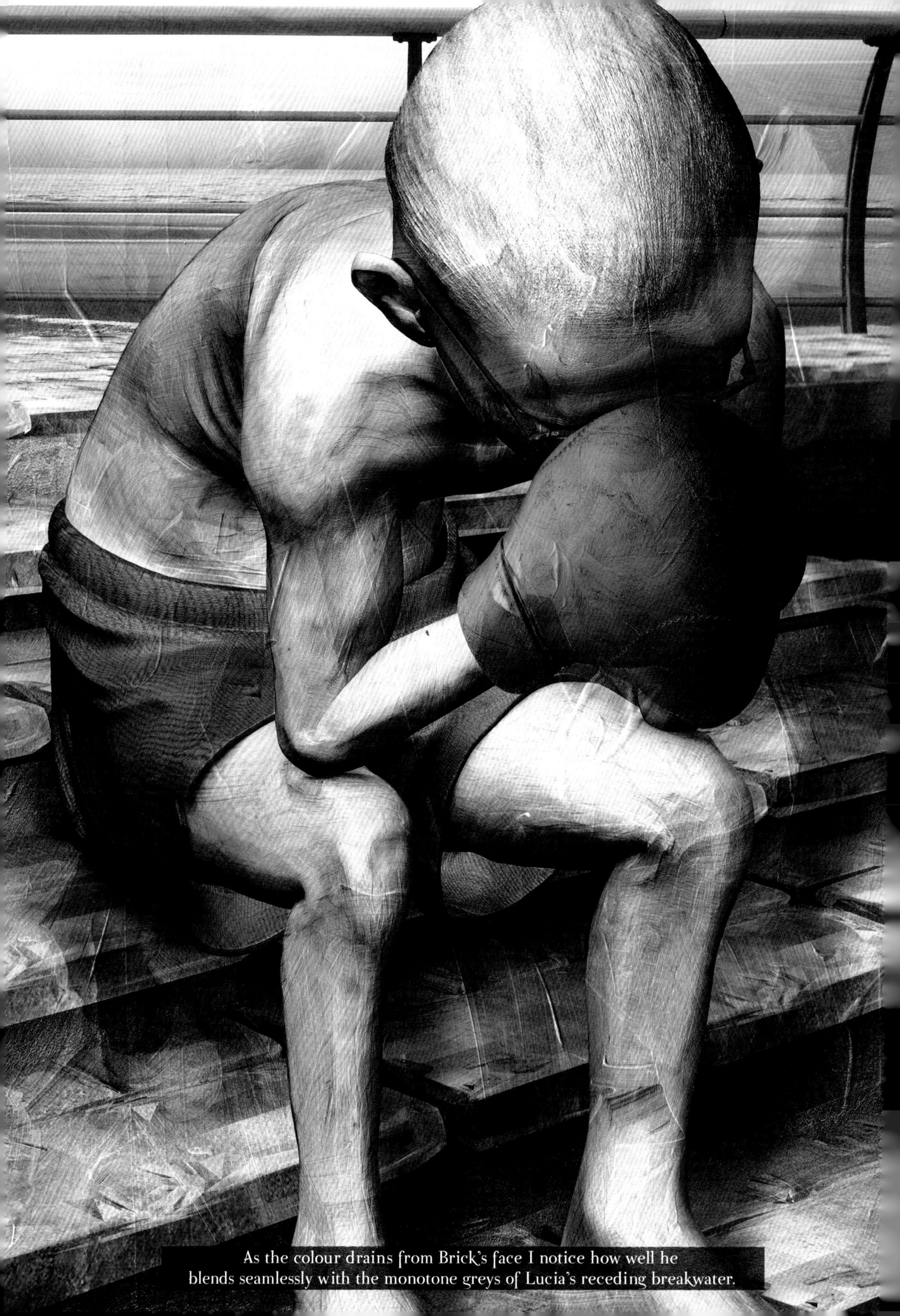

As the colour drains from Brick's face I notice how well he blends seamlessly with the monotone greys of Lucia's receding breakwater.

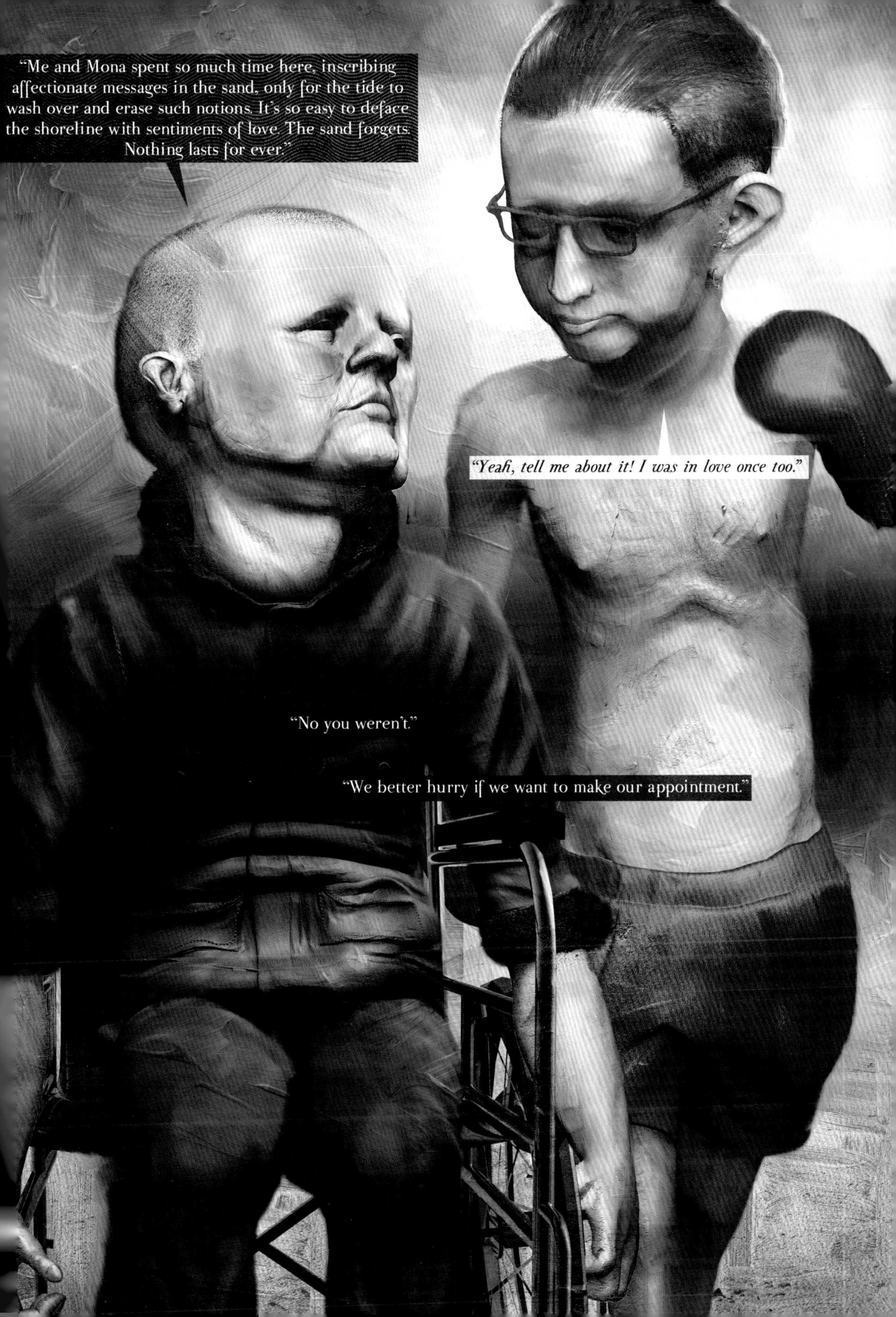
"Me and Mona spent so much time here, inscribing affectionate messages in the sand, only for the tide to wash over and erase such notions. It's so easy to deface the shoreline with sentiments of love. The sand forgets. Nothing lasts for ever."
"Yeah, tell me about it! I was in love once too."
"No you weren't."
"We better hurry if we want to make our appointment."

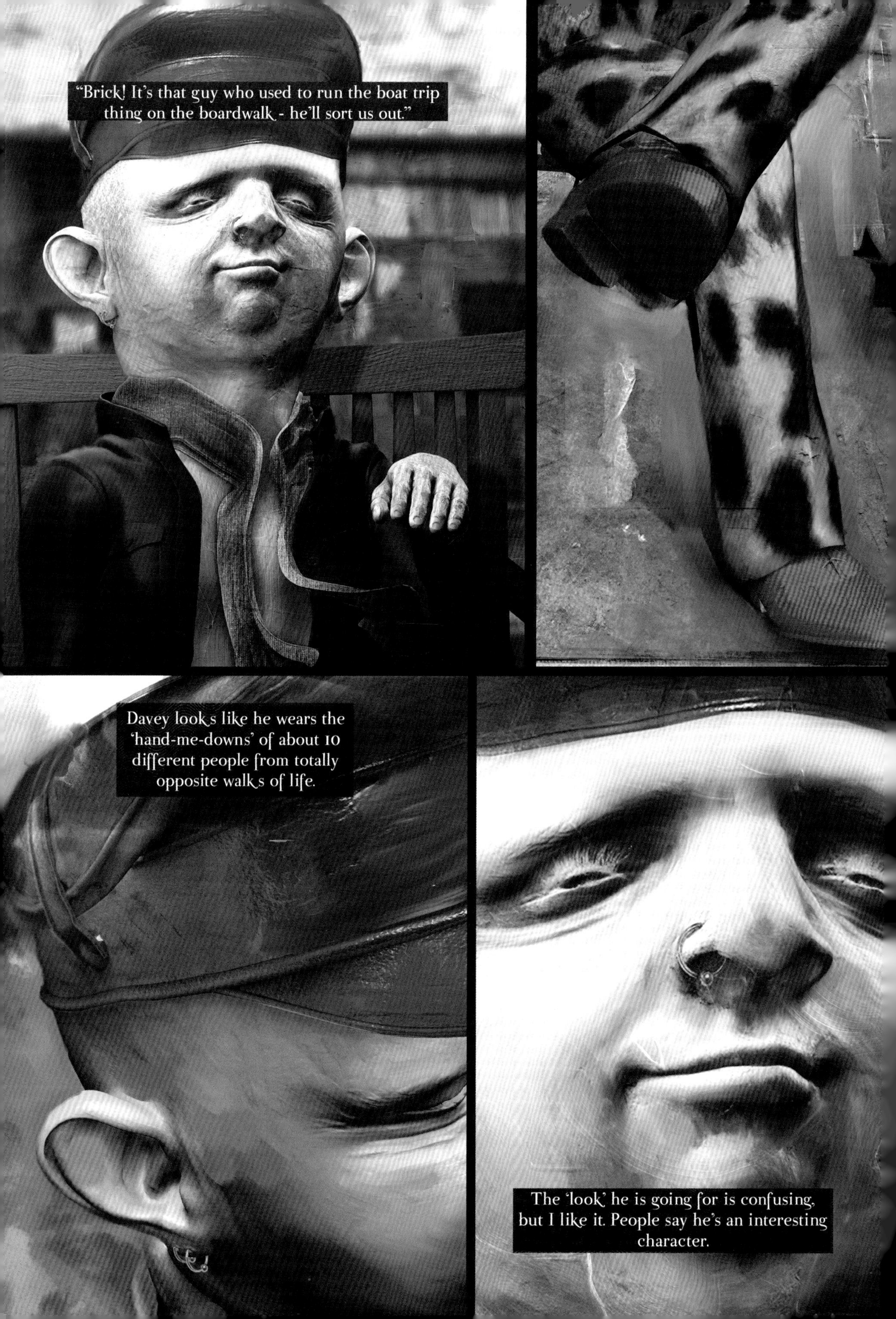
"Brick! It's that guy who used to run the boat trip thing on the boardwalk - he'll sort us out."
Davey looks like he wears the 'hand-me-downs' of about 10 different people from totally opposite walks of life.
The 'look' he is going for is confusing, but I like it. People say he's an interesting character.

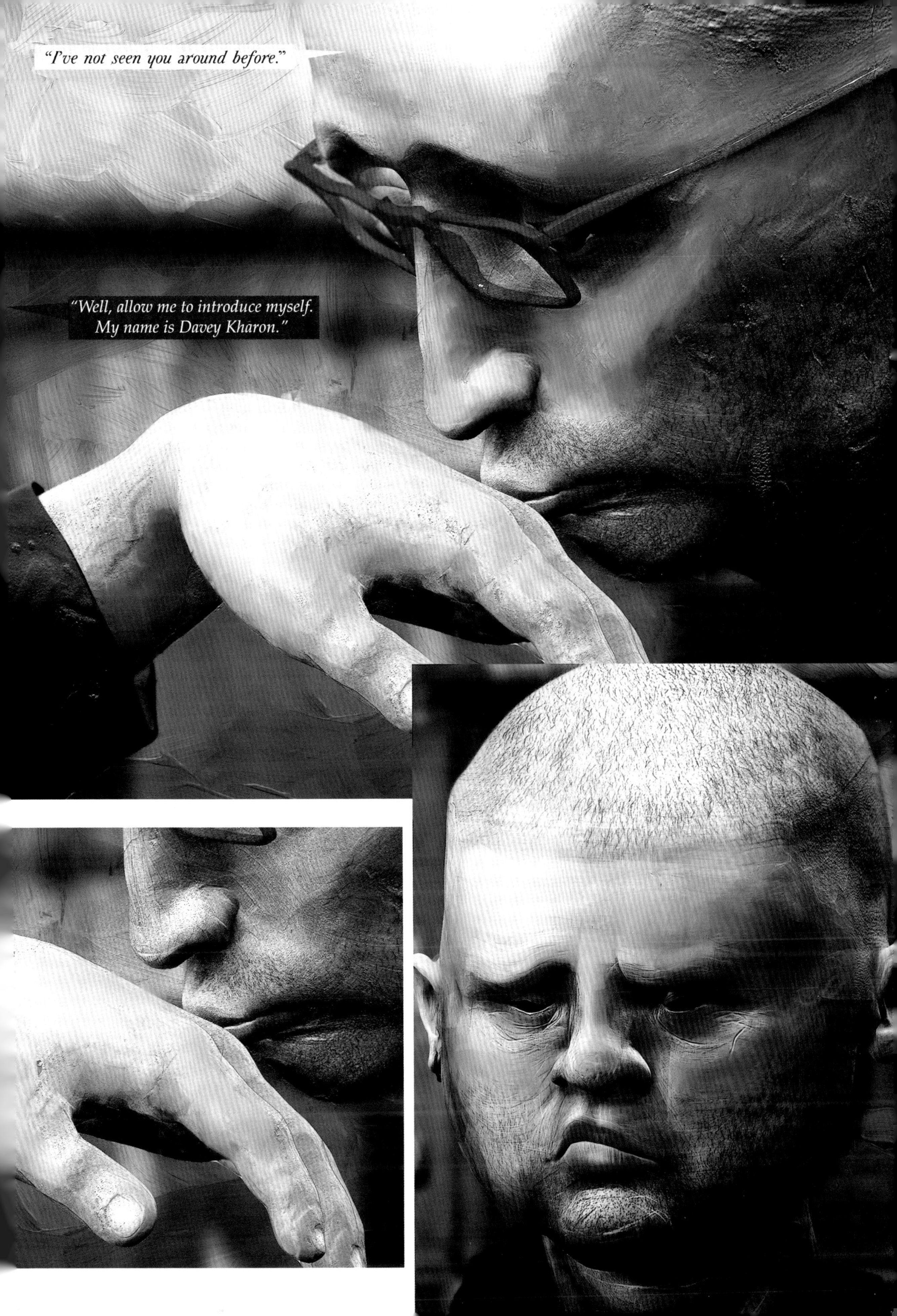
"I've not seen you around before."
"Well, allow me to introduce myself. My name is Davey Kharon."

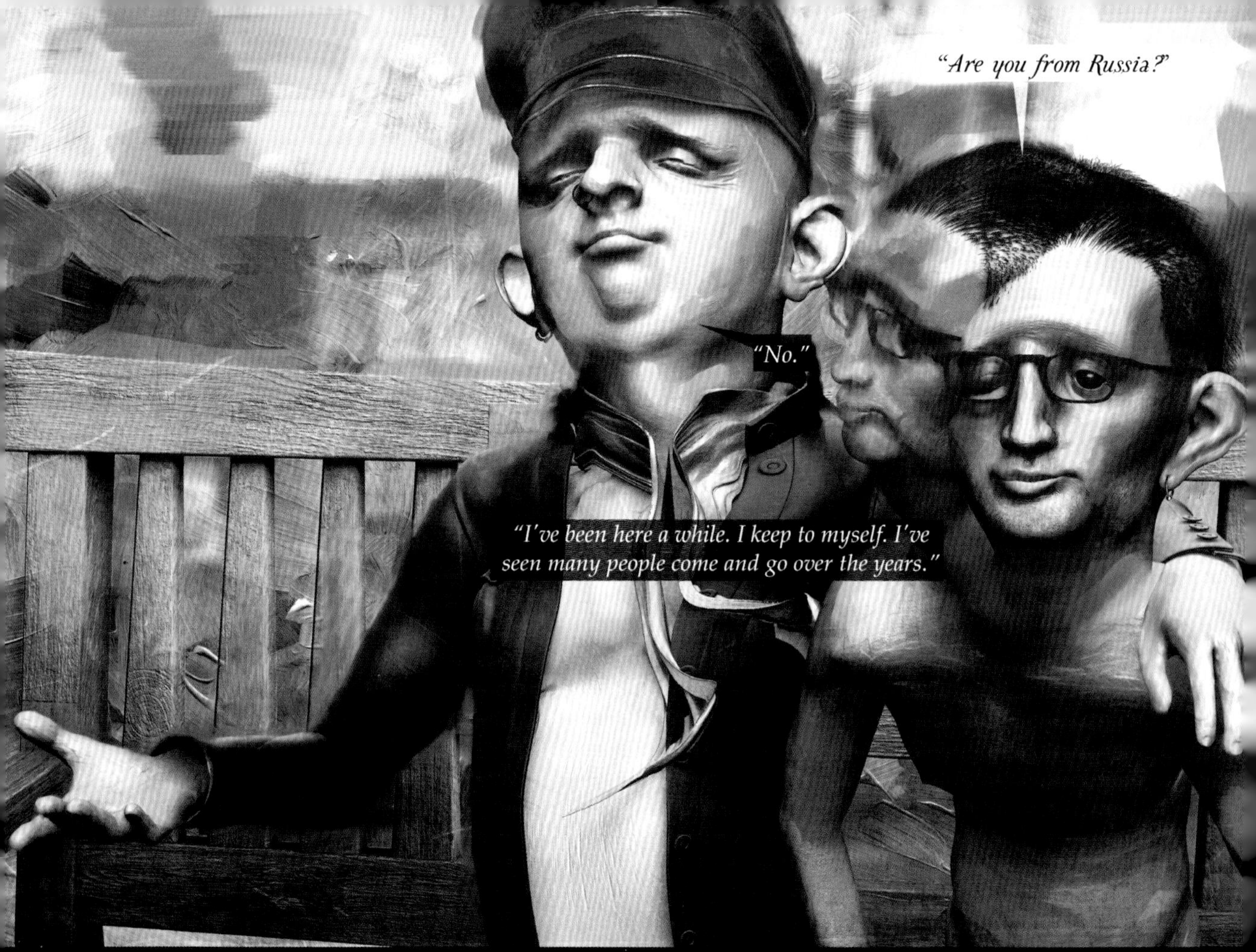
"Are you from Russia?"
"No."
"I've been here a while. I keep to myself. I've seen many people come and go over the years."

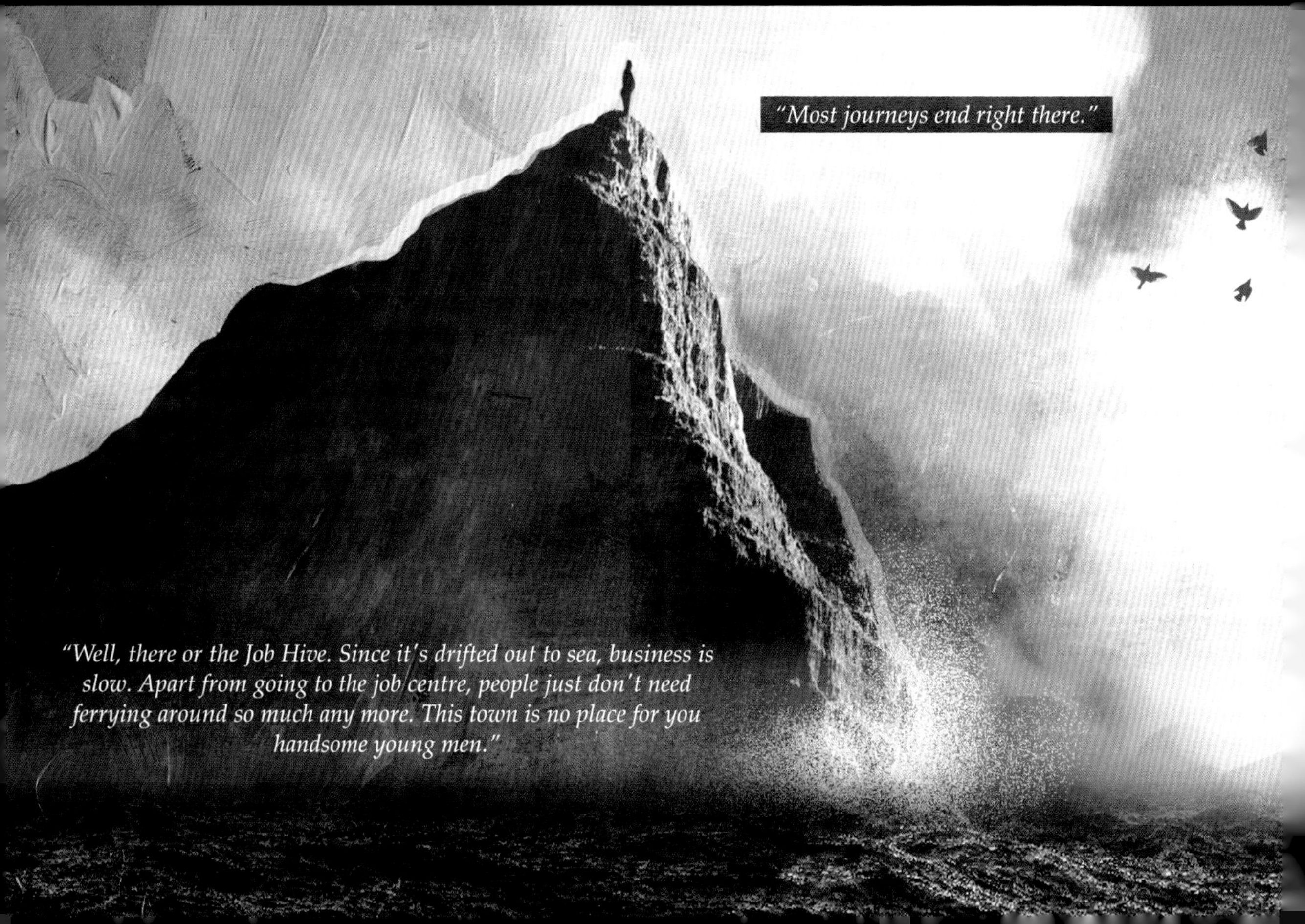
"Most journeys end right there."
"Well, there or the Job Hive. Since it's drifted out to sea, business is slow. Apart from going to the job centre, people just don't need ferrying around so much any more. This town is no place for you handsome young men."

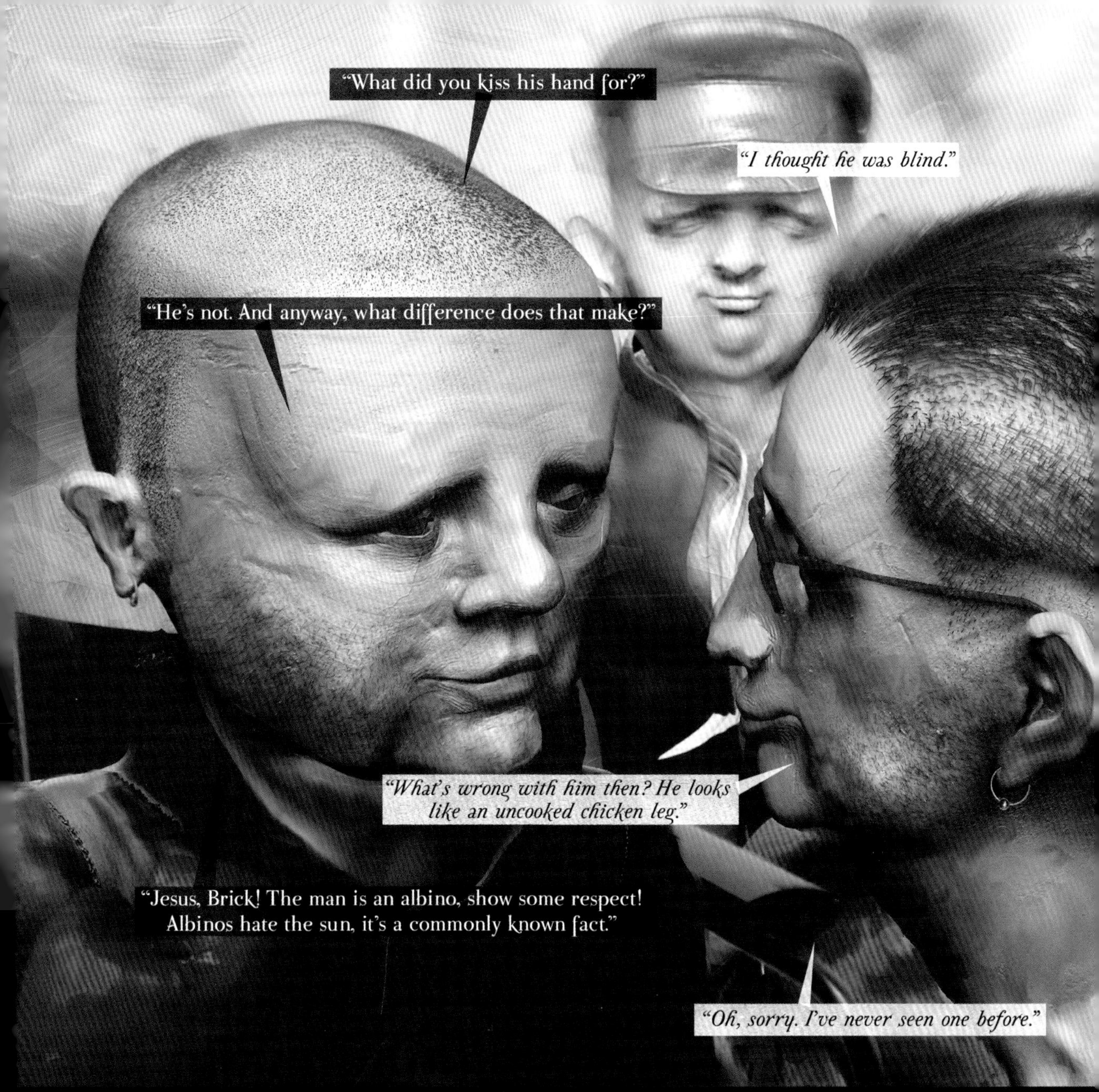
"What did you kiss his hand for?"
"I thought he was blind."
"He's not. And anyway, what difference does that make?"
"What's wrong with him then? He looks like an uncooked chicken leg."
"Jesus, Brick! The man is an albino, show some respect! Albinos hate the sun, it's a commonly known fact."
"Oh, sorry. I've never seen one before."

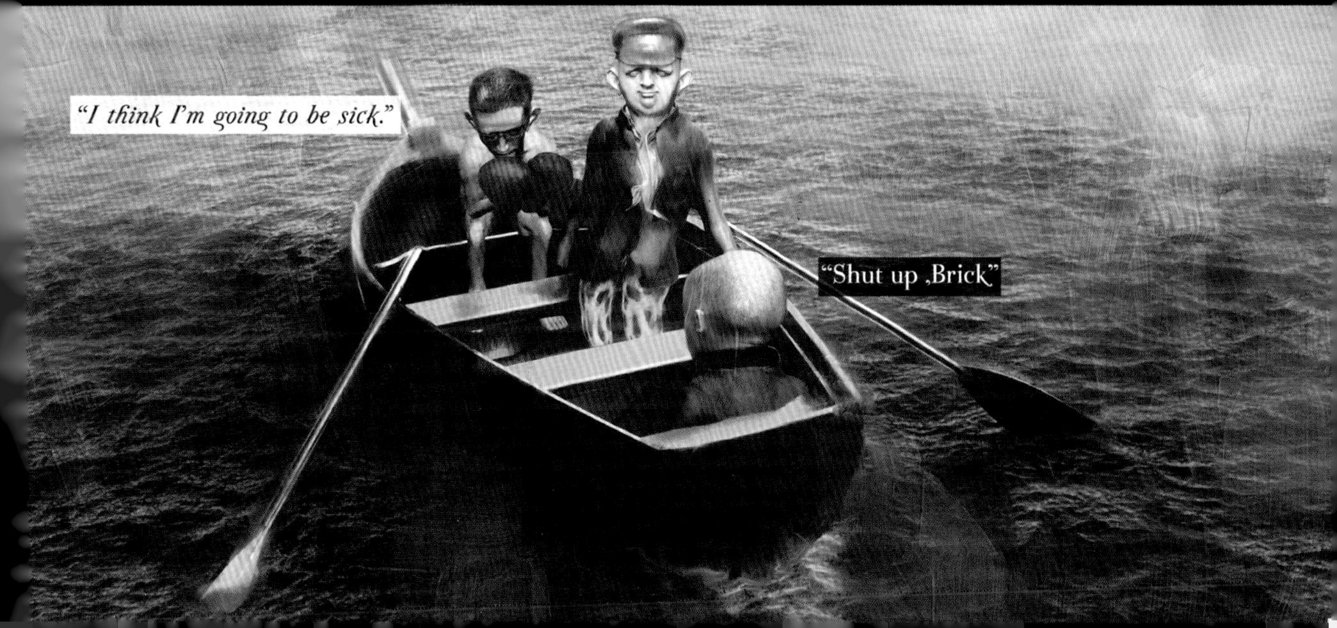
"I think I'm going to be sick."
"Shut up ,Brick."

The Job Hive in Lucia is perhaps the most unusual location in town, and the hardest to get to. Since I'm relegated to a wheelchair, me and Brick have always made sure our appointment times coincide. Brick assists me on the sometimes perilous journey across the sea to get there.

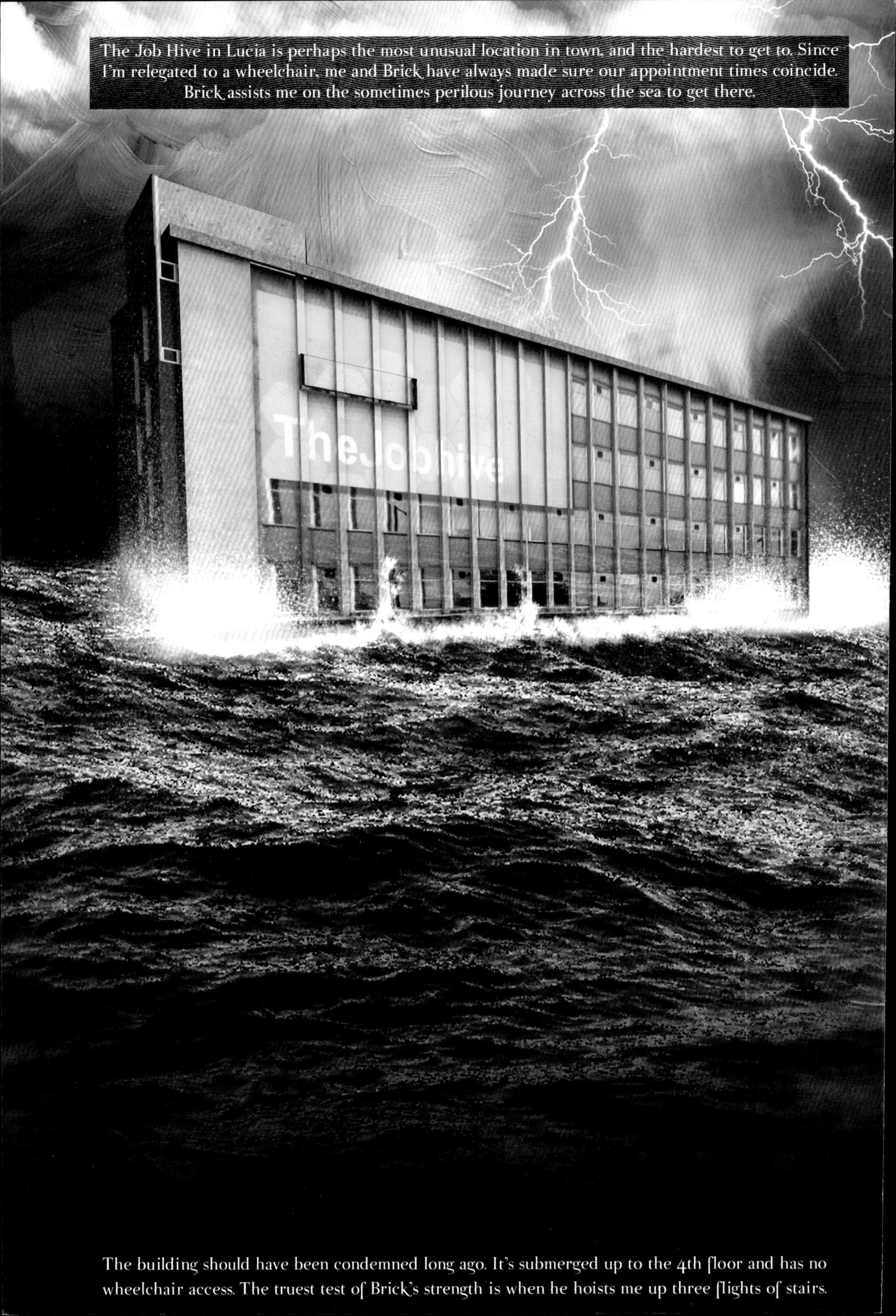
TheJobhive

The building should have been condemned long ago. It's submerged up to the 4th floor and has no wheelchair access. The truest test of Brick's strength is when he hoists me up three flights of stairs.

Ironic, really, that the only form of steady employment in Lucia is at the Job Hive. However, having said that, some of the employees just don't show up for work in the morning.

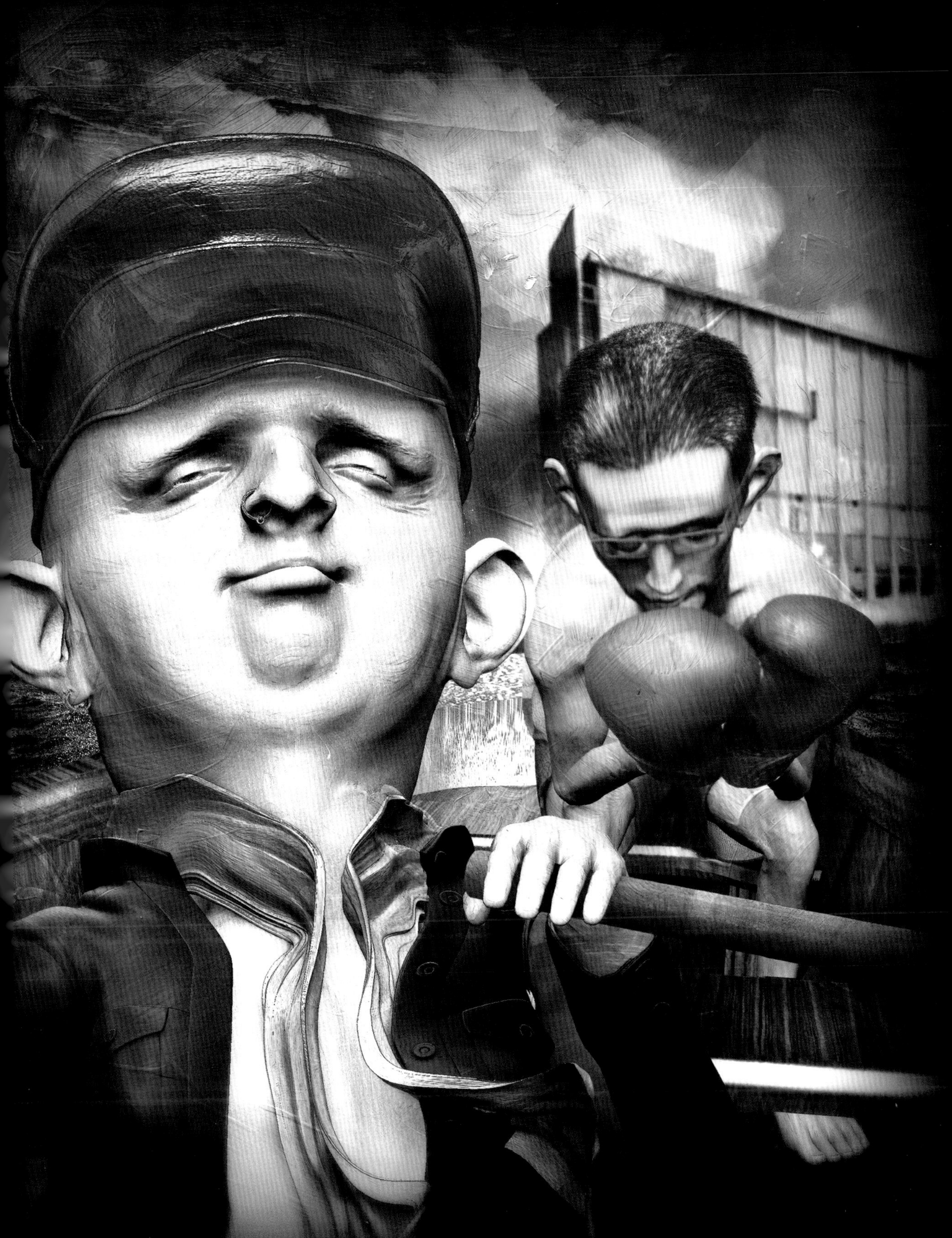

The sea is a dangerous place filled with all sorts of creatures and you need a decent guide. Davey came on good reputation and his age would suggest he has been doing something right. We haven't used his services before.

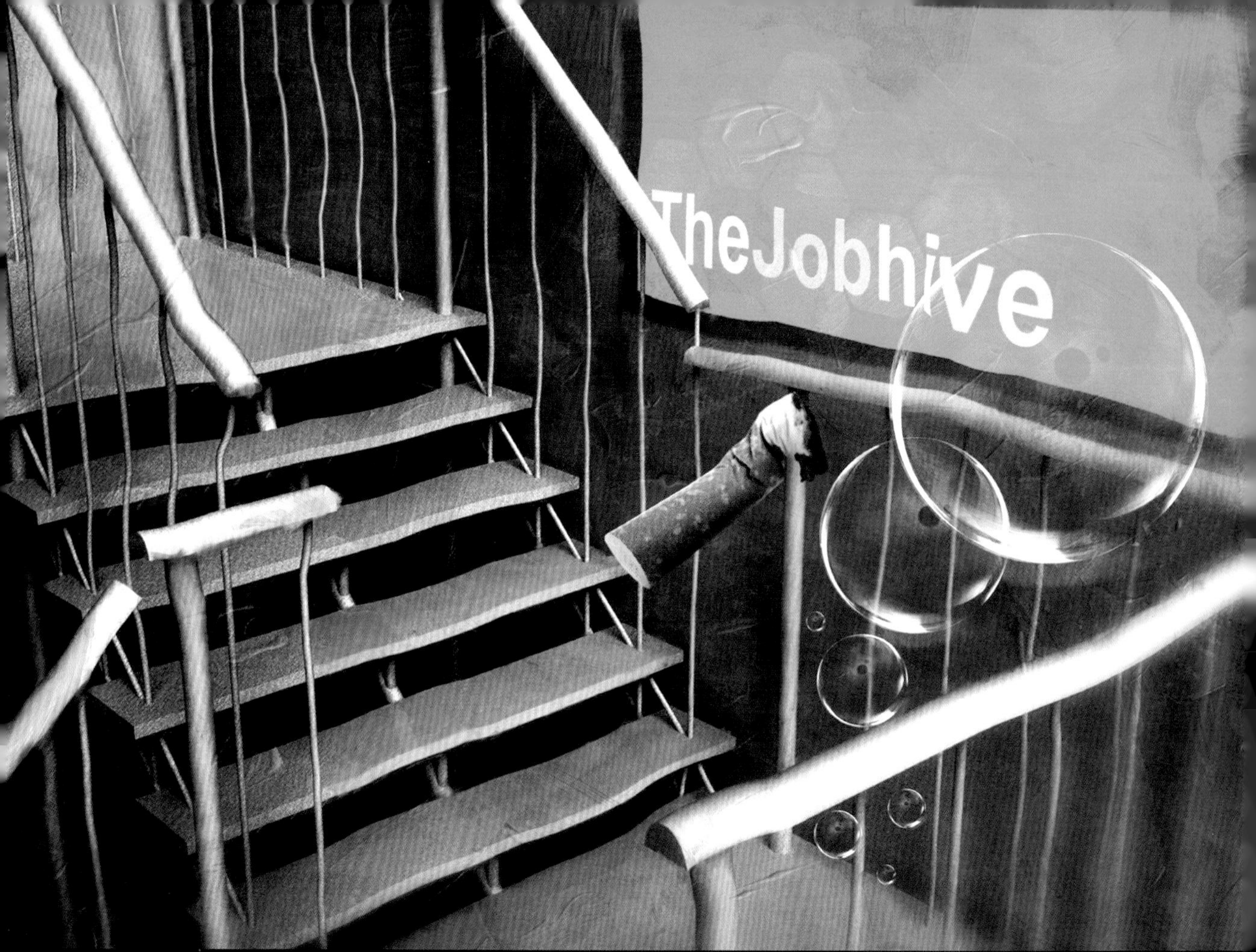
TheJobhive

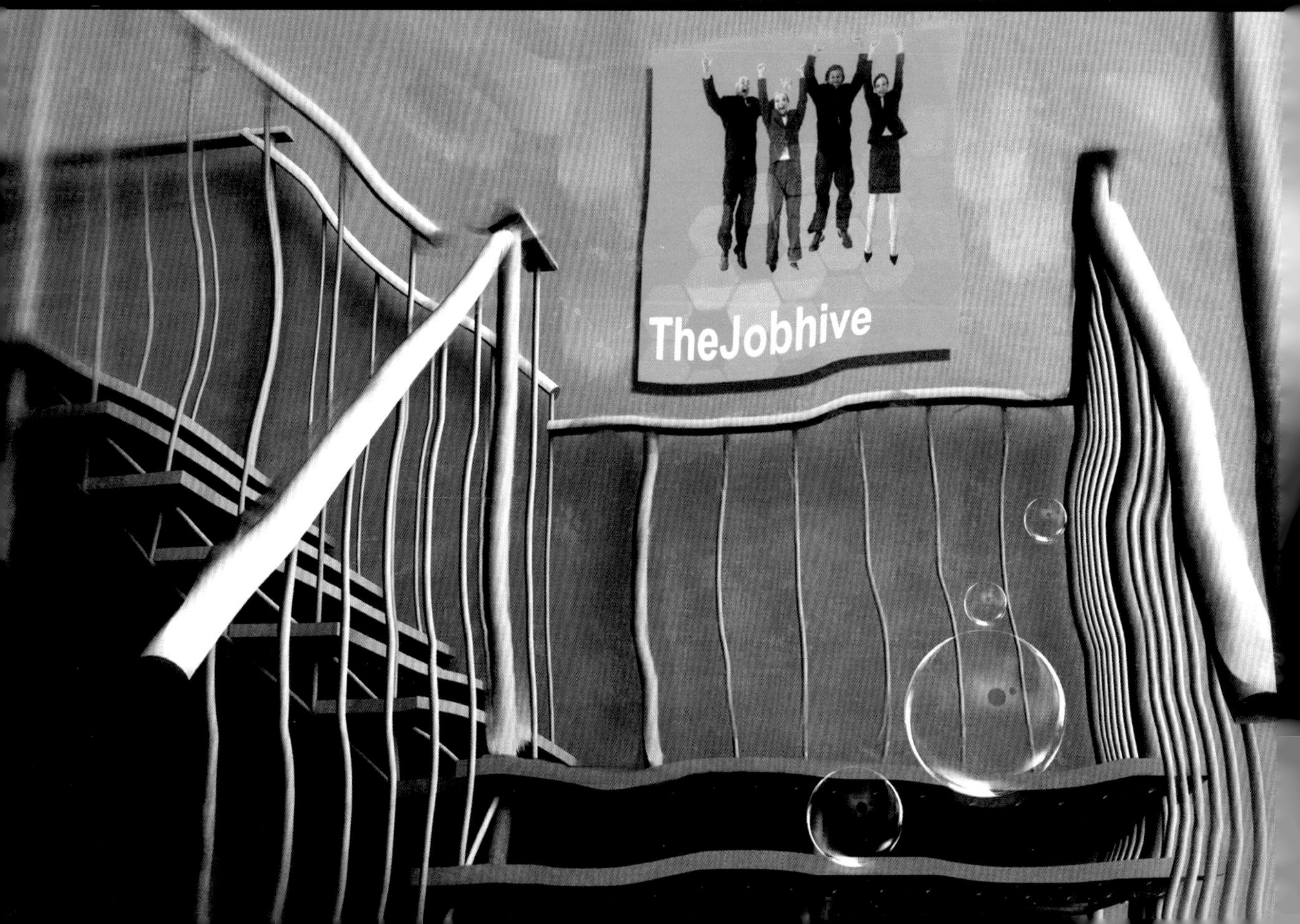
TheJobhive

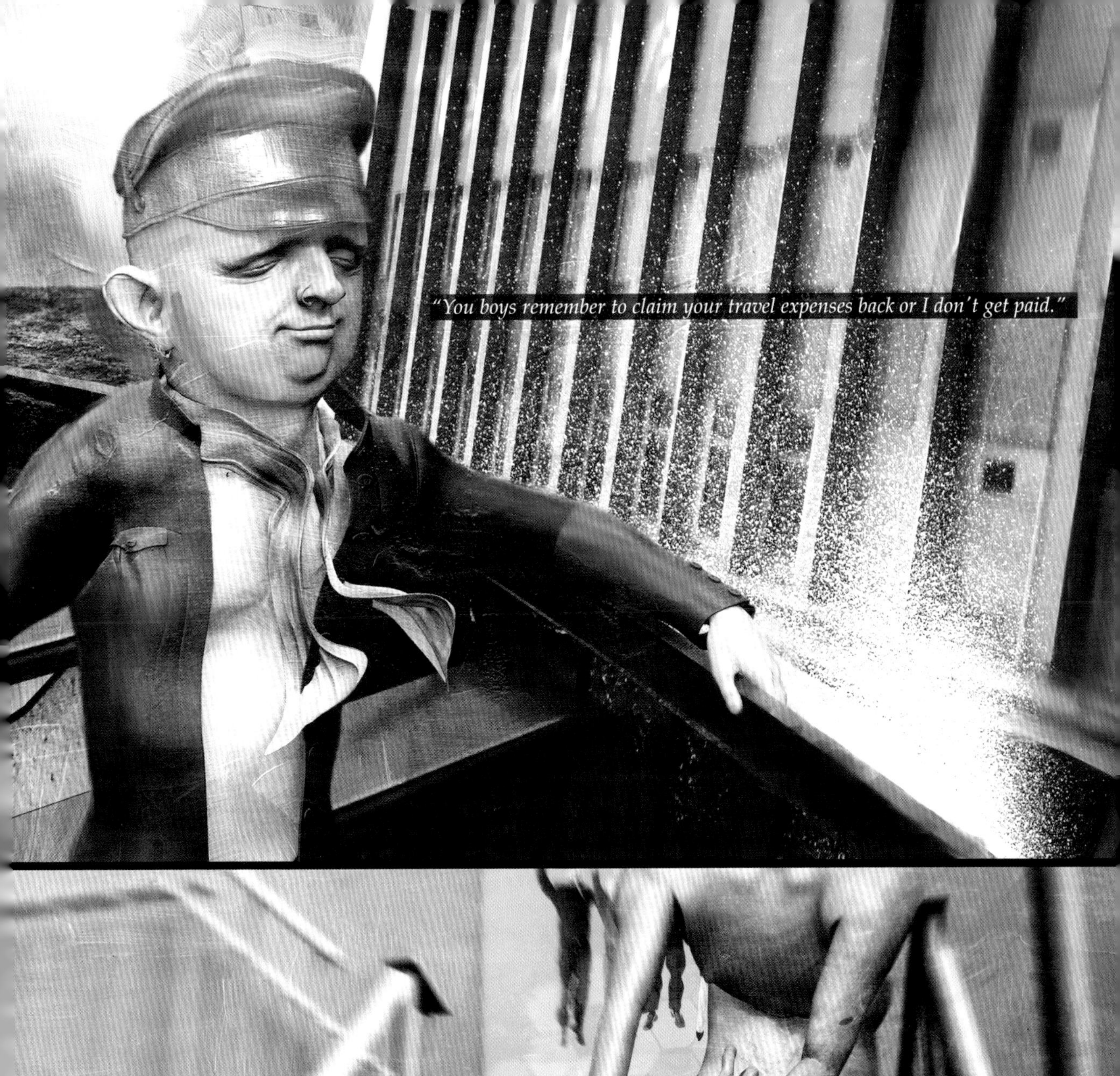
"You boys remember to claim your travel expenses back or I don't get paid."

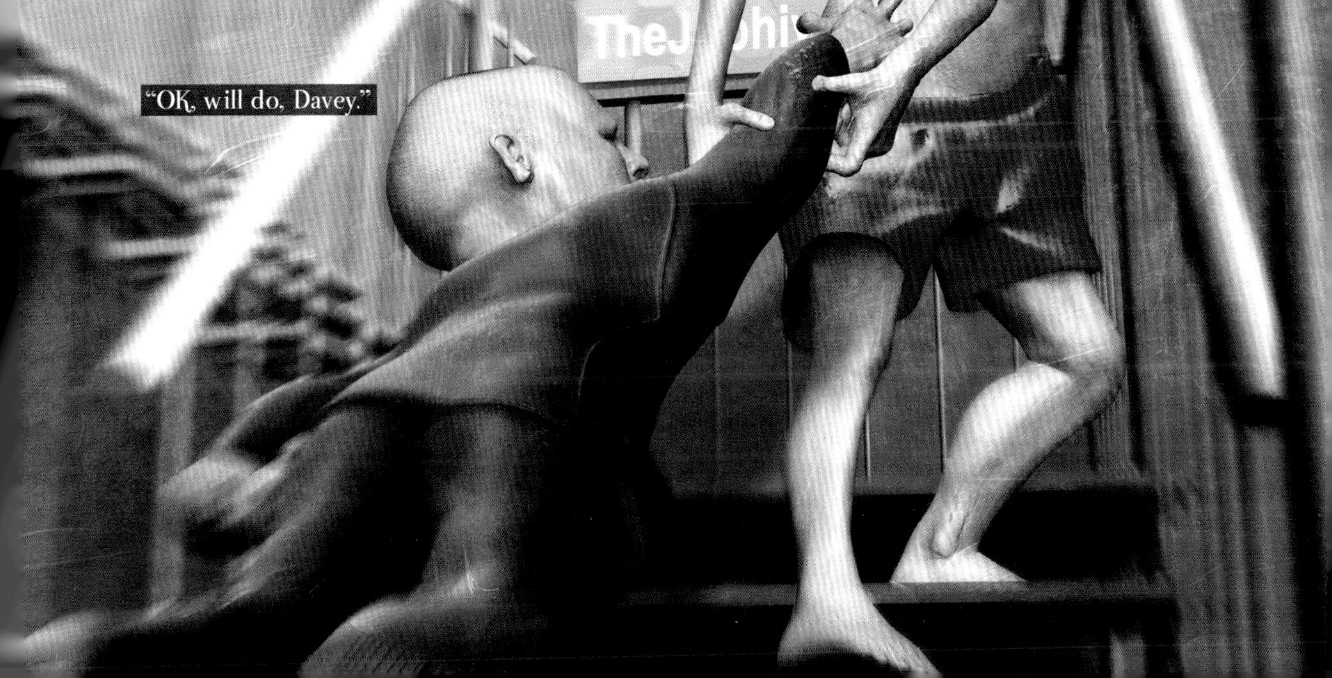
"OK, will do, Davey."

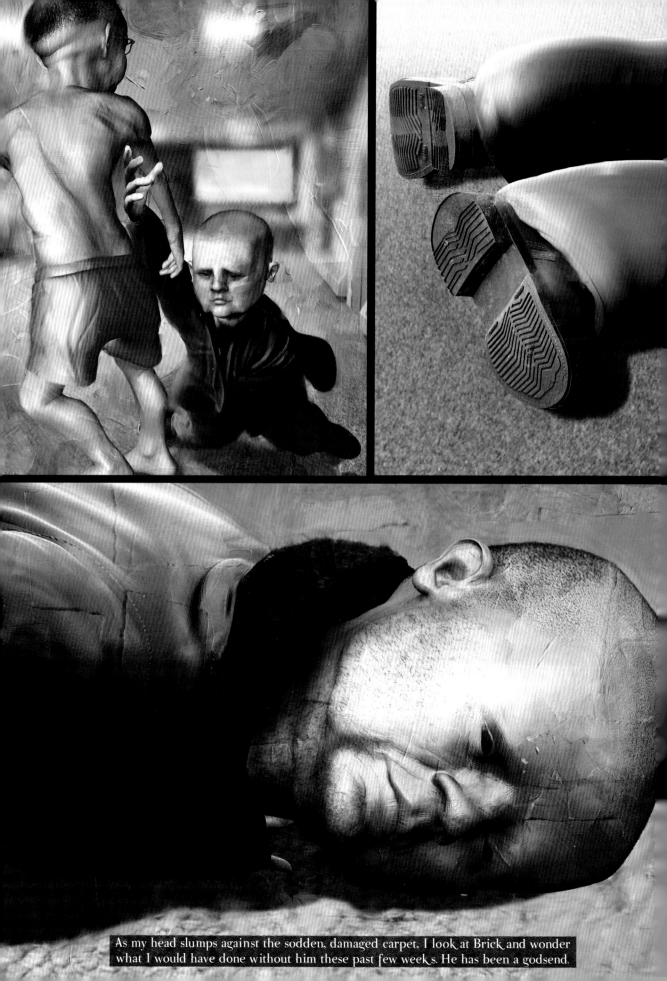

As my head slumps against the sodden, damaged carpet, I look at Brick and wonder what I would have done without him these past few weeks. He has been a godsend.

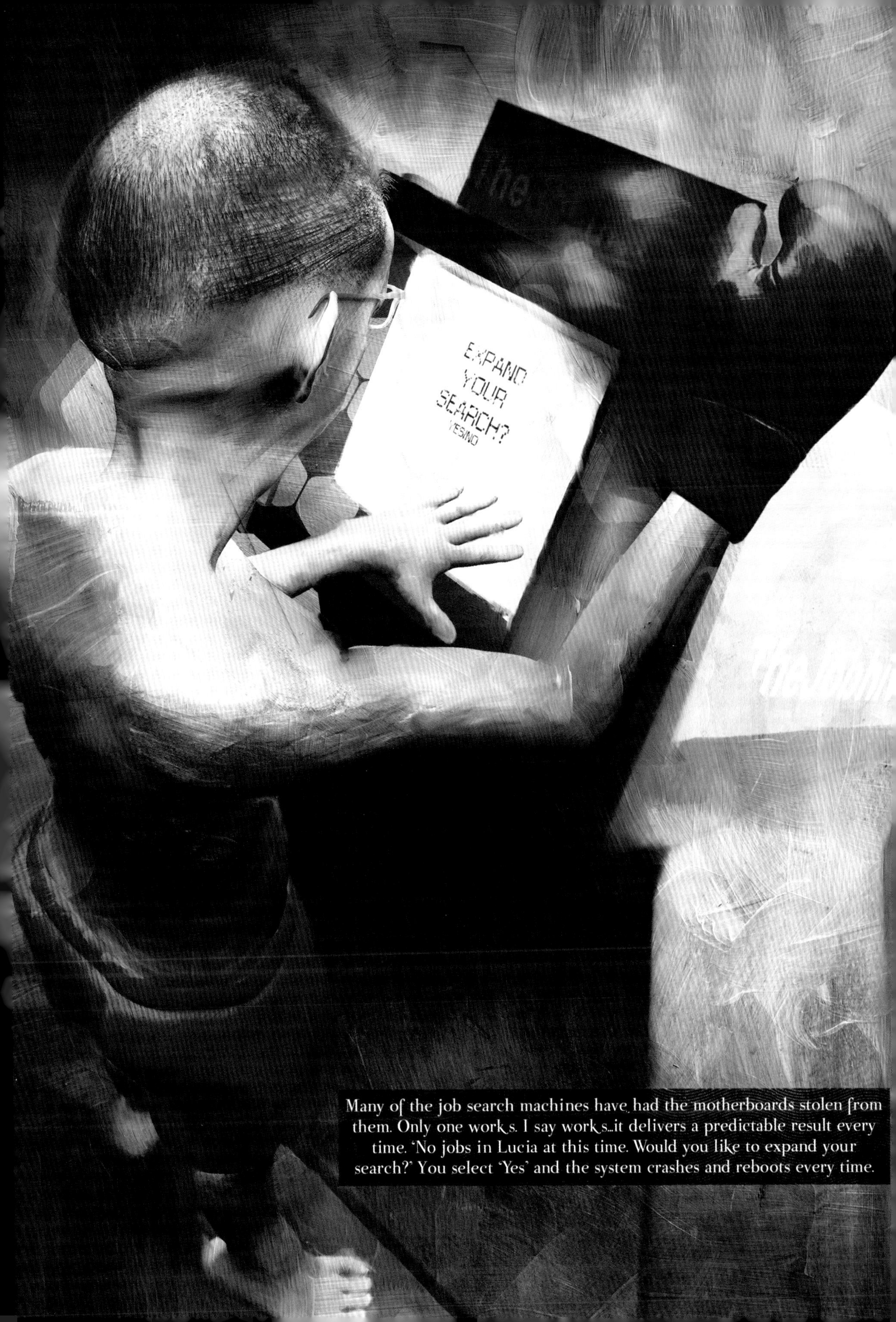
EXPAND YOUR SEARCH?
YES/NO
Many of the job search machines have had the motherboards stolen from them. Only one works. I say works...it delivers a predictable result every time. 'No jobs in Lucia at this time. Would you like to expand your search?' You select 'Yes' and the system crashes and reboots every time.

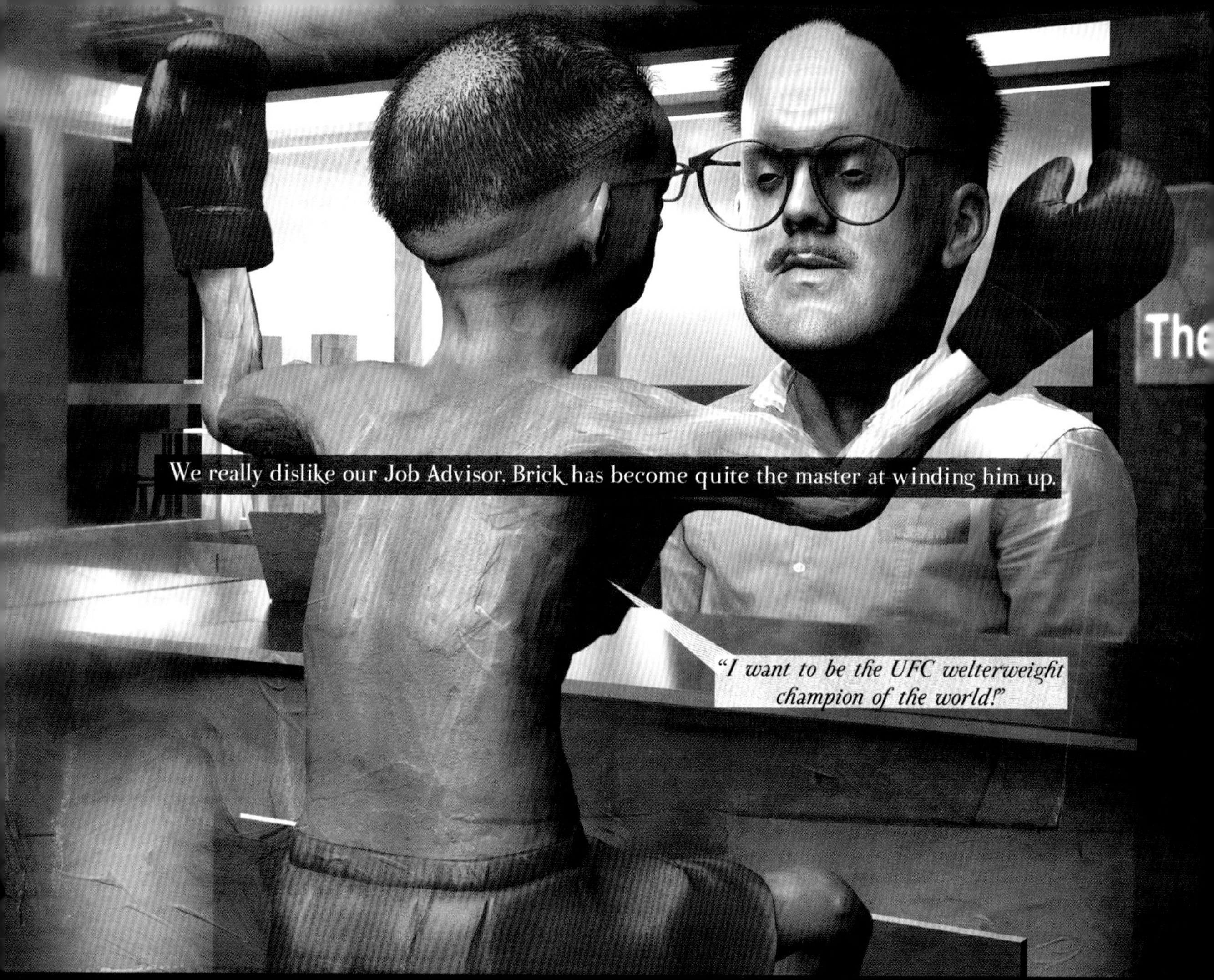
We really dislike our Job Advisor. Brick has become quite the master at winding him up.
"I want to be the UFC welterweight champion of the world!"

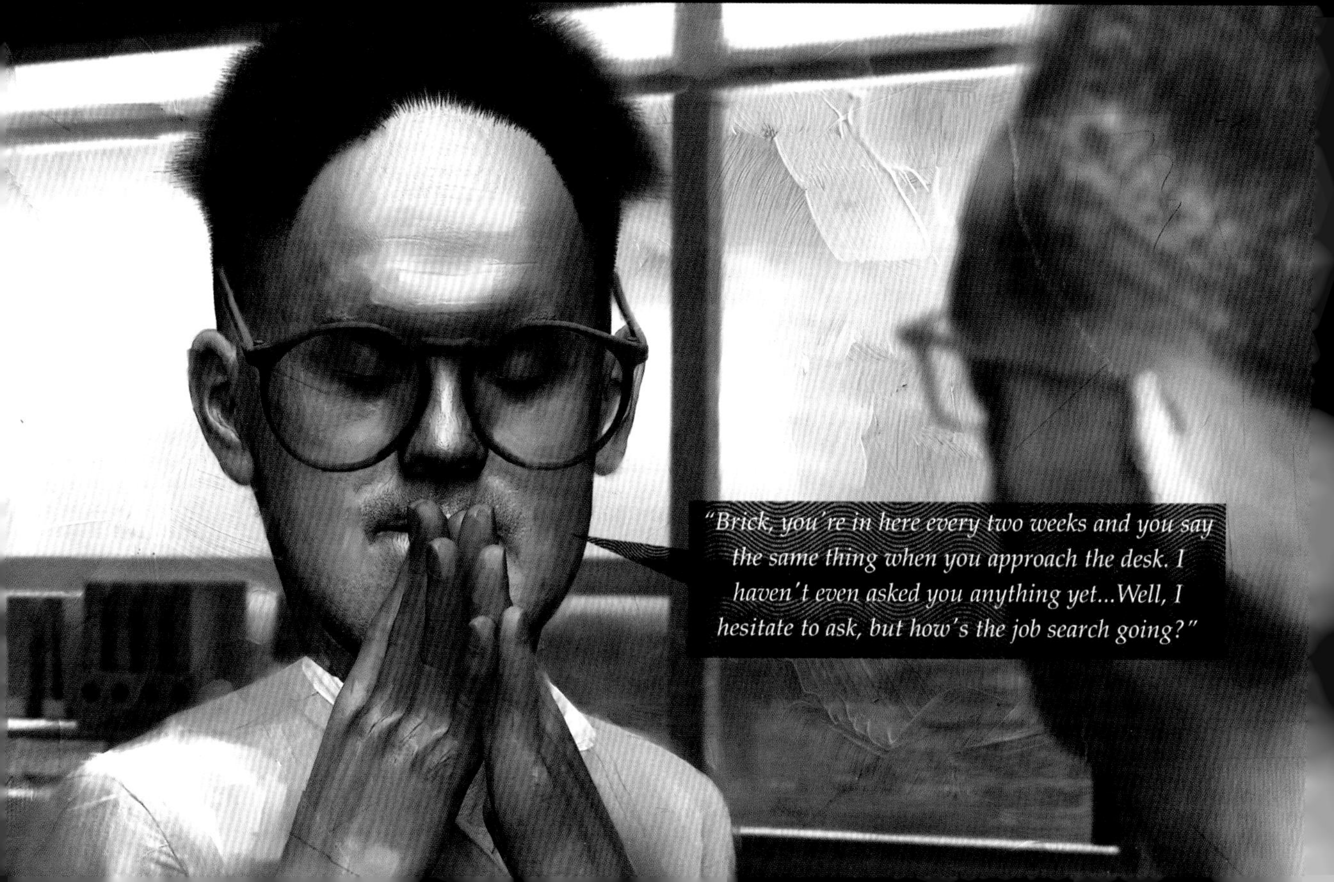
"Brick, you're in here every two weeks and you say the same thing when you approach the desk. I haven't even asked you anything yet...Well, I hesitate to ask, but how's the job search going?"

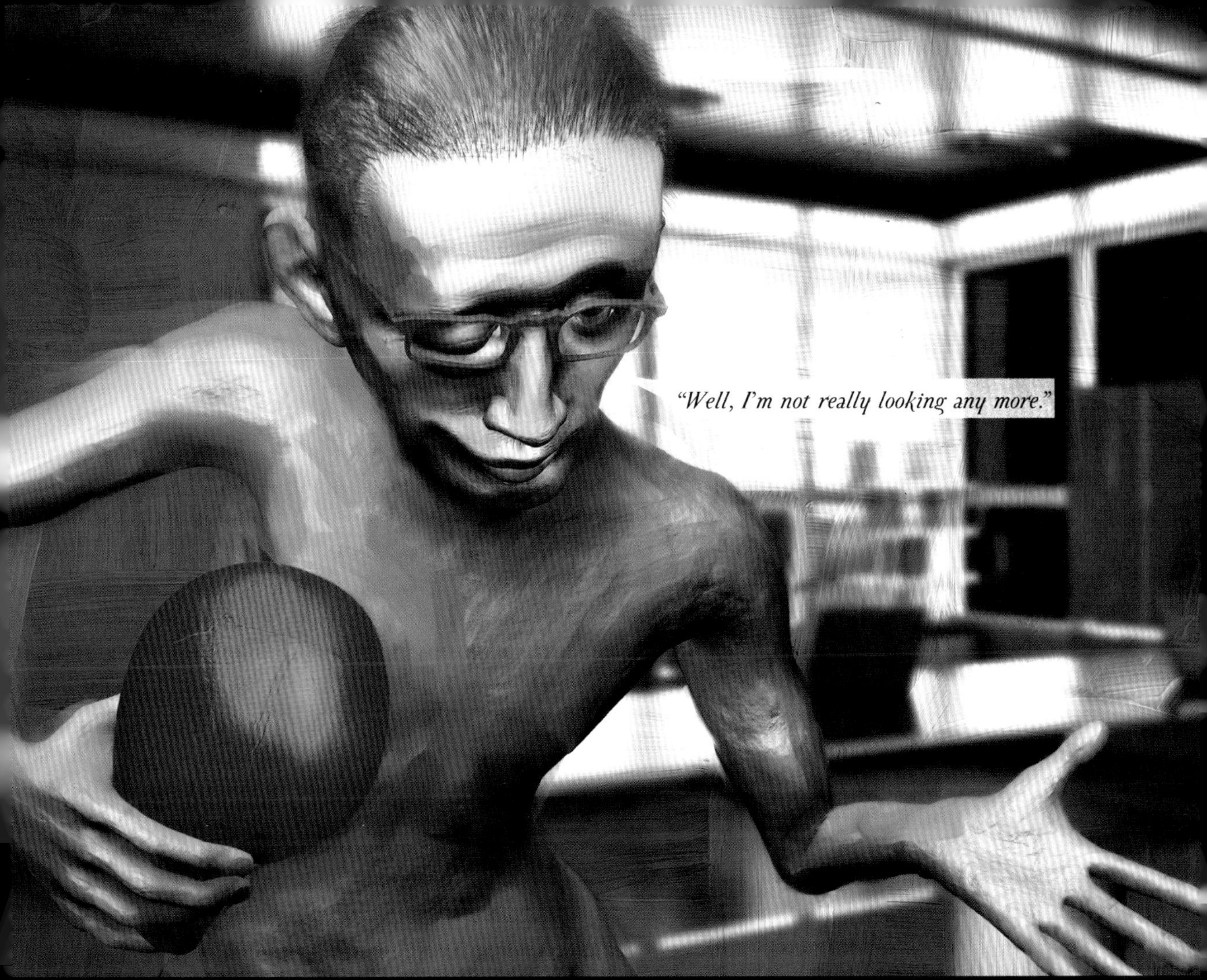
"Well, I'm not really looking any more."

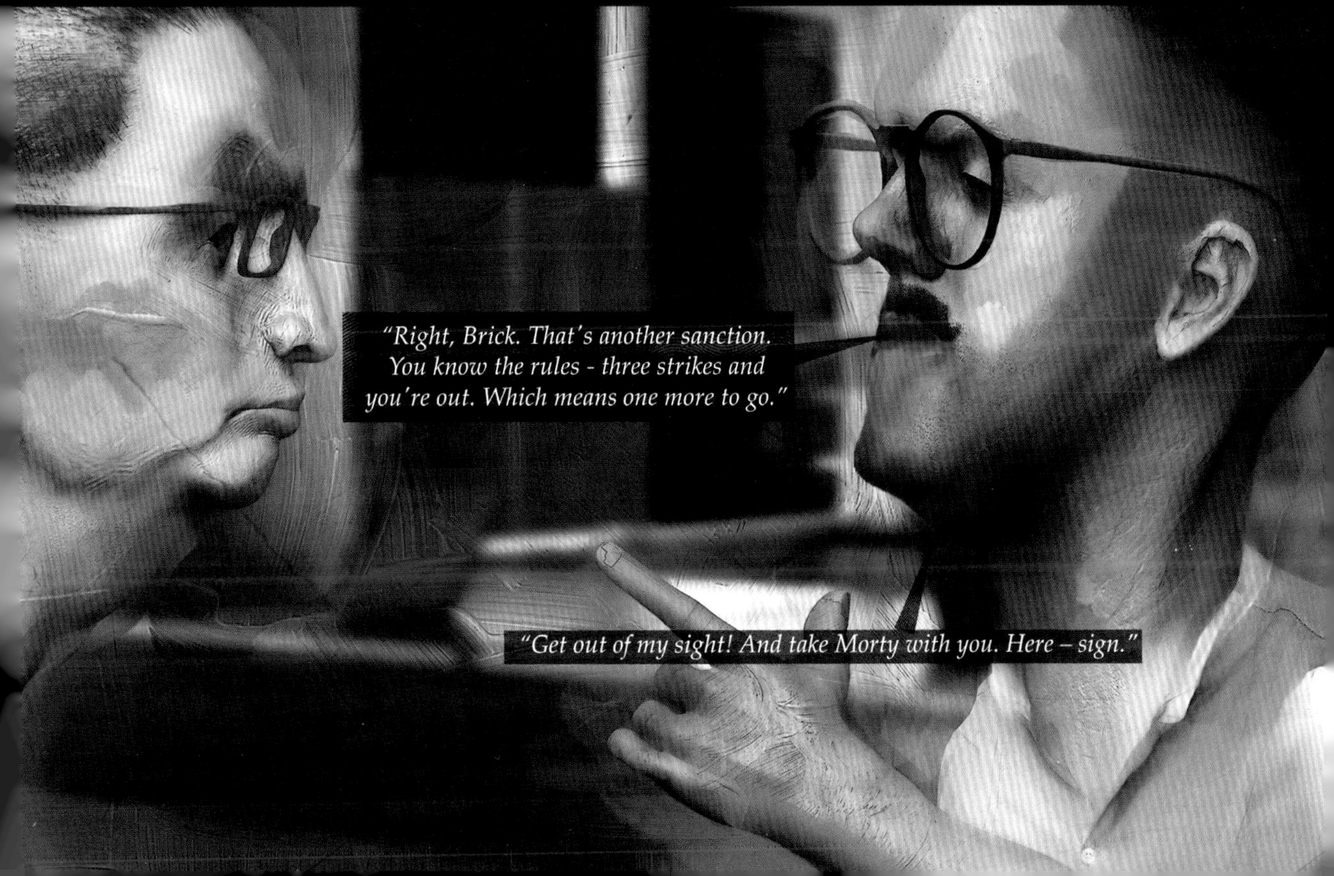
"Right, Brick. That's another sanction.
You know the rules - three strikes and
you're out. Which means one more to go."
"Get out of my sight! And take Morty with you. Here – sign."

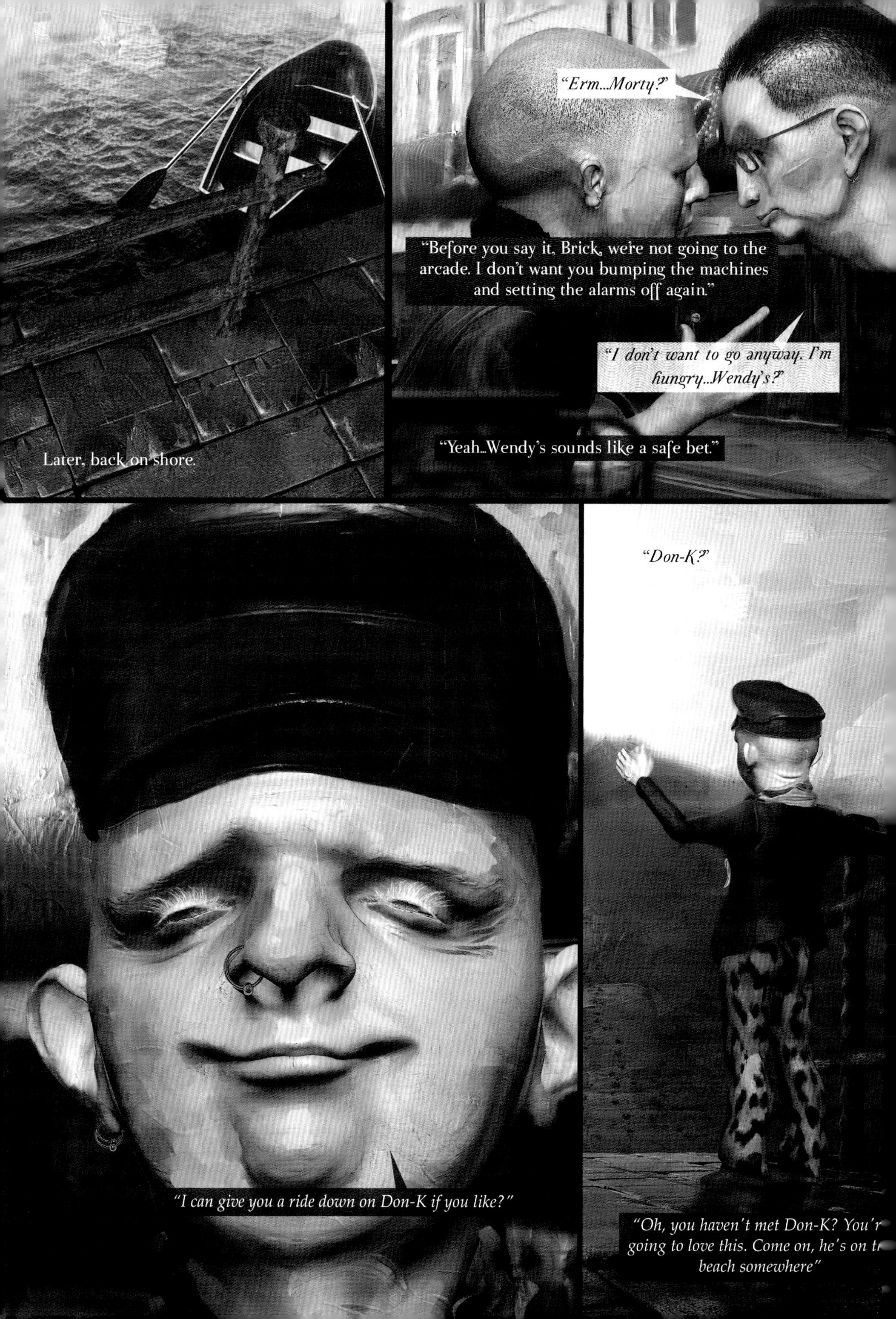
Later, back on shore.
"Erm...Morty?"
"Before you say it, Brick, we're not going to the arcade. I don't want you bumping the machines and setting the alarms off again."
"I don't want to go anyway. I'm hungry...Wendy's?"
"Yeah...Wendy's sounds like a safe bet."
"I can give you a ride down on Don-K if you like?"
"Don-K?"
"Oh, you haven't met Don-K? You'r going to love this. Come on, he's on t beach somewhere"

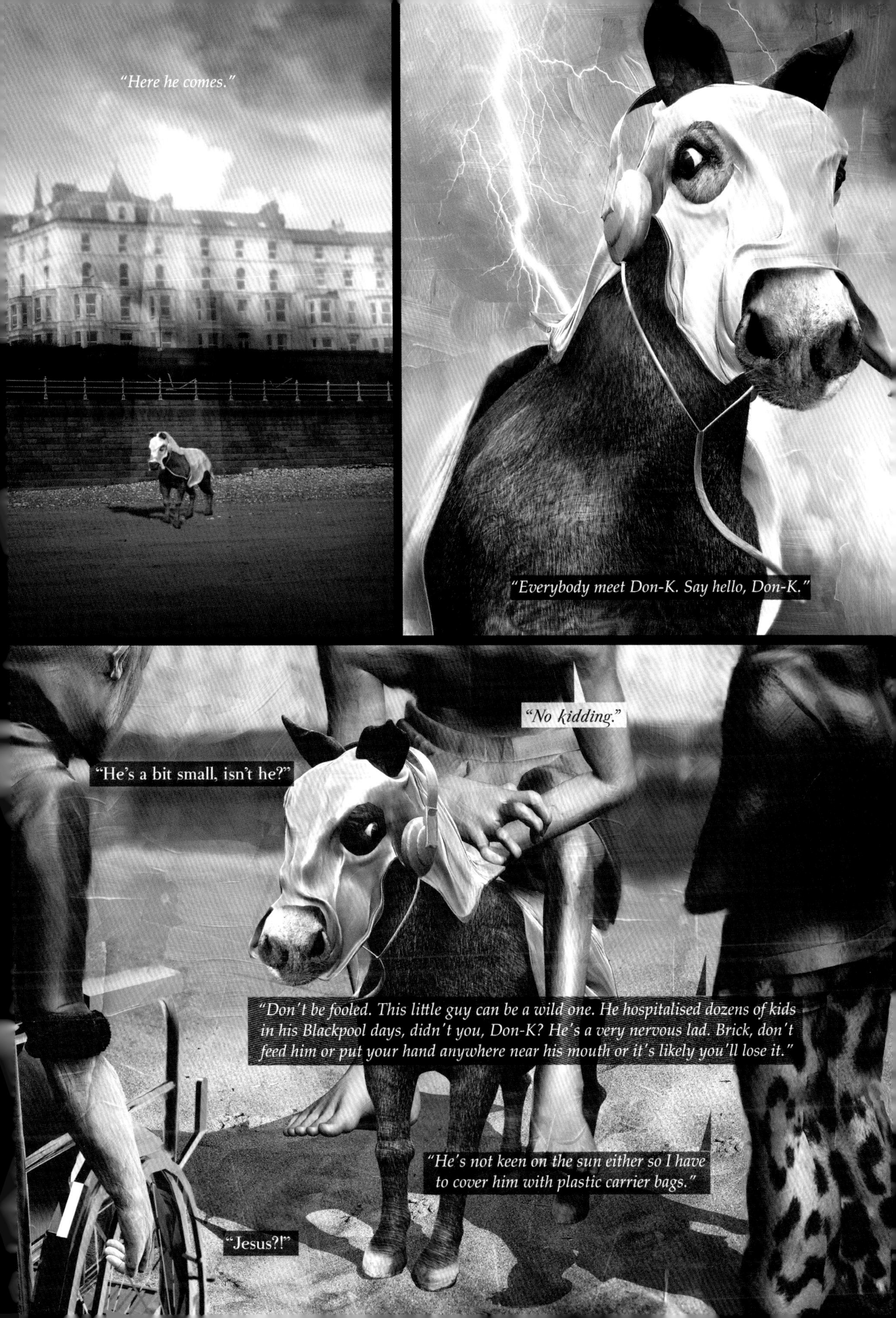
"Here he comes."
"Everybody meet Don-K. Say hello, Don-K."
"He's a bit small, isn't he?"
"No kidding."
"Don't be fooled. This little guy can be a wild one. He hospitalised dozens of kids in his Blackpool days, didn't you, Don-K? He's a very nervous lad. Brick, don't feed him or put your hand anywhere near his mouth or it's likely you'll lose it."
"He's not keen on the sun either so I have to cover him with plastic carrier bags."
"Jesus?!"

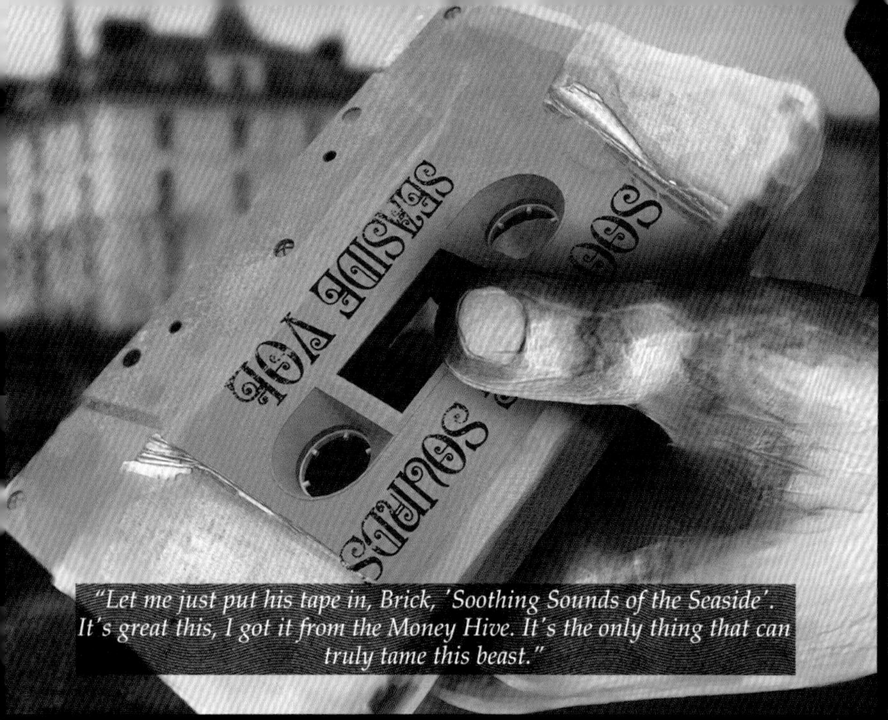
"Let me just put his tape in, Brick, 'Soothing Sounds of the Seaside'. It's great this, I got it from the Money Hive. It's the only thing that can truly tame this beast."

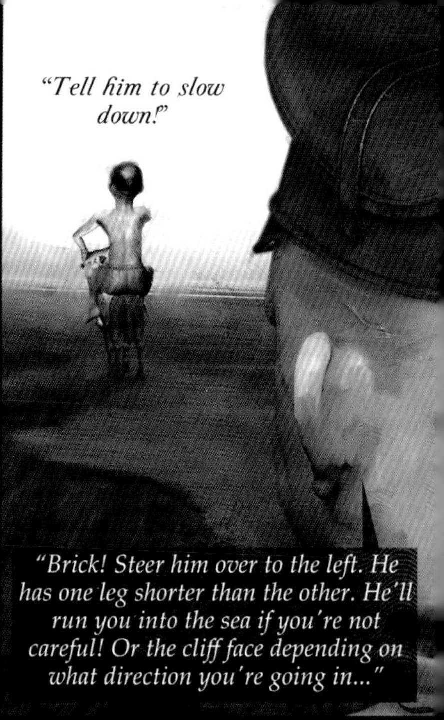
"Tell him to slow down!"
"Brick! Steer him over to the left. He has one leg shorter than the other. He'll run you into the sea if you're not careful! Or the cliff face depending on what direction you're going in..."

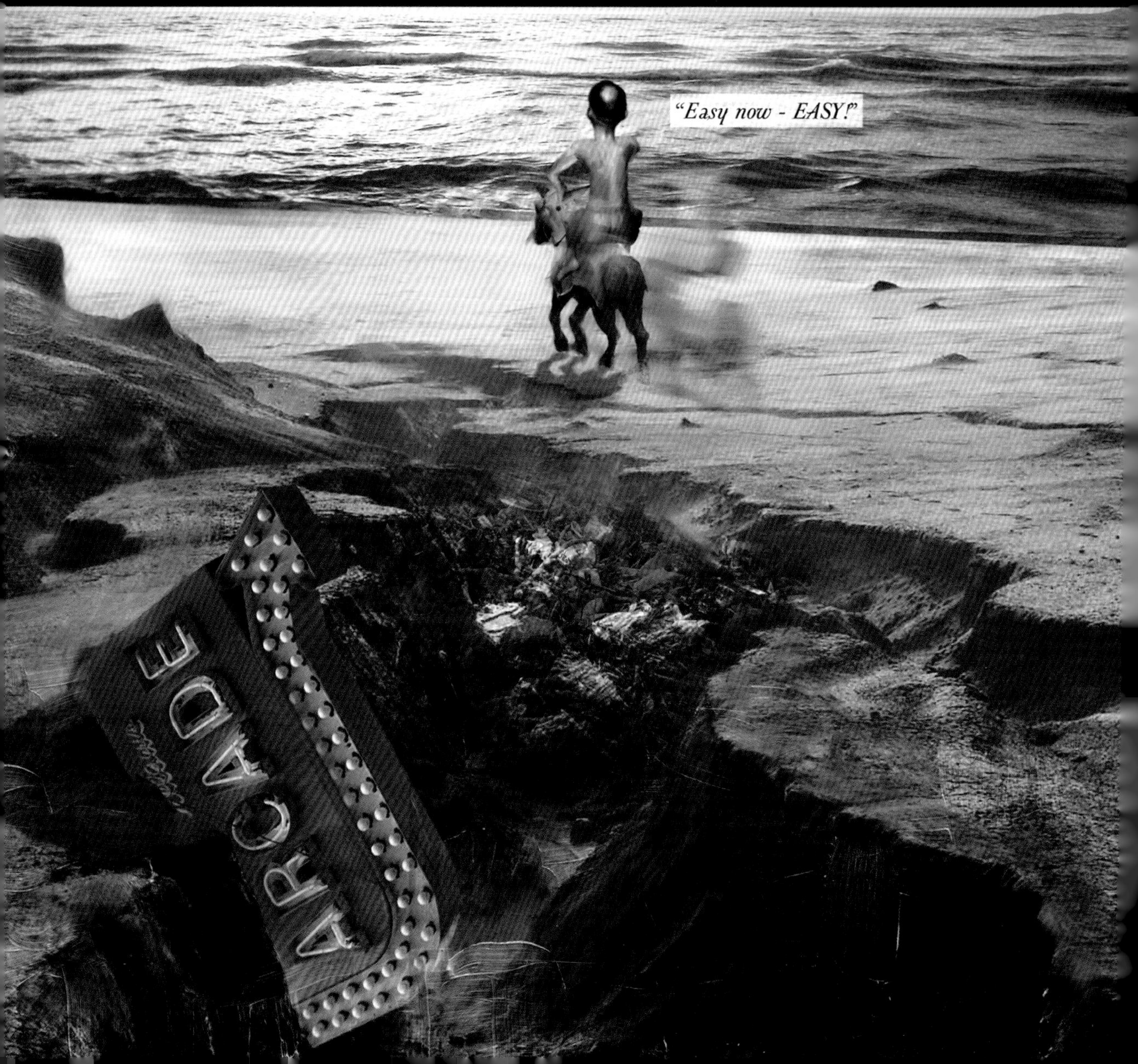
"Easy now - EASY!"
ARCADE

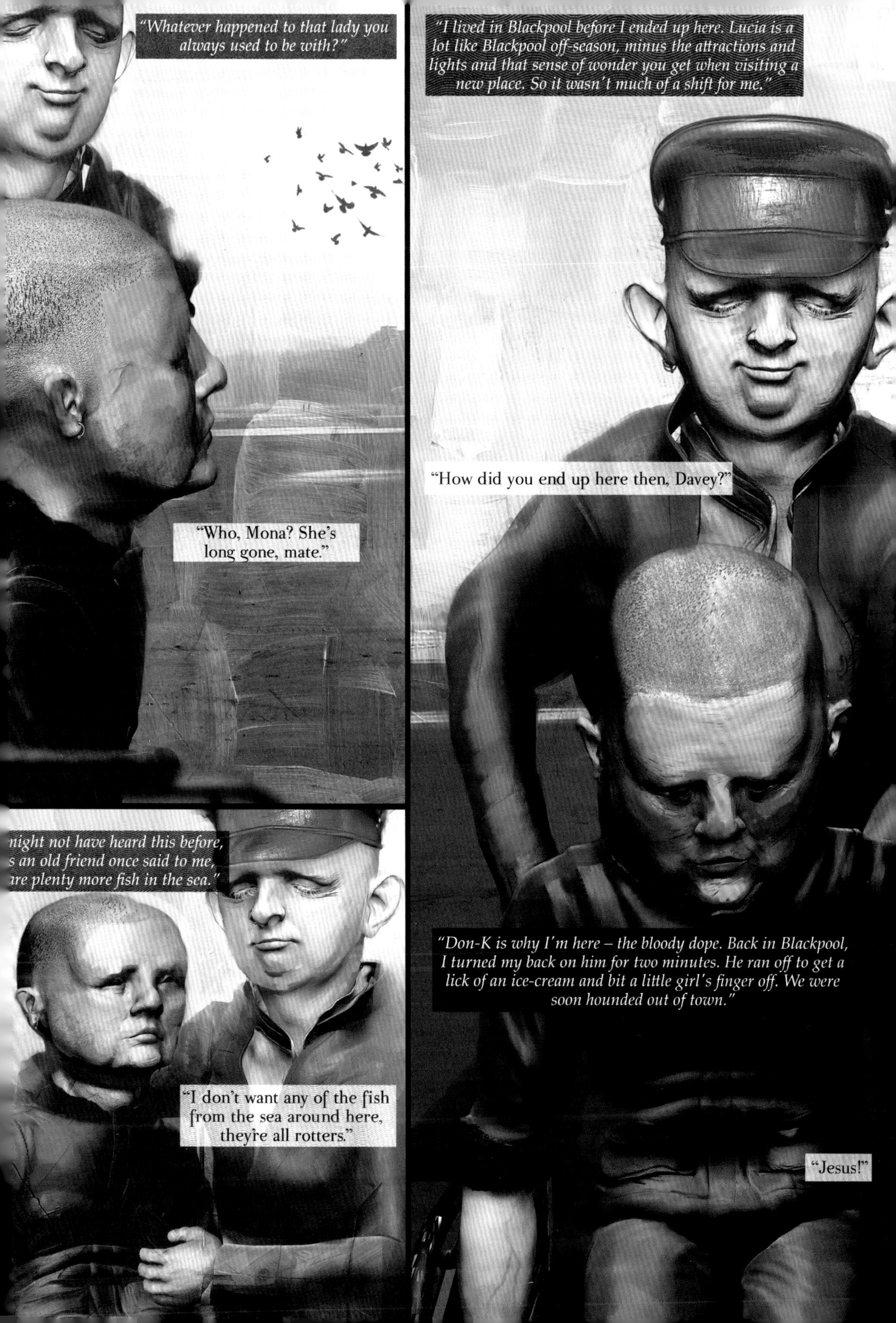
"Whatever happened to that lady you always used to be with?"
"Who, Mona? She's long gone, mate."
night not have heard this before, s an old friend once said to me, are plenty more fish in the sea."
"I don't want any of the fish from the sea around here, they're all rotters."
"I lived in Blackpool before I ended up here. Lucia is a lot like Blackpool off-season, minus the attractions and lights and that sense of wonder you get when visiting a new place. So it wasn't much of a shift for me."
"How did you end up here then, Davey?"
"Don-K is why I'm here – the bloody dope. Back in Blackpool, I turned my back on him for two minutes. He ran off to get a lick of an ice-cream and bit a little girl's finger off. We were soon hounded out of town."
"Jesus!"

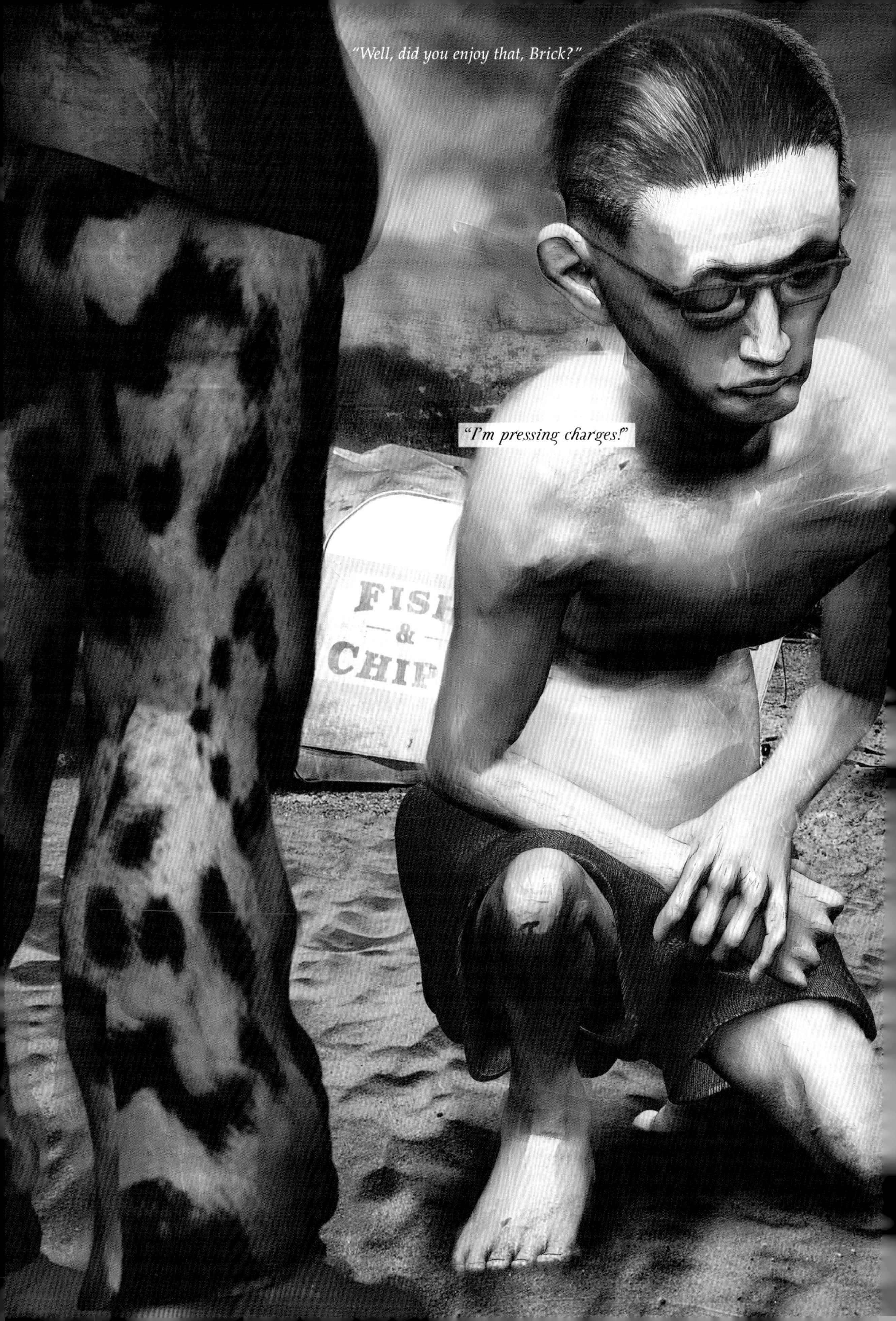
"Well, did you enjoy that, Brick?"
"I'm pressing charges!"
FISH
&
CHIP

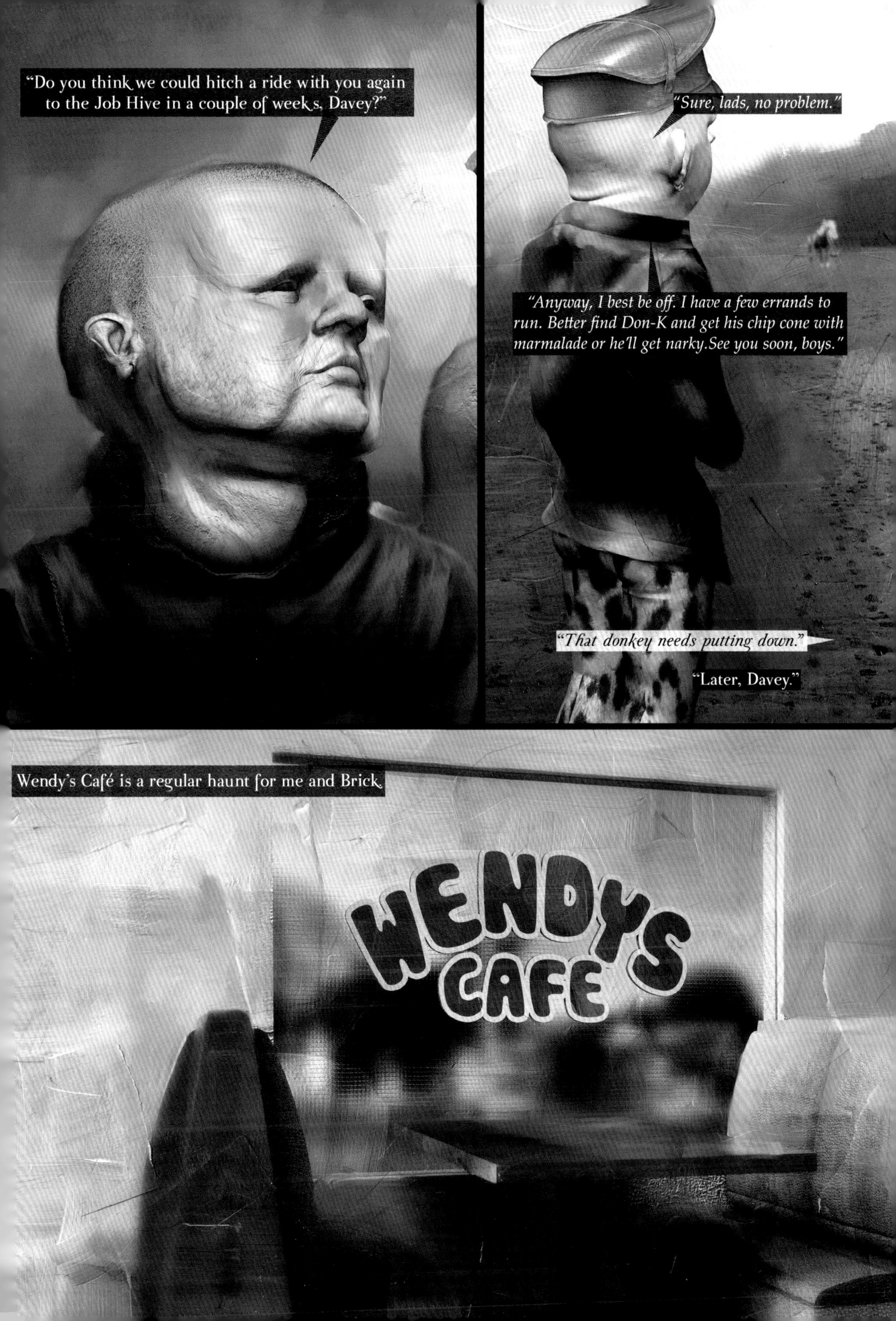
"Do you think we could hitch a ride with you again to the Job Hive in a couple of weeks, Davey?"
"Sure, lads, no problem."
"Anyway, I best be off. I have a few errands to run. Better find Don-K and get his chip cone with marmalade or he'll get narky. See you soon, boys."
"That donkey needs putting down."
"Later, Davey."
Wendy's Café is a regular haunt for me and Brick.
WENDYS CAFE

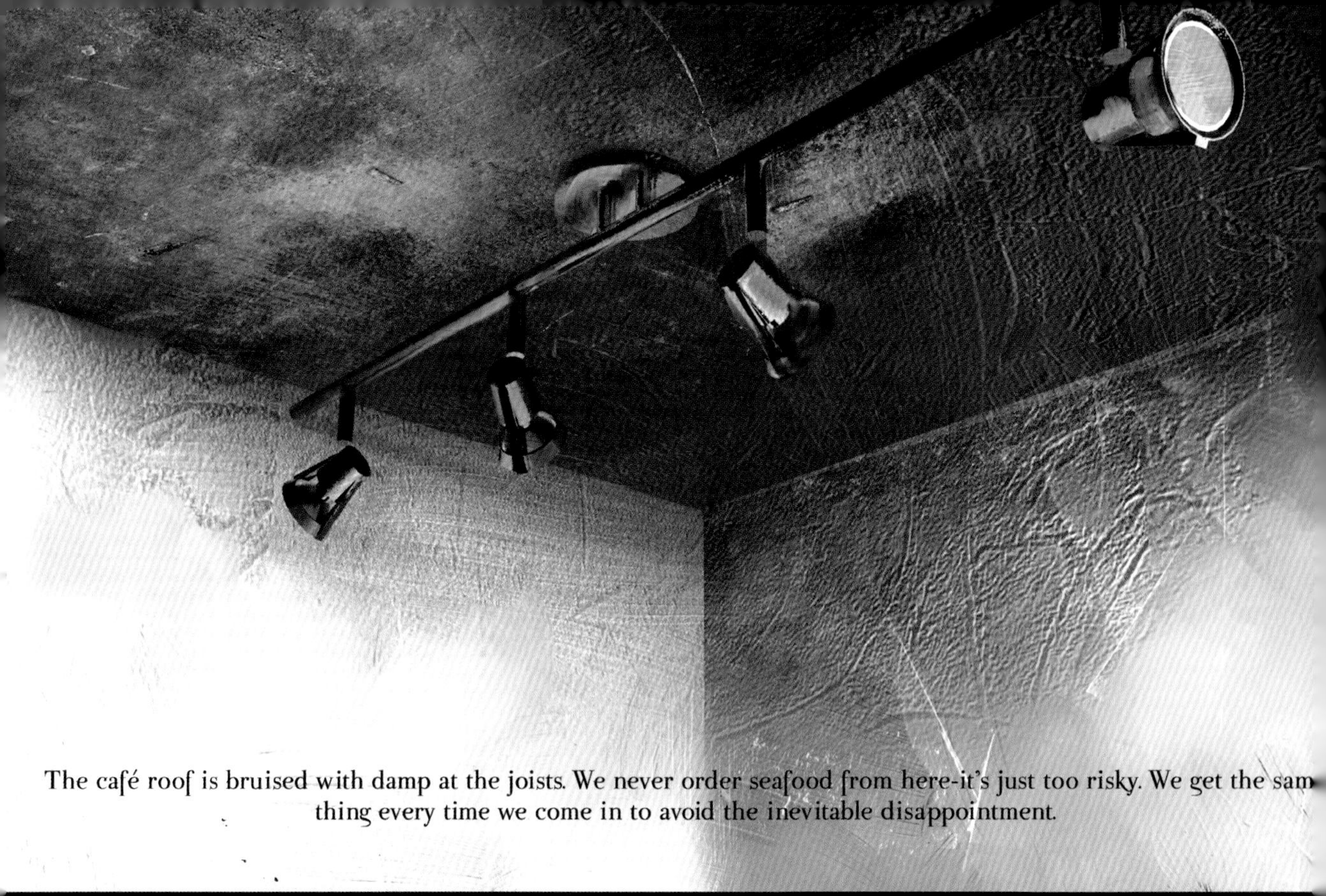

The café roof is bruised with damp at the joists. We never order seafood from here-it's just too risky. We get the sam thing every time we come in to avoid the inevitable disappointment.

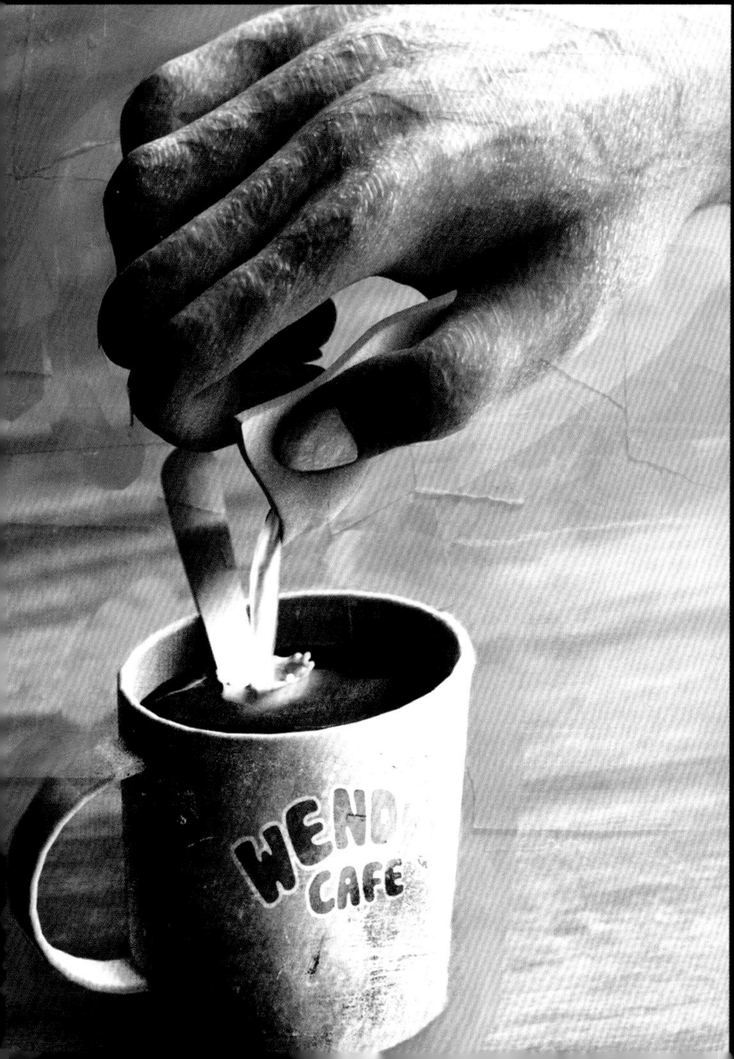
WEND
CAFE

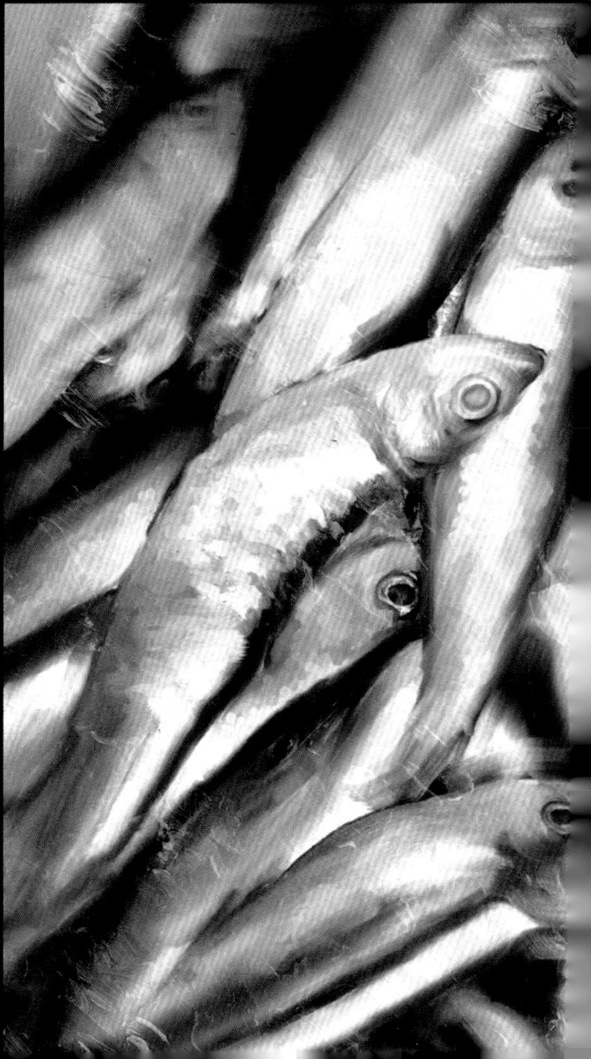

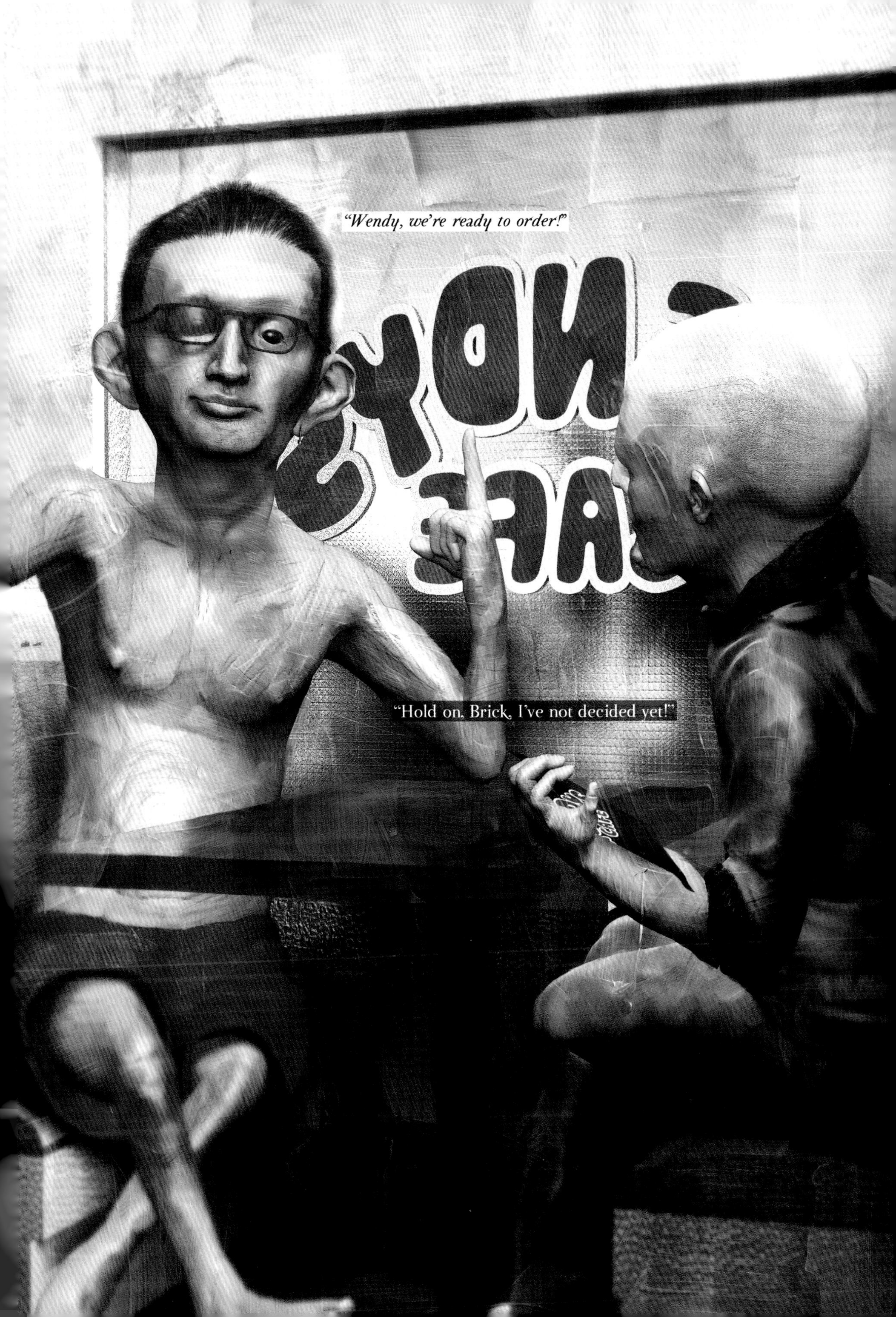
"Wendy, we're ready to order!"
"Hold on, Brick, I've not decided yet!"

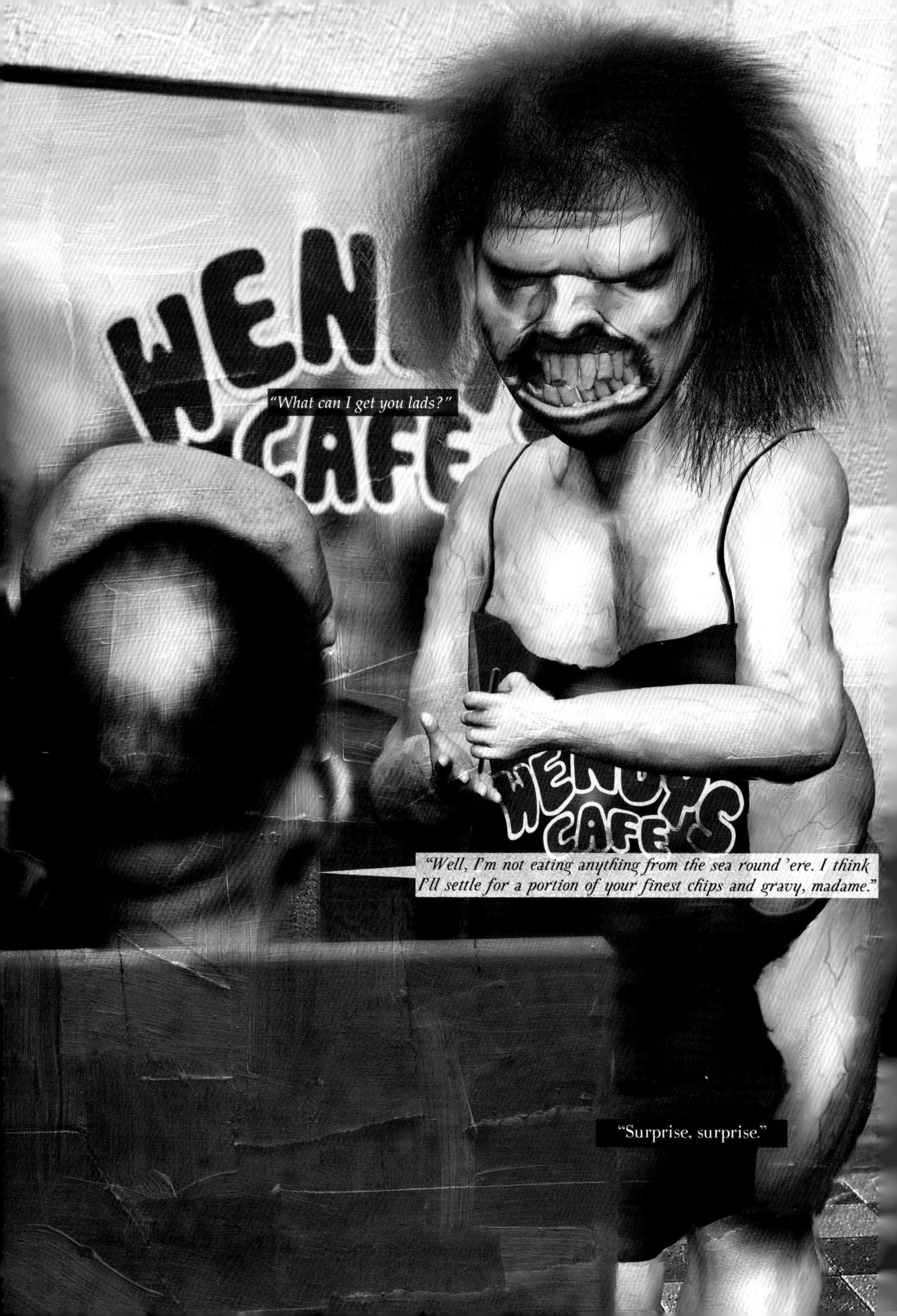
WENDY'S CAFE
"What can I get you lads?"
WENDY'S CAFE
"Well, I'm not eating anything from the sea round 'ere. I think I'll settle for a portion of your finest chips and gravy, madame."
"Surprise, surprise."

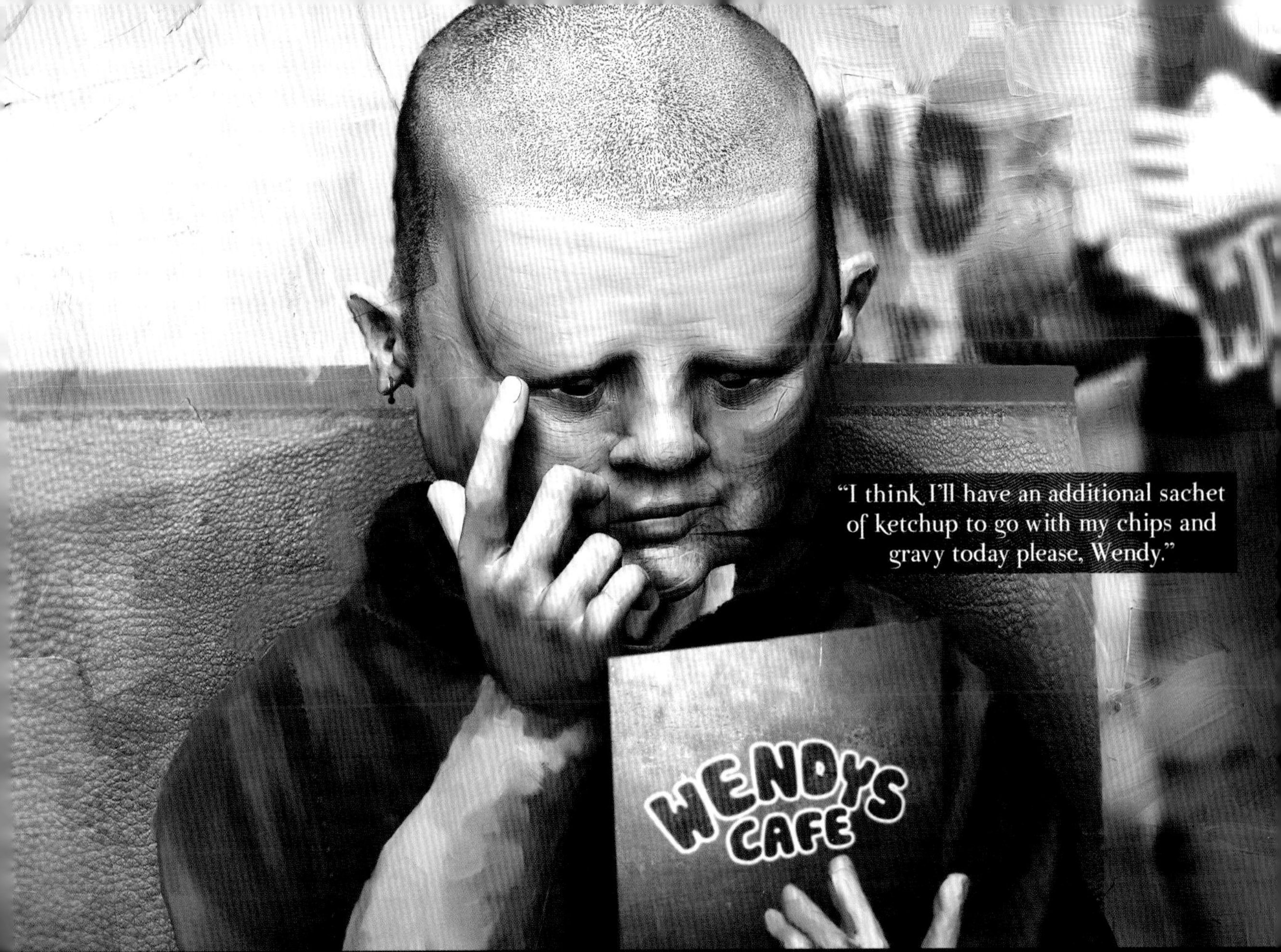

NO
WENDYS CAFE
"I think I'll have an additional sachet of ketchup to go with my chips and gravy today please, Wendy."

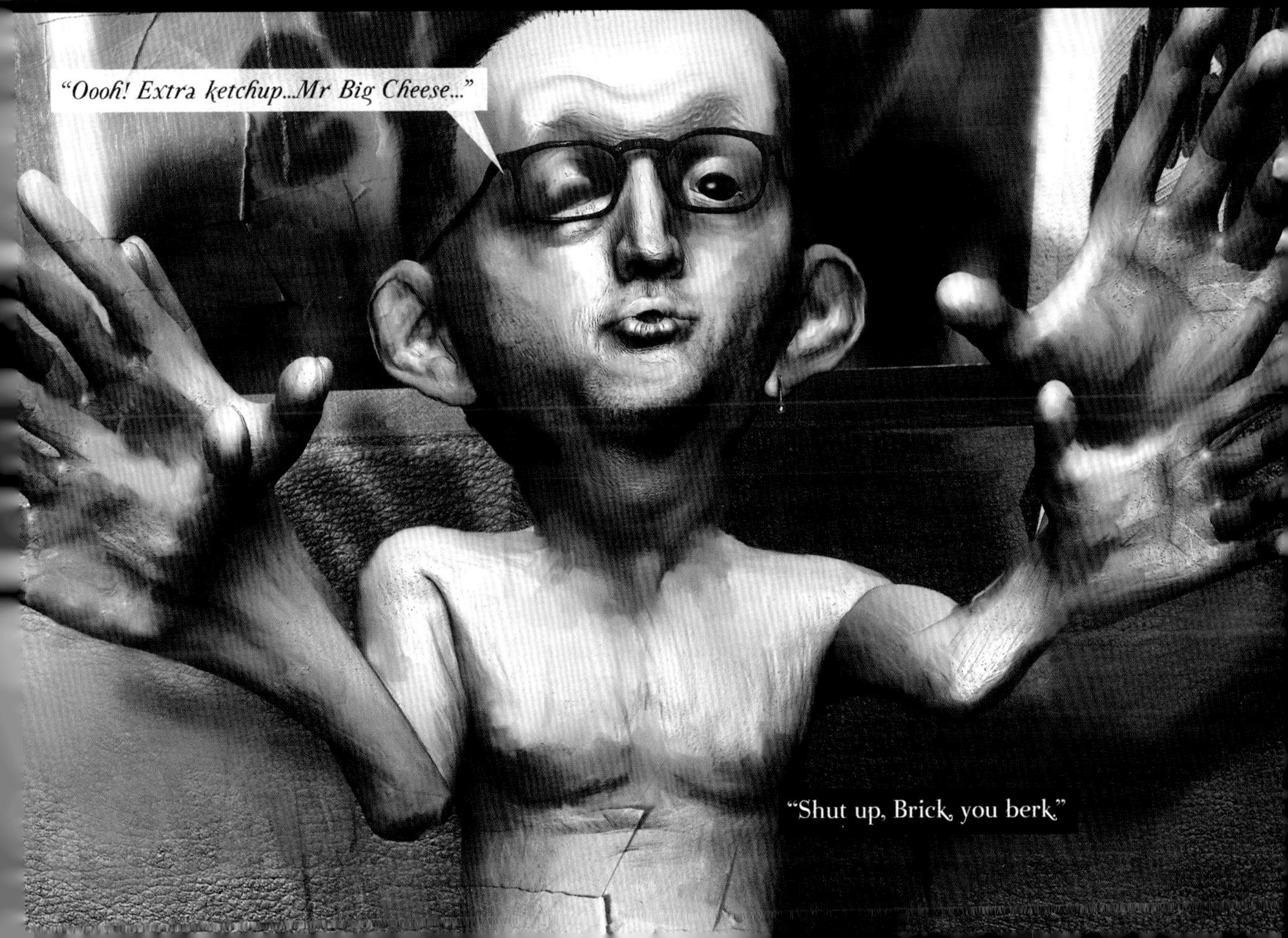

"Oooh! Extra ketchup...Mr Big Cheese..."
"Shut up, Brick, you berk."

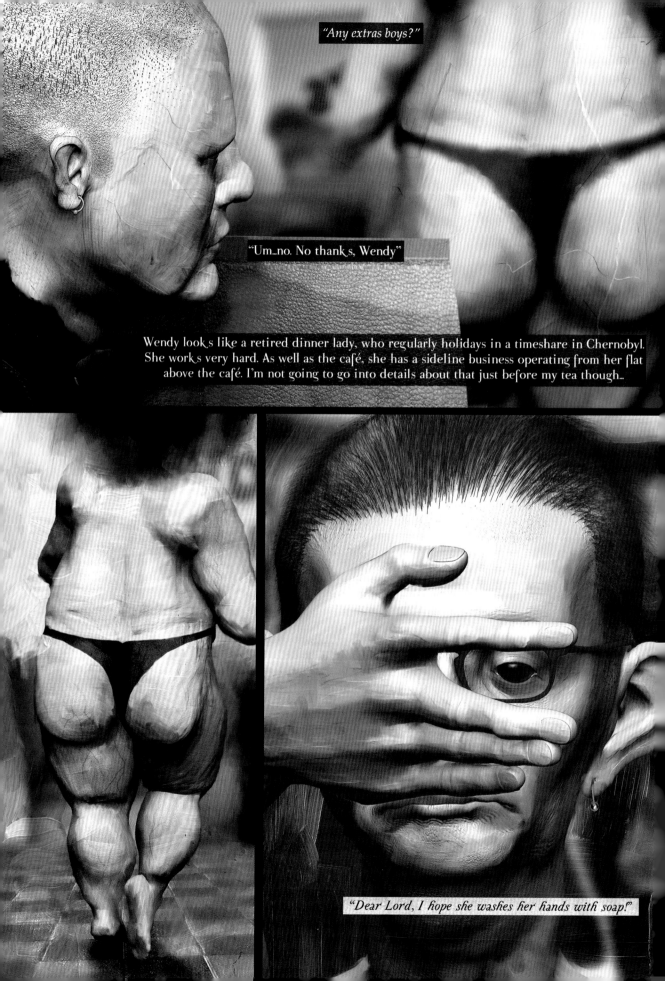

"Any extras boys?"

"Um...no. No thanks, Wendy"

Wendy looks like a retired dinner lady, who regularly holidays in a timeshare in Chernobyl. She works very hard. As well as the café, she has a sideline business operating from her flat above the café. I'm not going to go into details about that just before my tea though...

"Dear Lord, I hope she washes her hands with soap!"

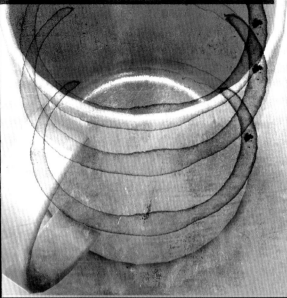

The level of cleanliness at Wendy's is indicated by the coffee tidemarks that circumference the inside of the cups. I wonder what people thought about when they paused long enough to etch a stain and make their mark.

I wonder...

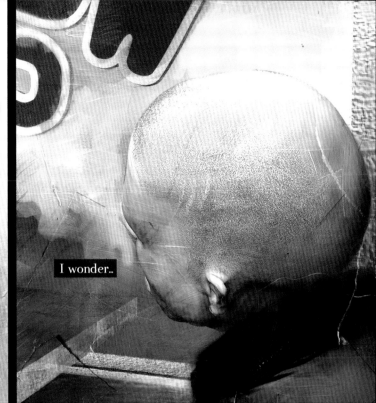

I wonder...

"Hey, Morty...I was wondering, do you think a bee can catch diabetes, you know because of the sugar they eat every day?"

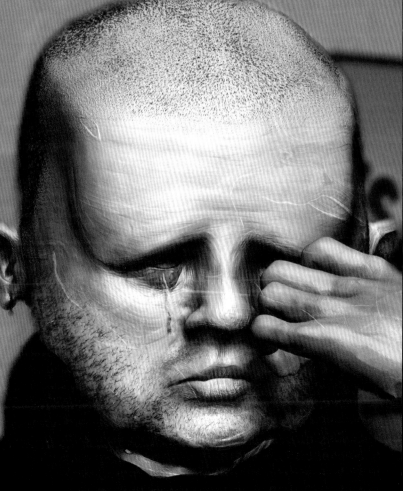

"Diabeeeties!"

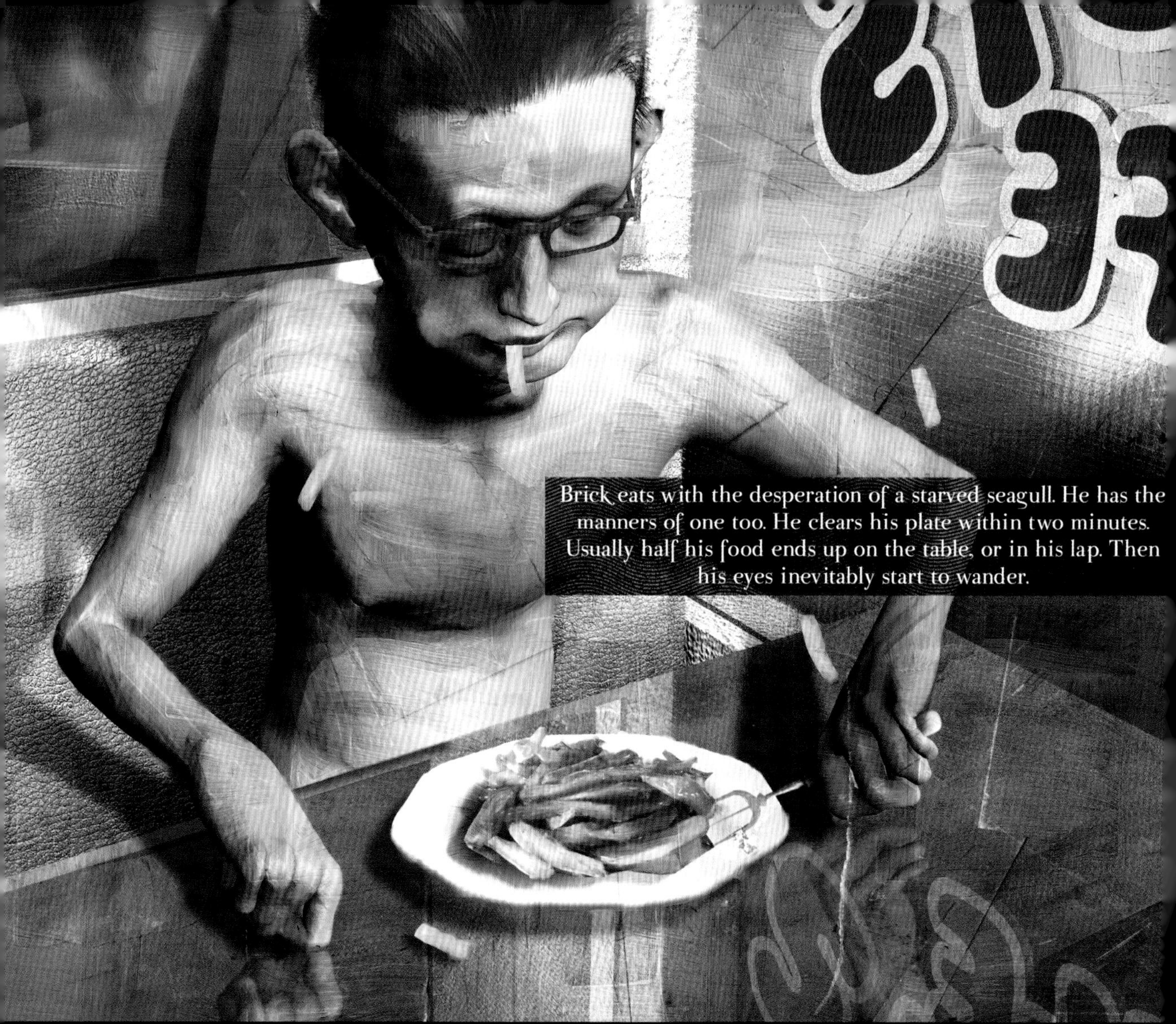
Brick eats with the desperation of a starved seagull. He has the manners of one too. He clears his plate within two minutes. Usually half his food ends up on the table, or in his lap. Then his eyes inevitably start to wander.

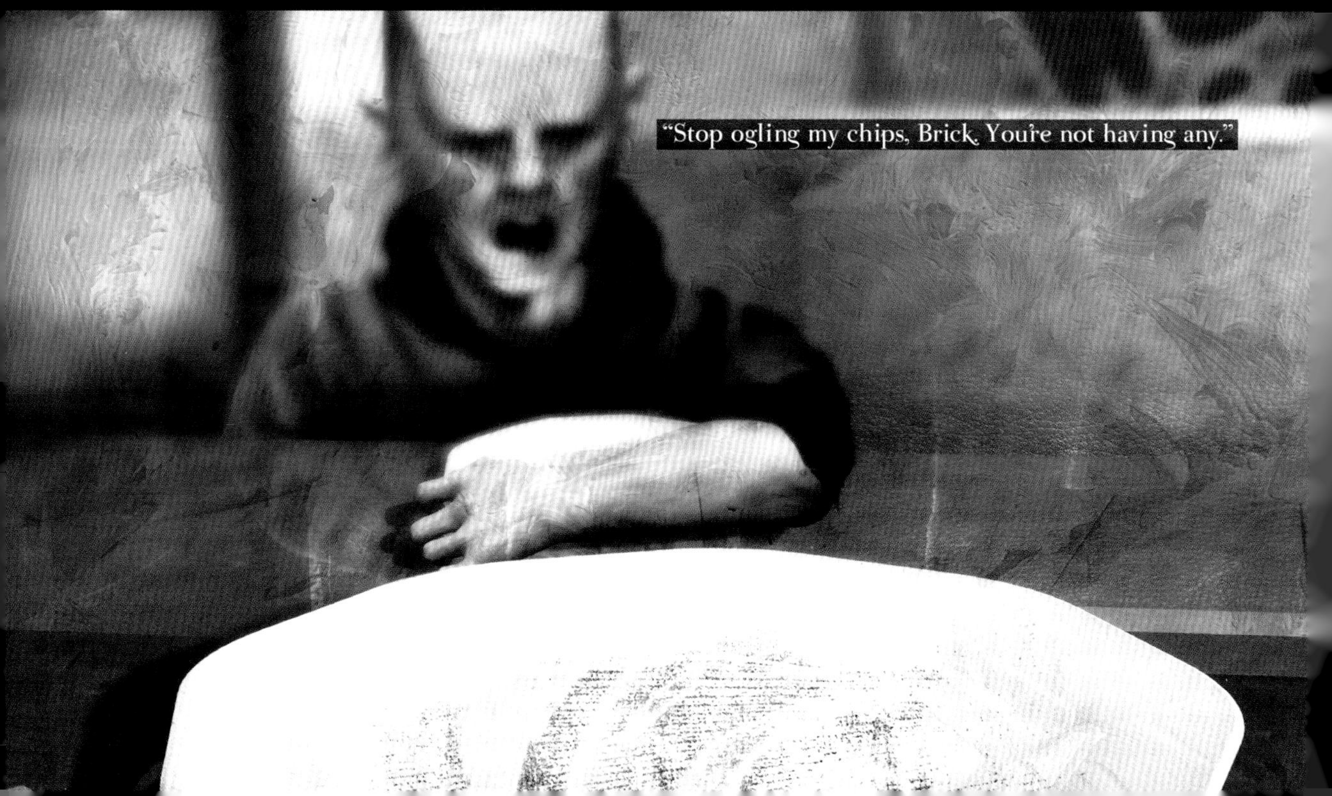
"Stop ogling my chips, Brick. You're not having any."

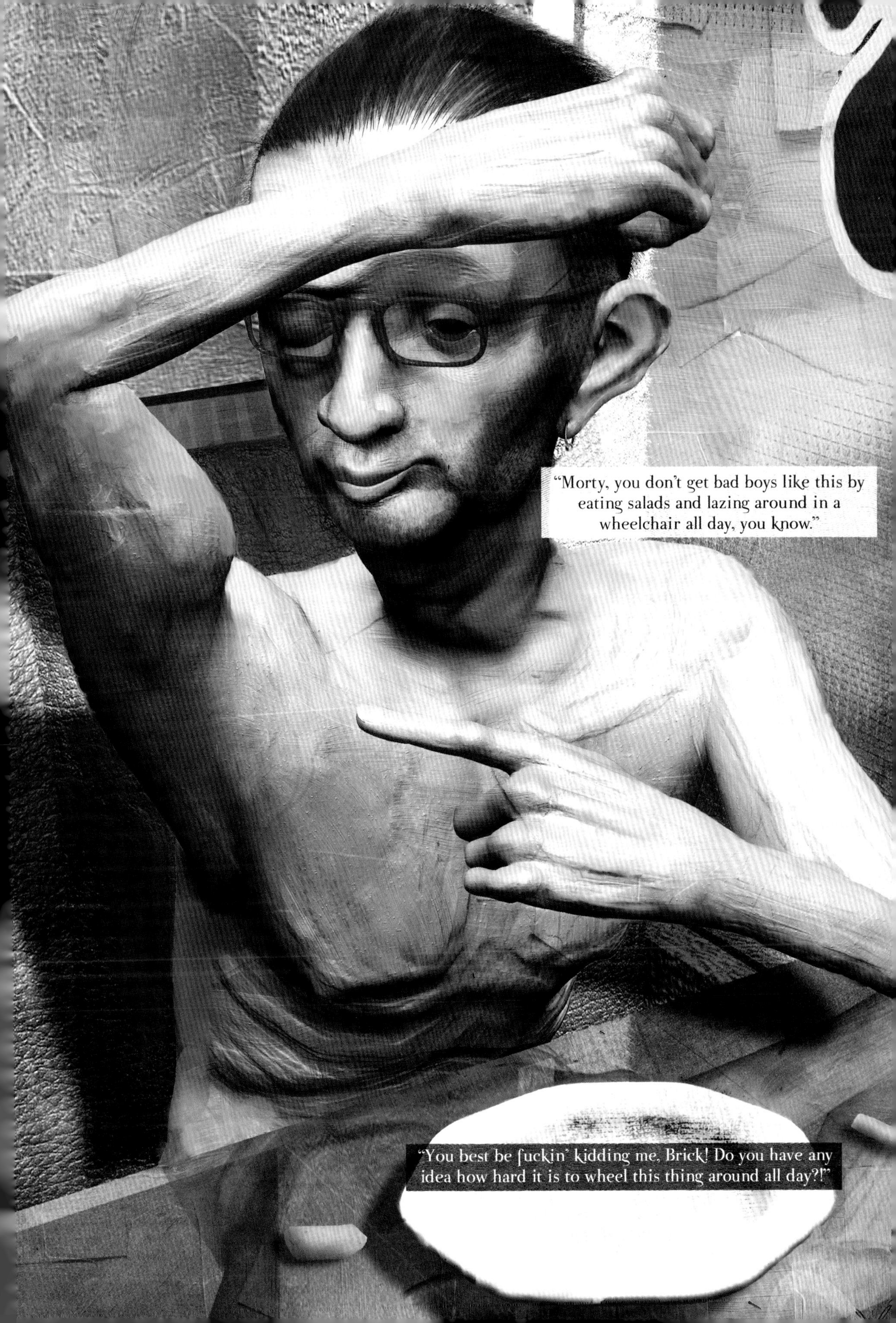
"Morty, you don't get bad boys like this by eating salads and lazing around in a wheelchair all day, you know."
"You best be fuckin' kidding me, Brick! Do you have any idea how hard it is to wheel this thing around all day?!"

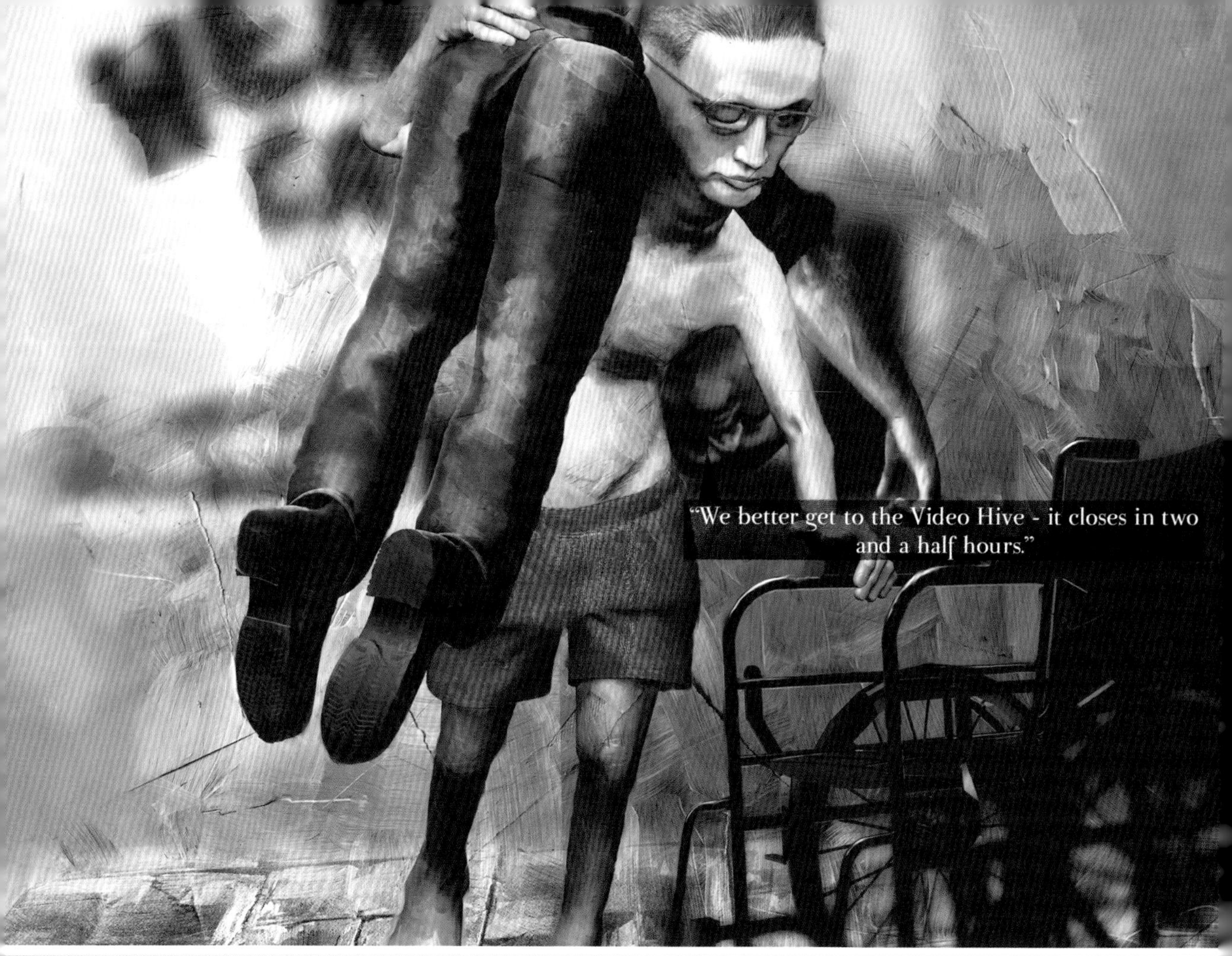
"We better get to the Video Hive - it closes in two and a half hours."

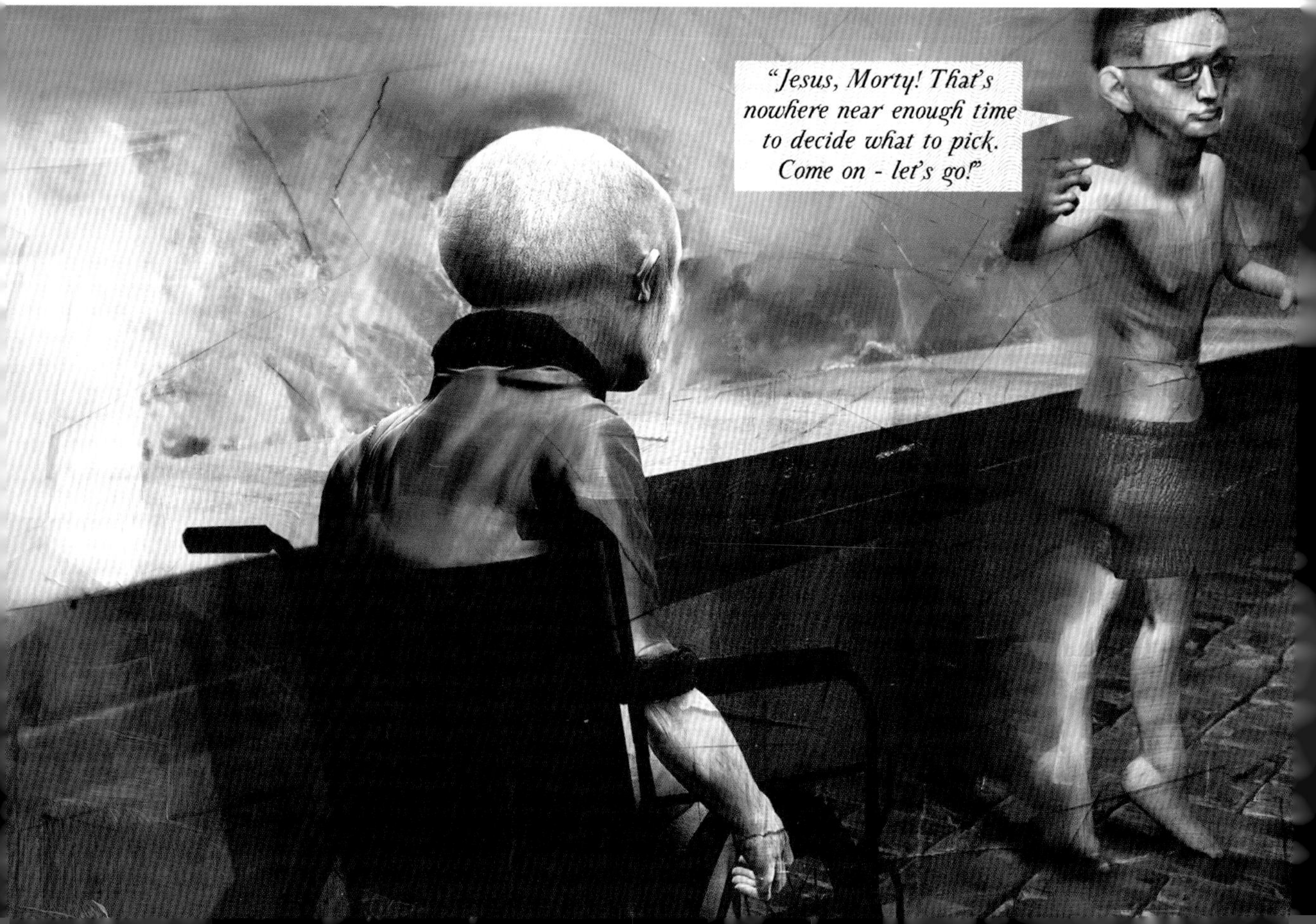
"Jesus, Morty! That's nowhere near enough time to decide what to pick. Come on - let's go!"

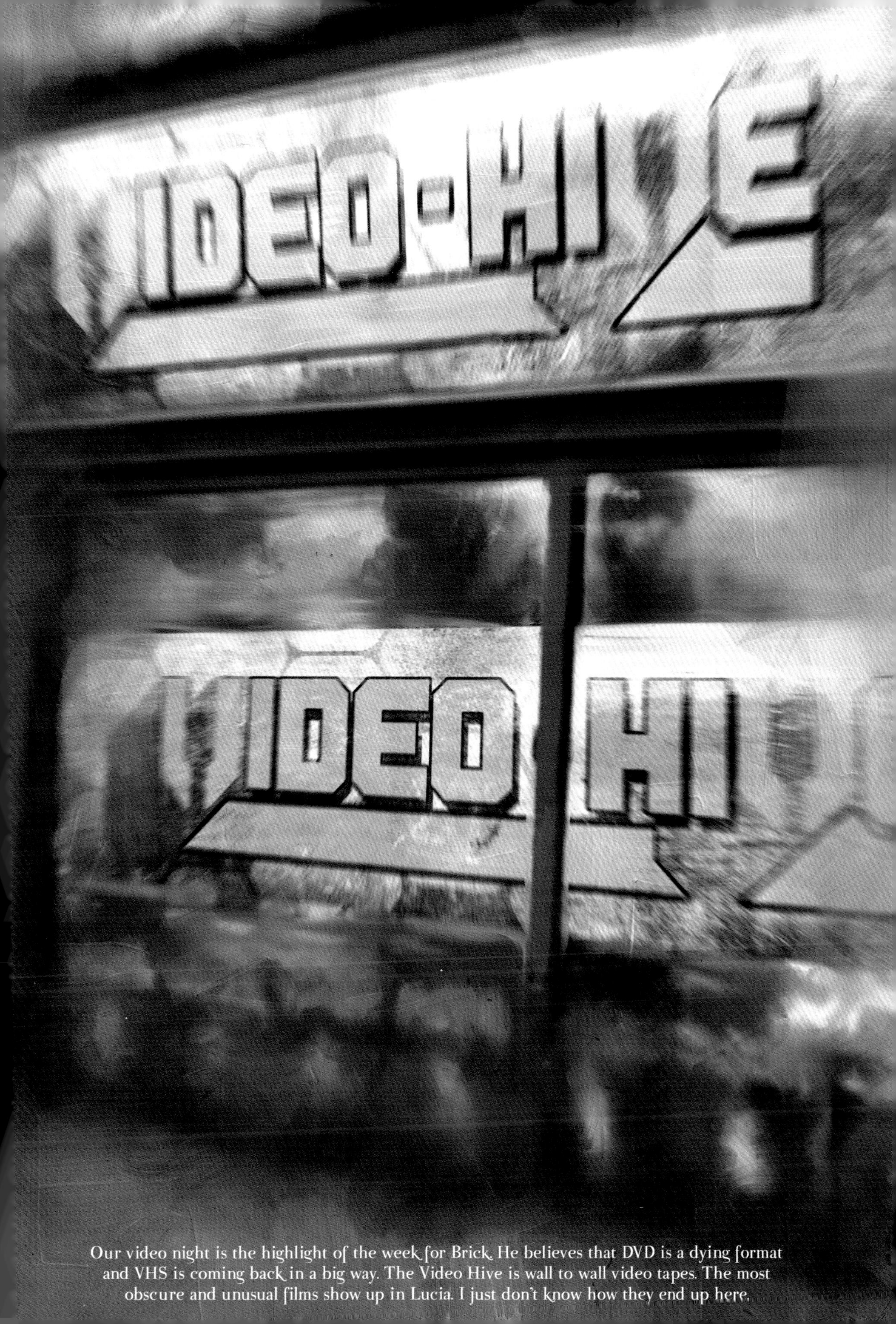
VIDEO HIVE
VIDEO HI

Our video night is the highlight of the week for Brick. He believes that DVD is a dying format and VHS is coming back in a big way. The Video Hive is wall to wall video tapes. The most obscure and unusual films show up in Lucia. I just don't know how they end up here.

Colin has worked at the Video Hive for as long as I can remember. He sees us coming a mile off. He is an opportunist. He romanticises VHS cassettes and puts ridiculous ideas in Brick's head about opening a huge supermarket, stuffed to the brim with their worthless tapes. Brick, of course, considers this a valid business venture for the future.

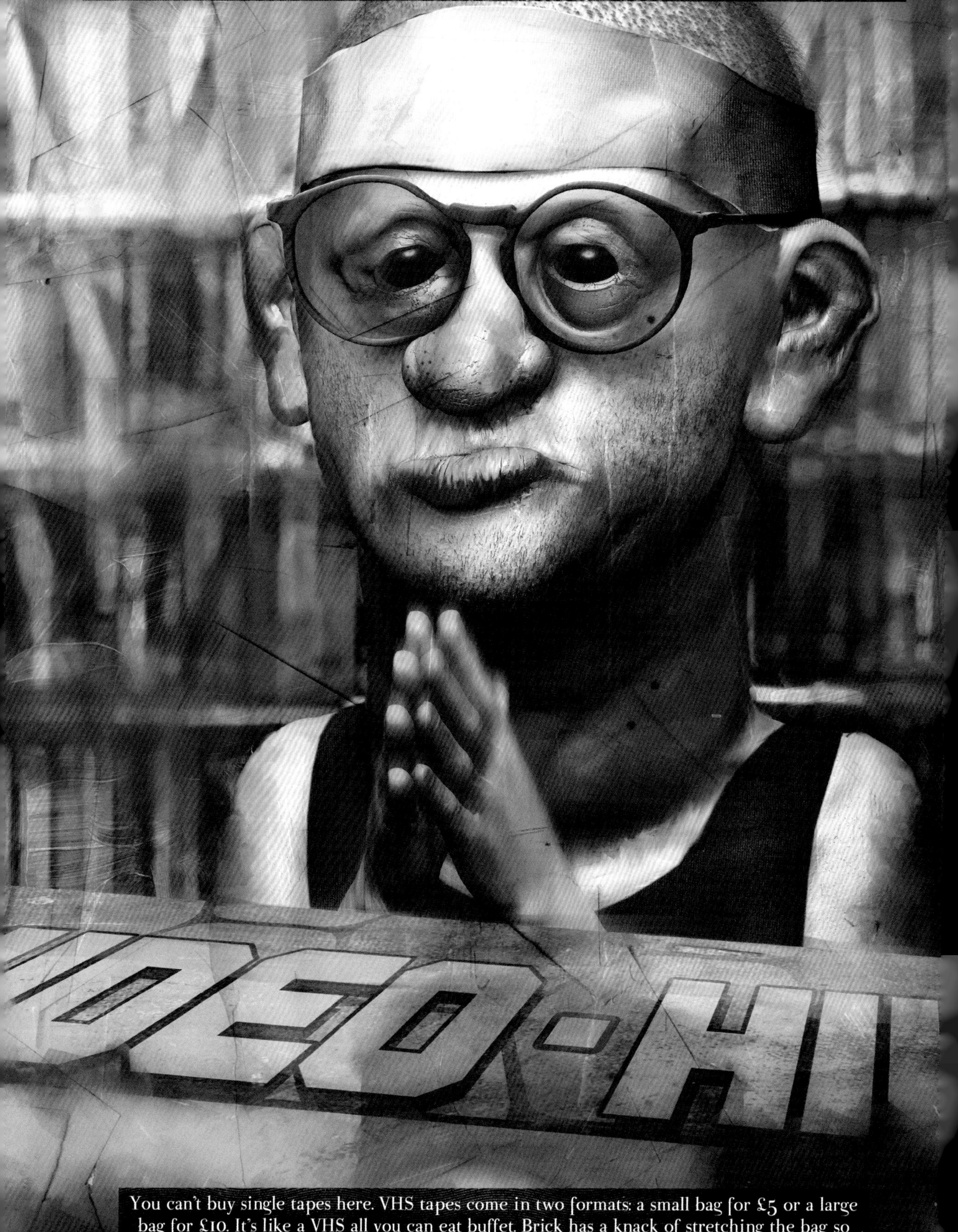

You can't buy single tapes here. VHS tapes come in two formats: a small bag for £5 or a large bag for £10. It's like a VHS all you can eat buffet. Brick has a knack of stretching the bag so we can fit even more in. I don't think I'll ever be rid of these worthless bits of crap.

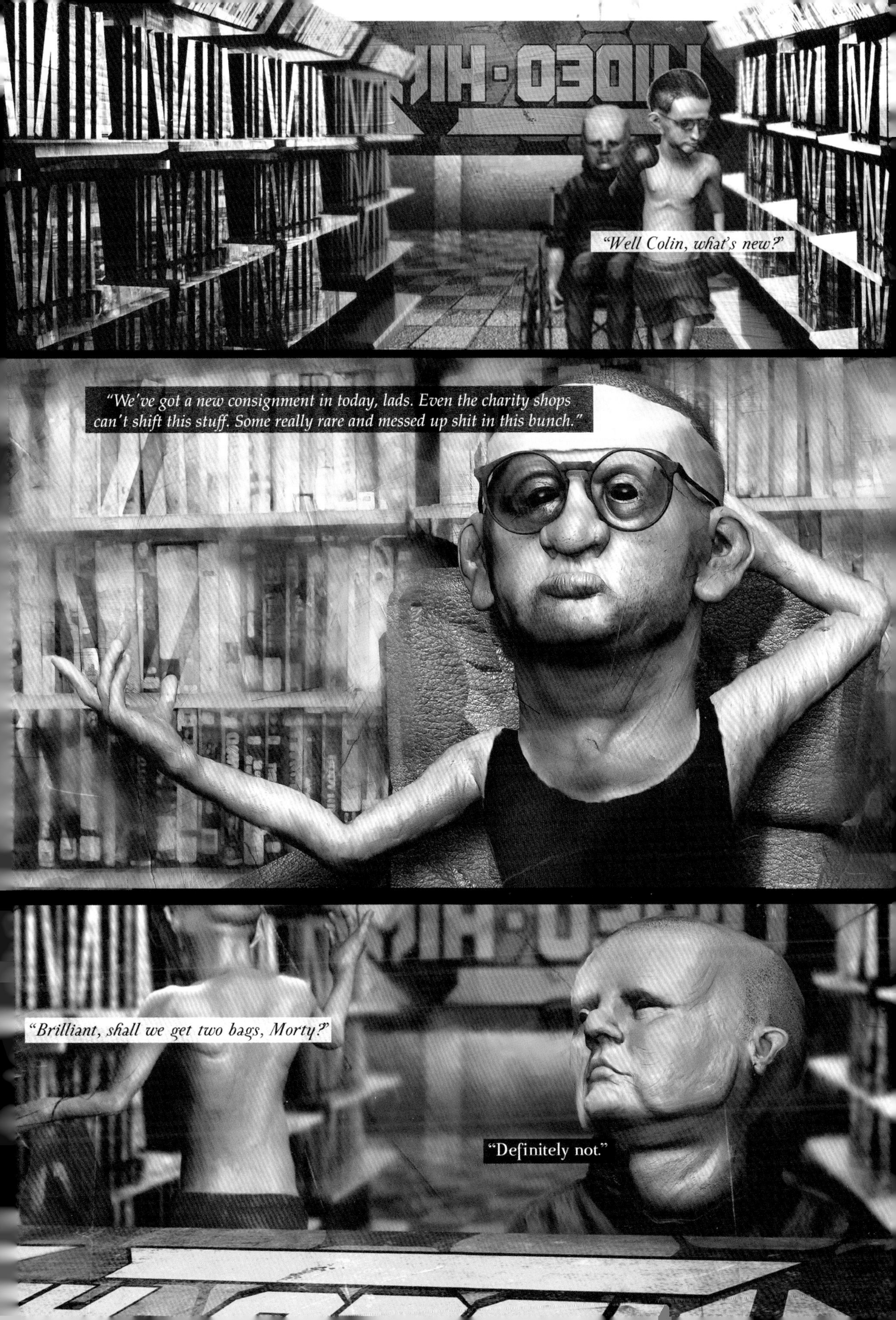
"Well Colin, what's new?"
"We've got a new consignment in today, lads. Even the charity shops can't shift this stuff. Some really rare and messed up shit in this bunch."
"Brilliant, shall we get two bags, Morty?"
"Definitely not."

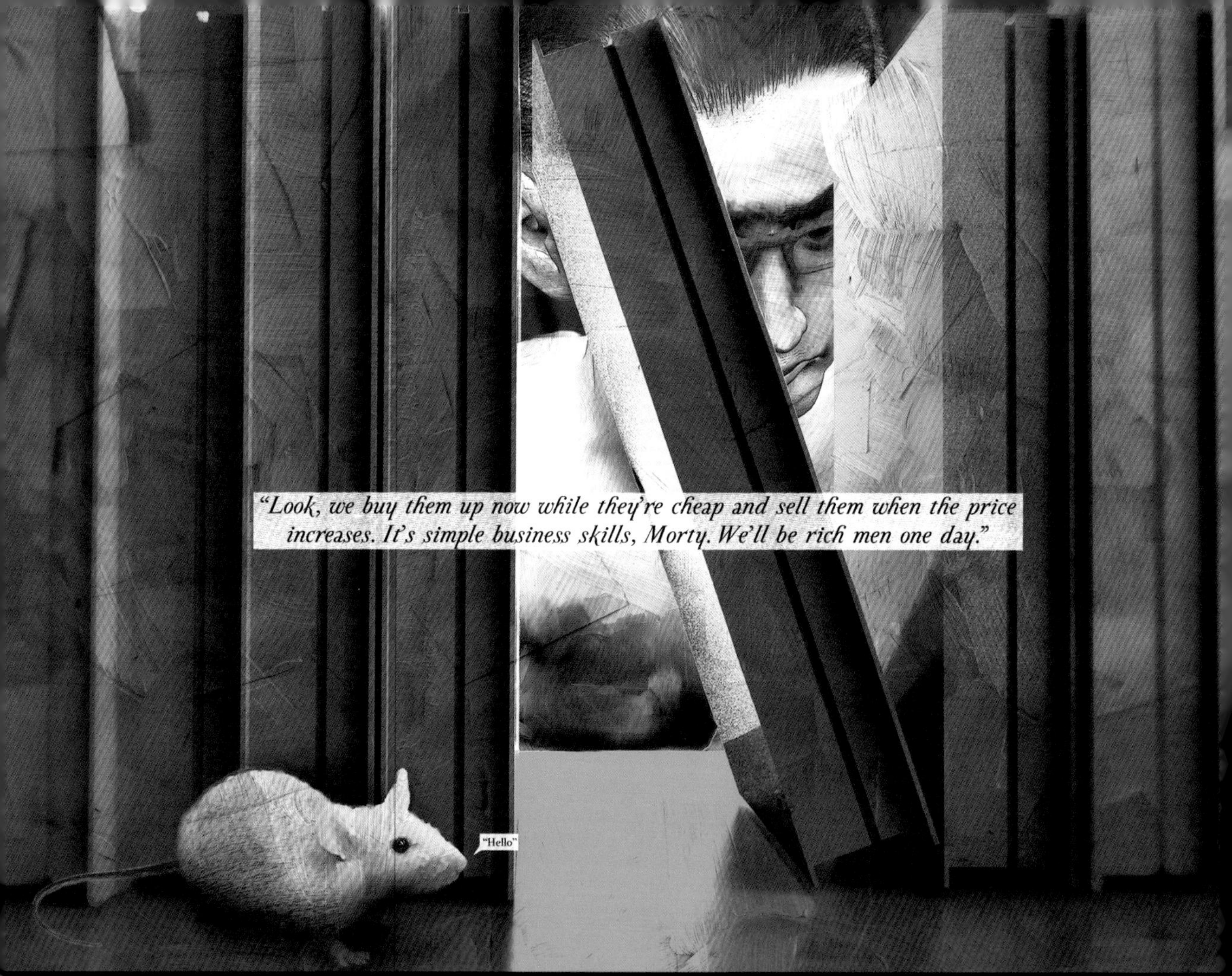
"Look, we buy them up now while they're cheap and sell them when the price increases. It's simple business skills, Morty. We'll be rich men one day."
"Hello"
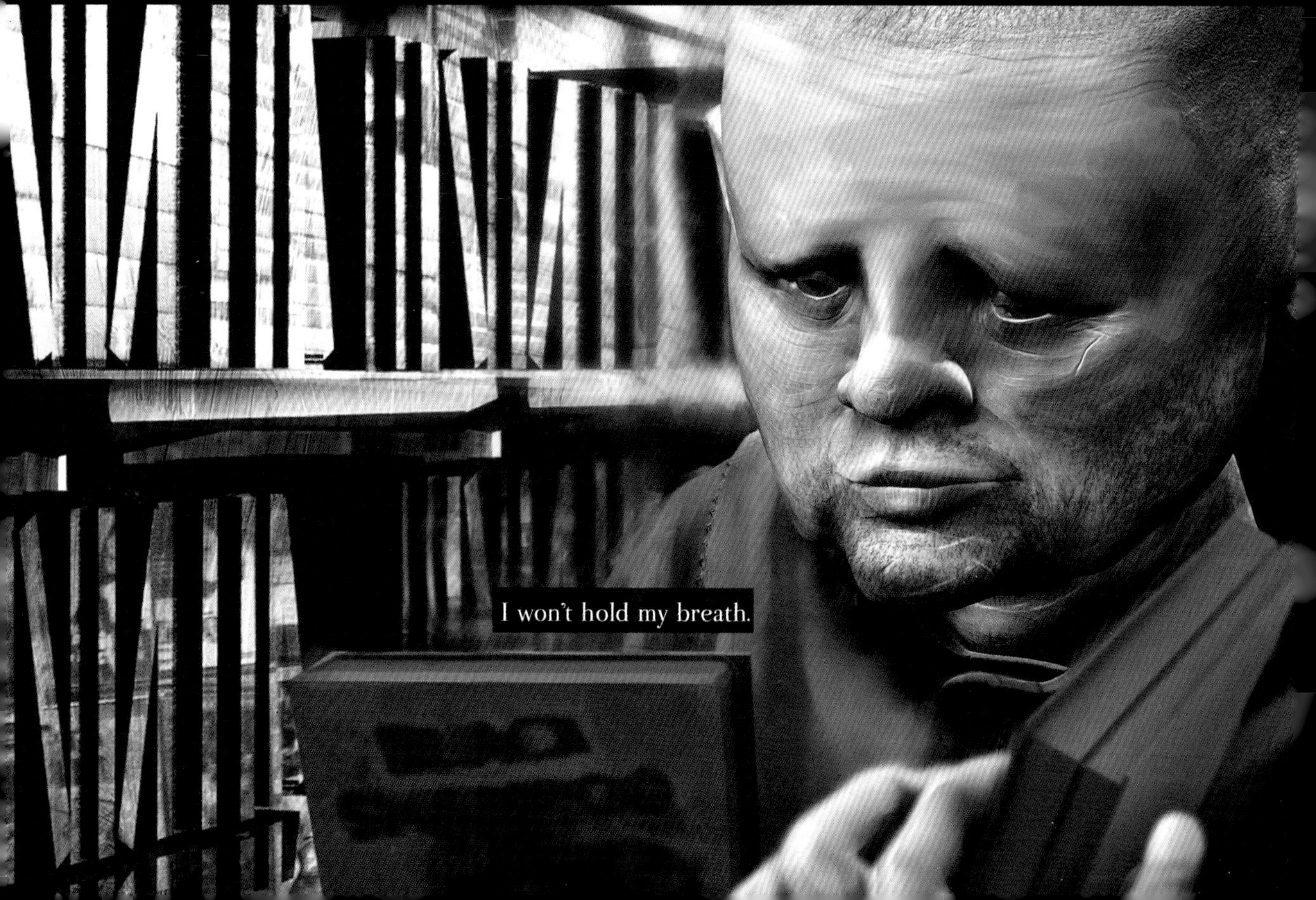
I won't hold my breath.

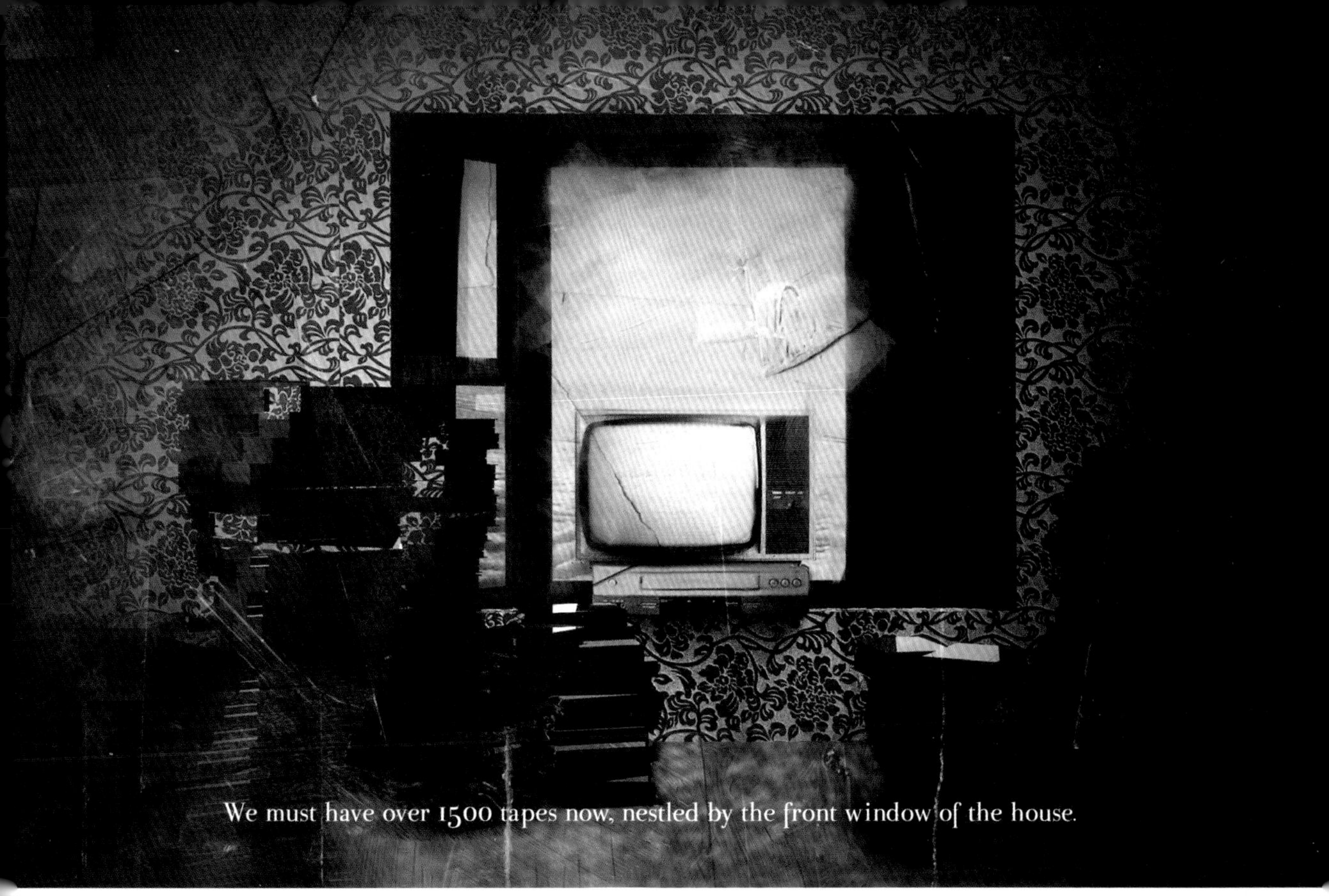
We must have over 1500 tapes now, nestled by the front window of the house.

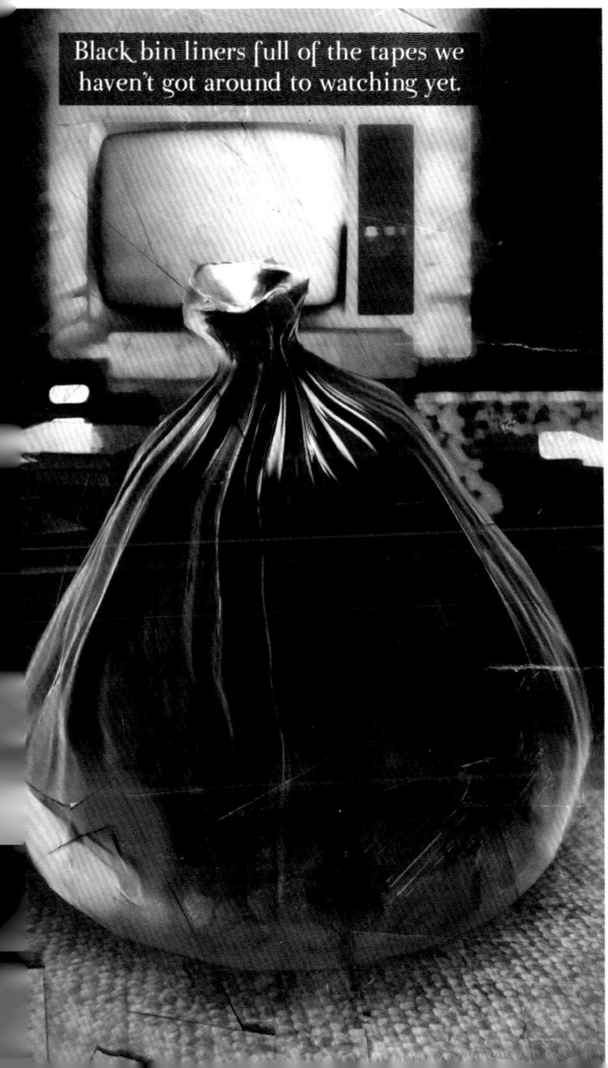
Black bin liners full of the tapes we haven't got around to watching yet.

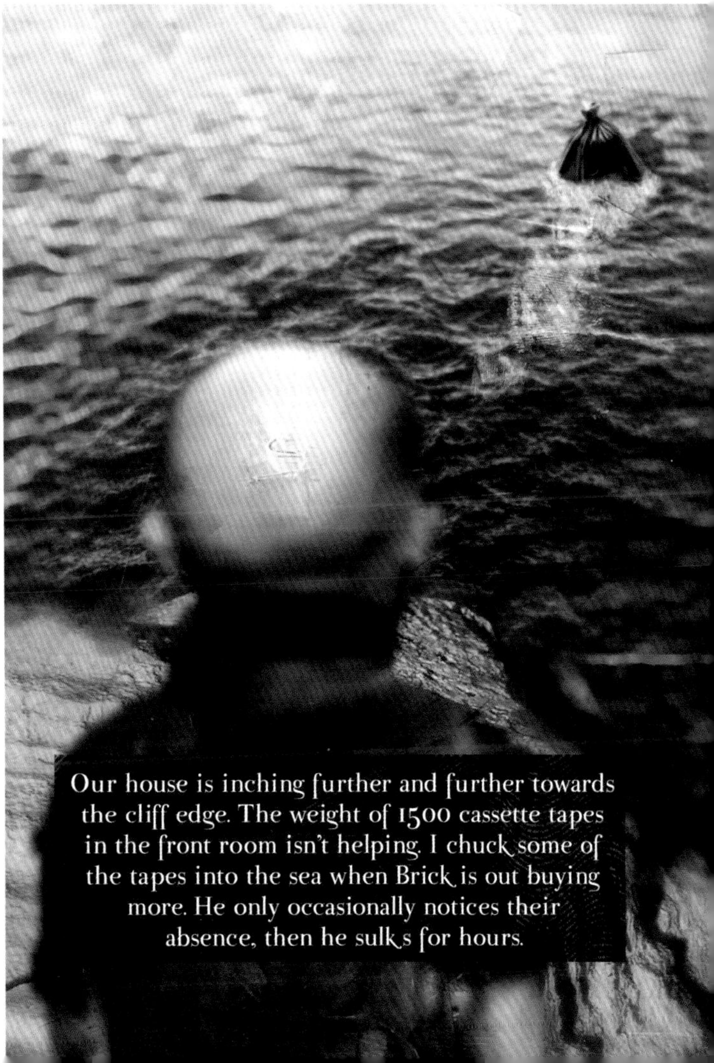
Our house is inching further and further towards the cliff edge. The weight of 1500 cassette tapes in the front room isn't helping. I chuck some of the tapes into the sea when Brick is out buying more. He only occasionally notices their absence, then he sulks for hours.

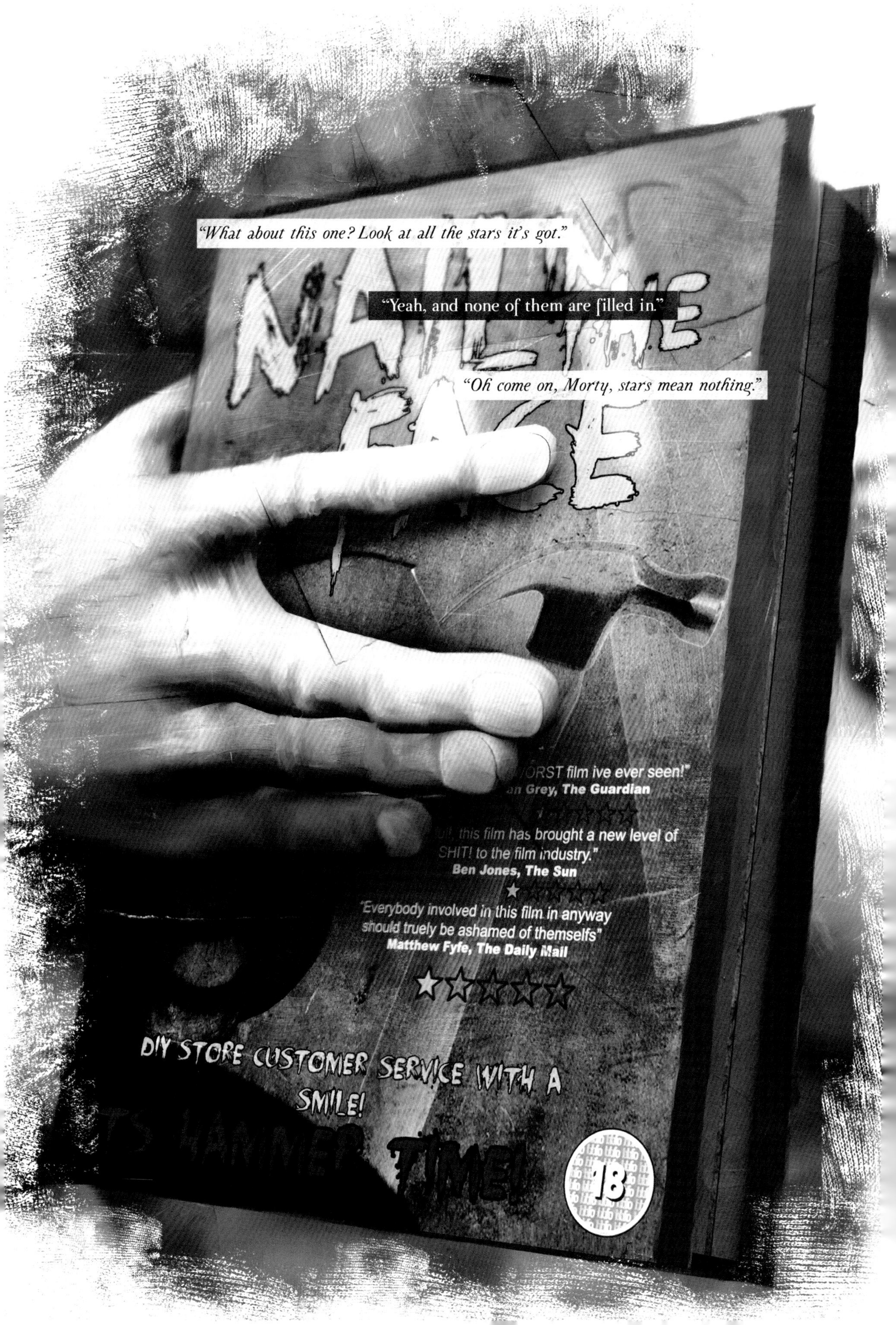

"What about this one? Look at all the stars it's got."
"Yeah, and none of them are filled in."
"Oh come on, Morty, stars mean nothing."
this film has brought a new level of SHIT! to the film industry."
Ben Jones, The Sun
"Everybody involved in this film in anyway should truely be ashamed of themselfs"
Matthew Fyfe, The Daily Mail
DIY STORE CUSTOMER SERVICE WITH A SMILE!
18

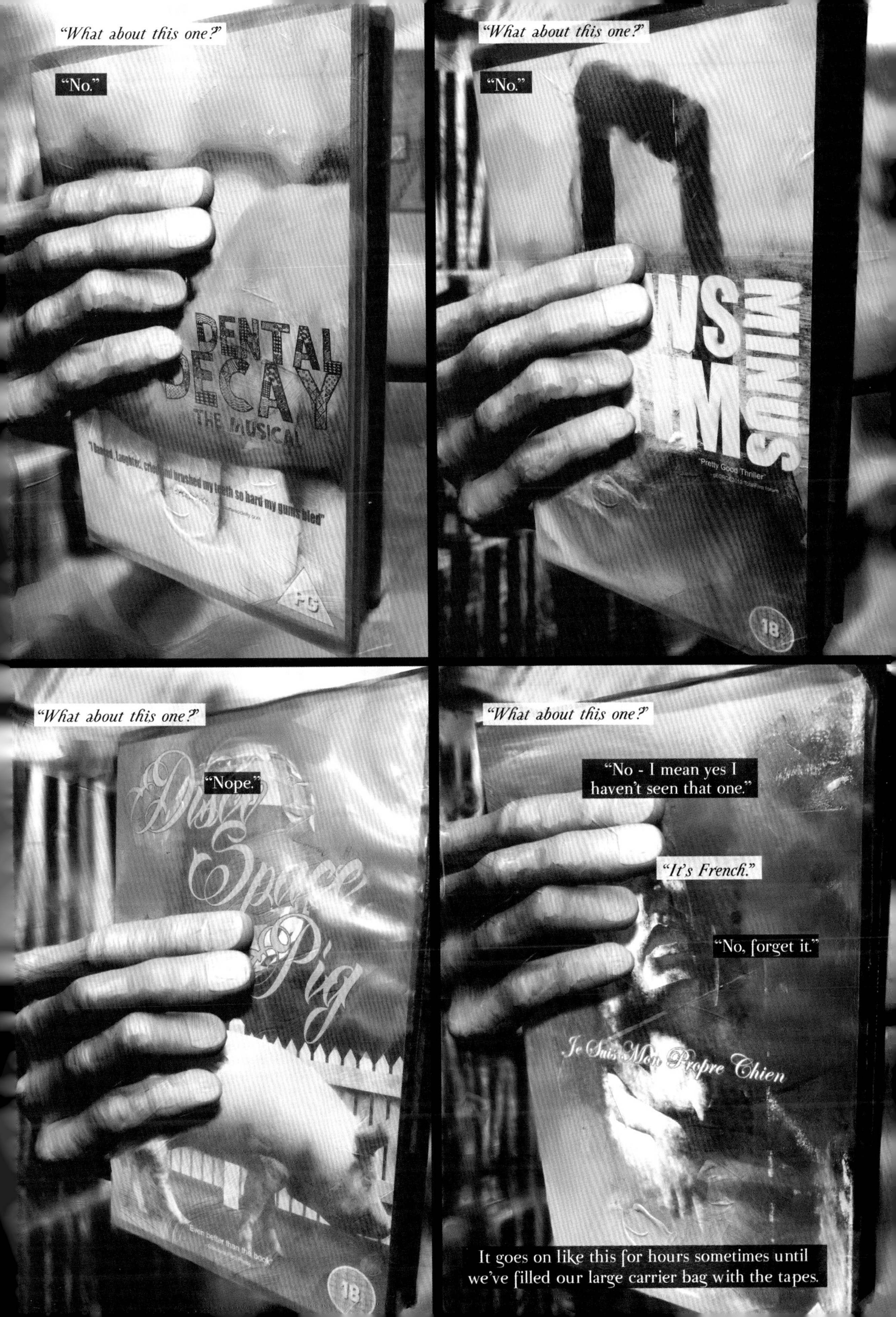
"What about this one?"
"No."
DENTAL DECAY
THE MUSICAL
PG
"What about this one?"
"No."
MINUS
"Pretty Good Thriller"
18
"What about this one?"
"Nope."
Disco Space Pig
Even better than the book
18
"What about this one?"
"No - I mean yes I haven't seen that one."
"It's French."
"No, forget it."
Je Suis Mon Propre Chien
It goes on like this for hours sometimes until we've filled our large carrier bag with the tapes.

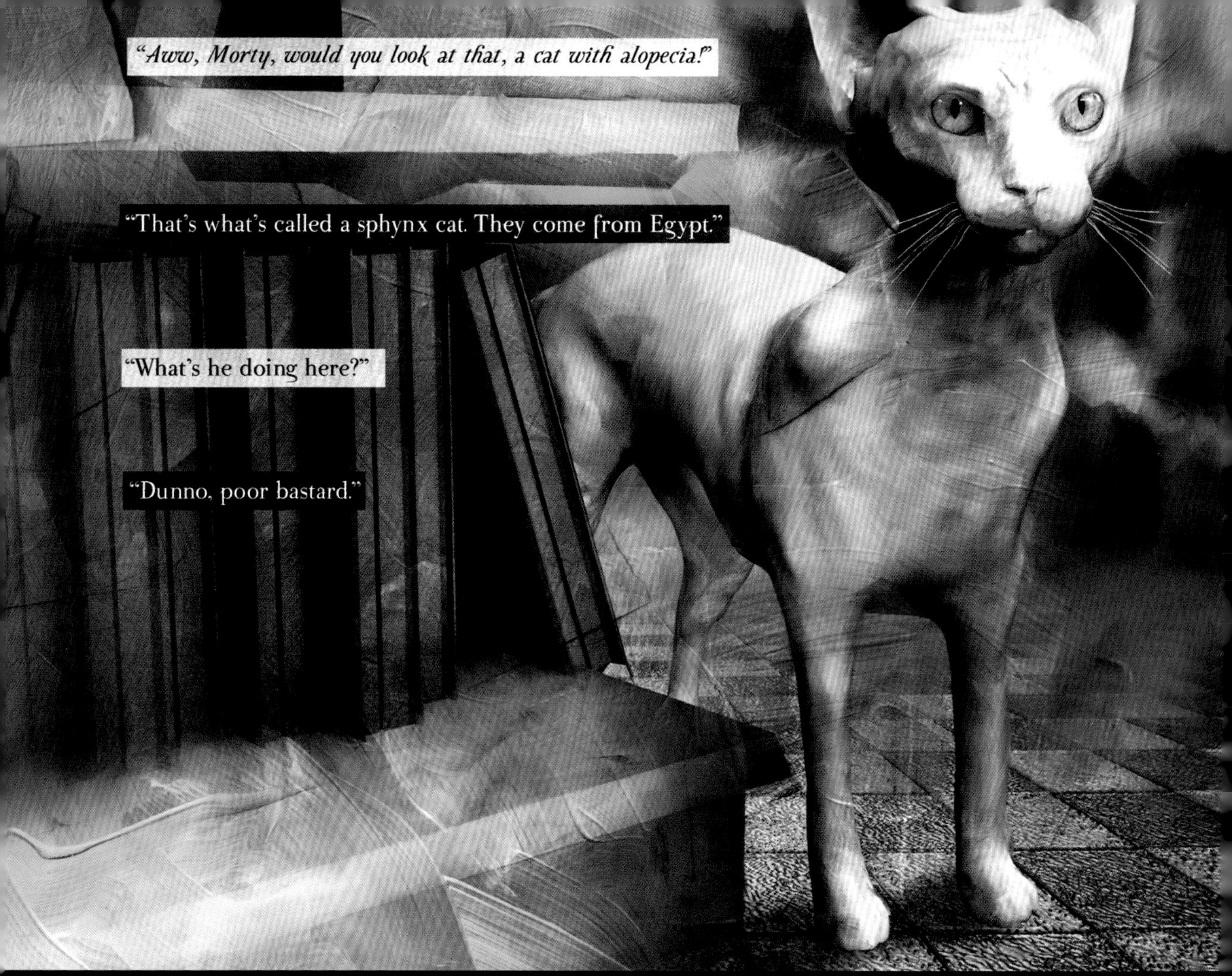
"Aww, Morty, would you look at that, a cat with alopecia!"
"That's what's called a sphynx cat. They come from Egypt."
"What's he doing here?"
"Dunno, poor bastard."

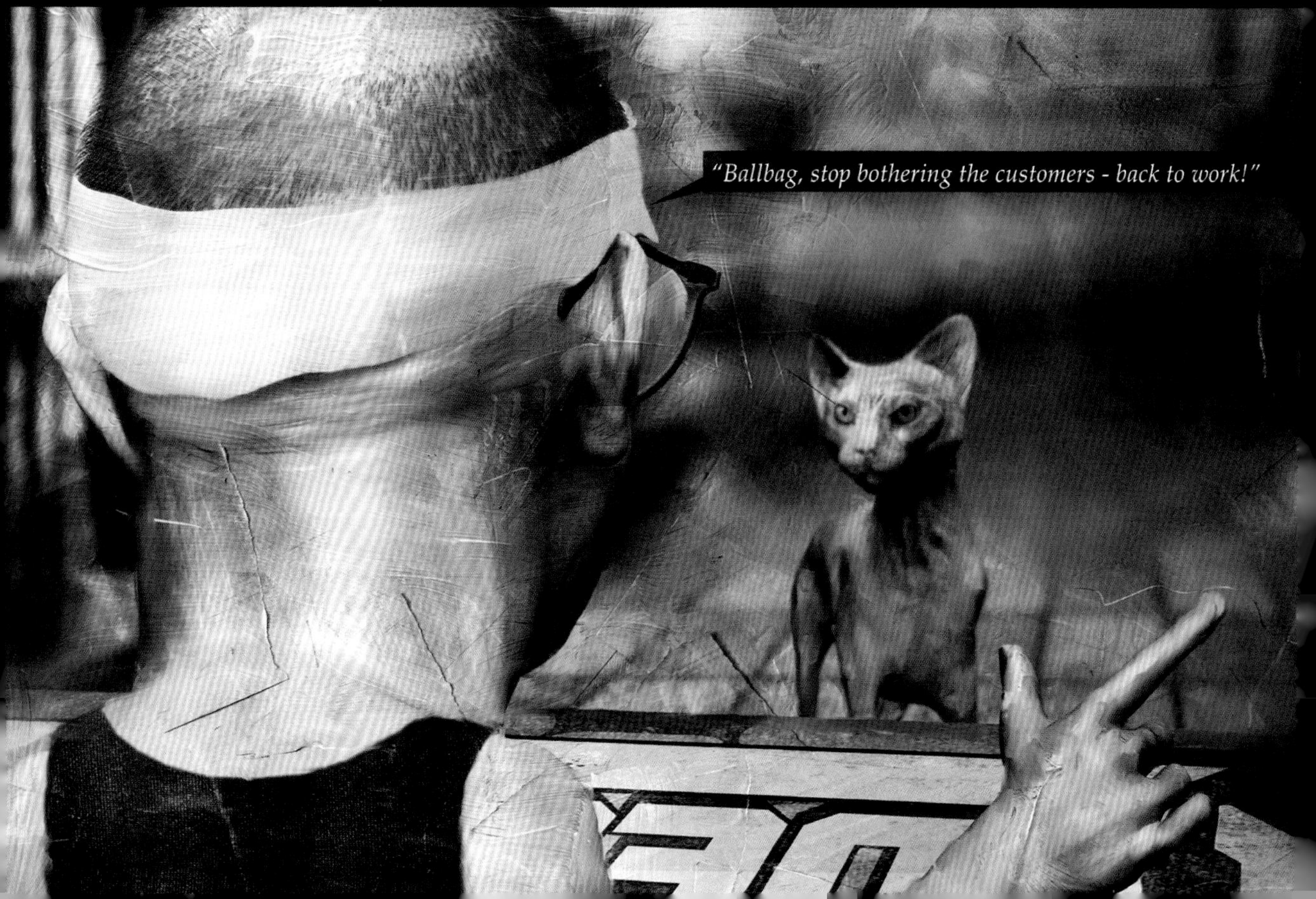
"Ballbag, stop bothering the customers - back to work!"

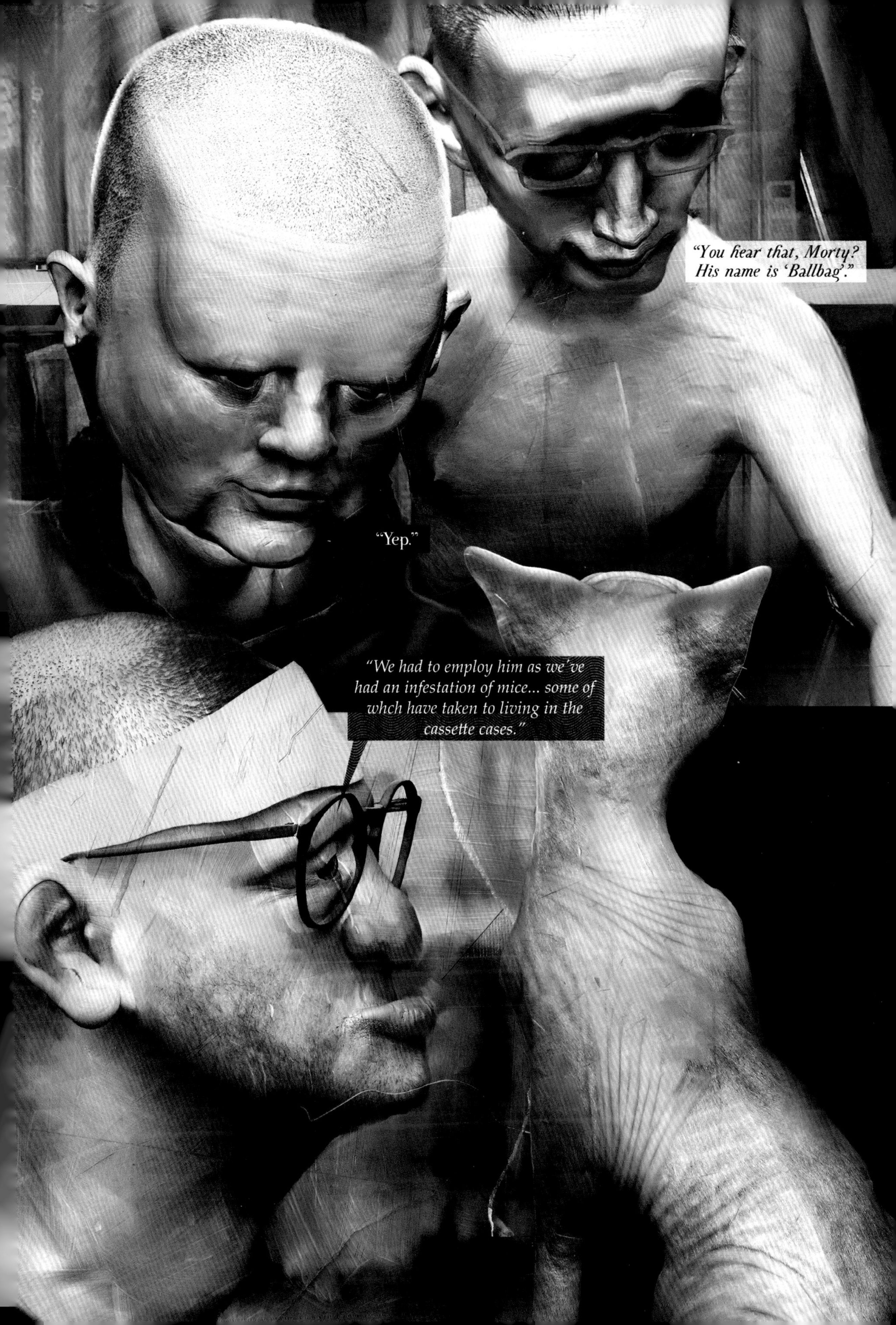
"You hear that, Morty? His name is 'Ballbag'."
"Yep."
"We had to employ him as we've had an infestation of mice... some of whch have taken to living in the cassette cases."

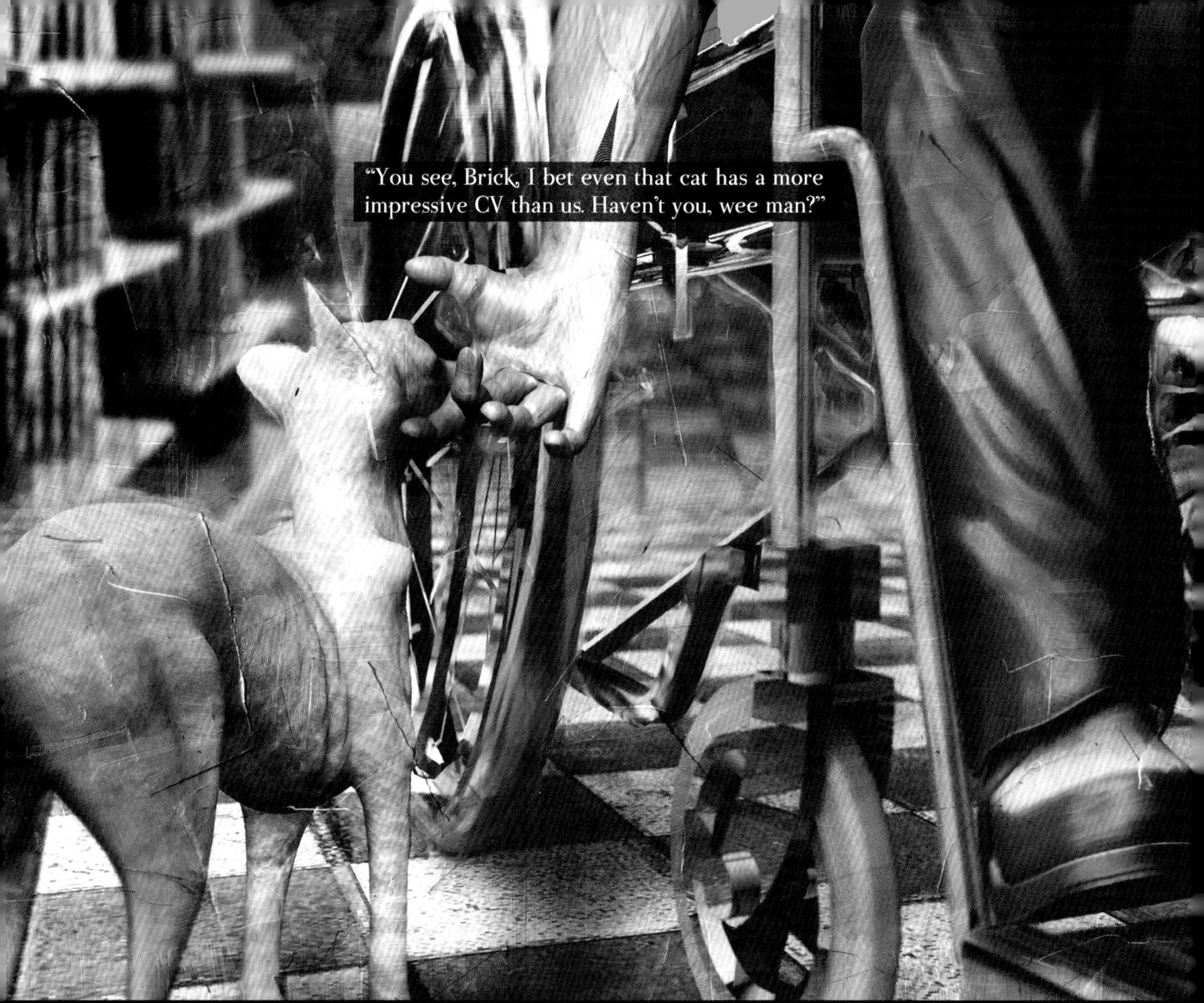
"You see, Brick, I bet even that cat has a more impressive CV than us. Haven't you, wee man?"

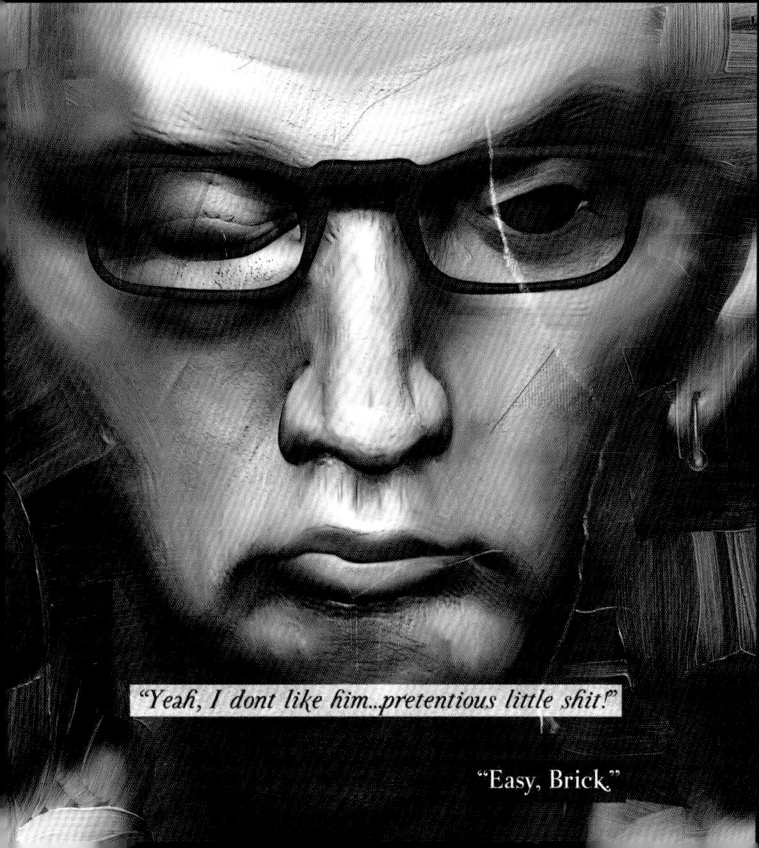
"Yeah, I dont like him...pretentious little shit!"
"Easy, Brick."

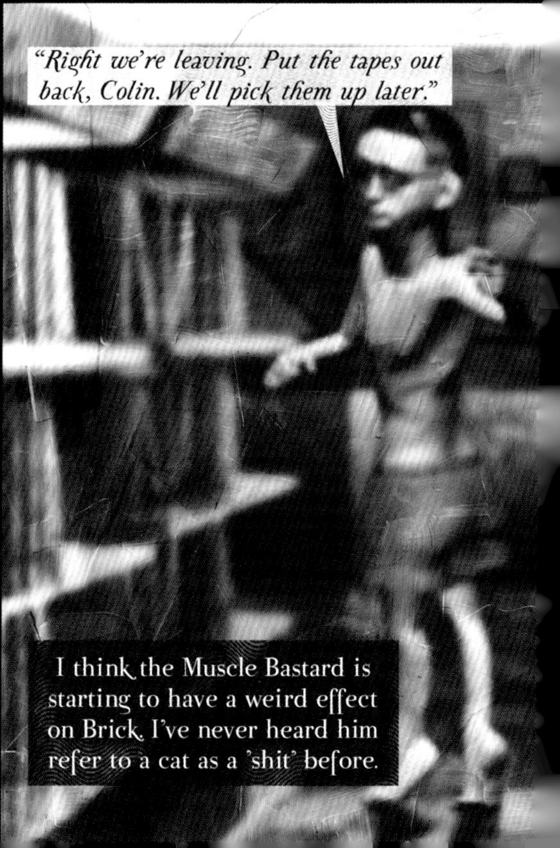
"Right we're leaving. Put the tapes out back, Colin. We'll pick them up later."
I think the Muscle Bastard is starting to have a weird effect on Brick. I've never heard him refer to a cat as a 'shit' before.

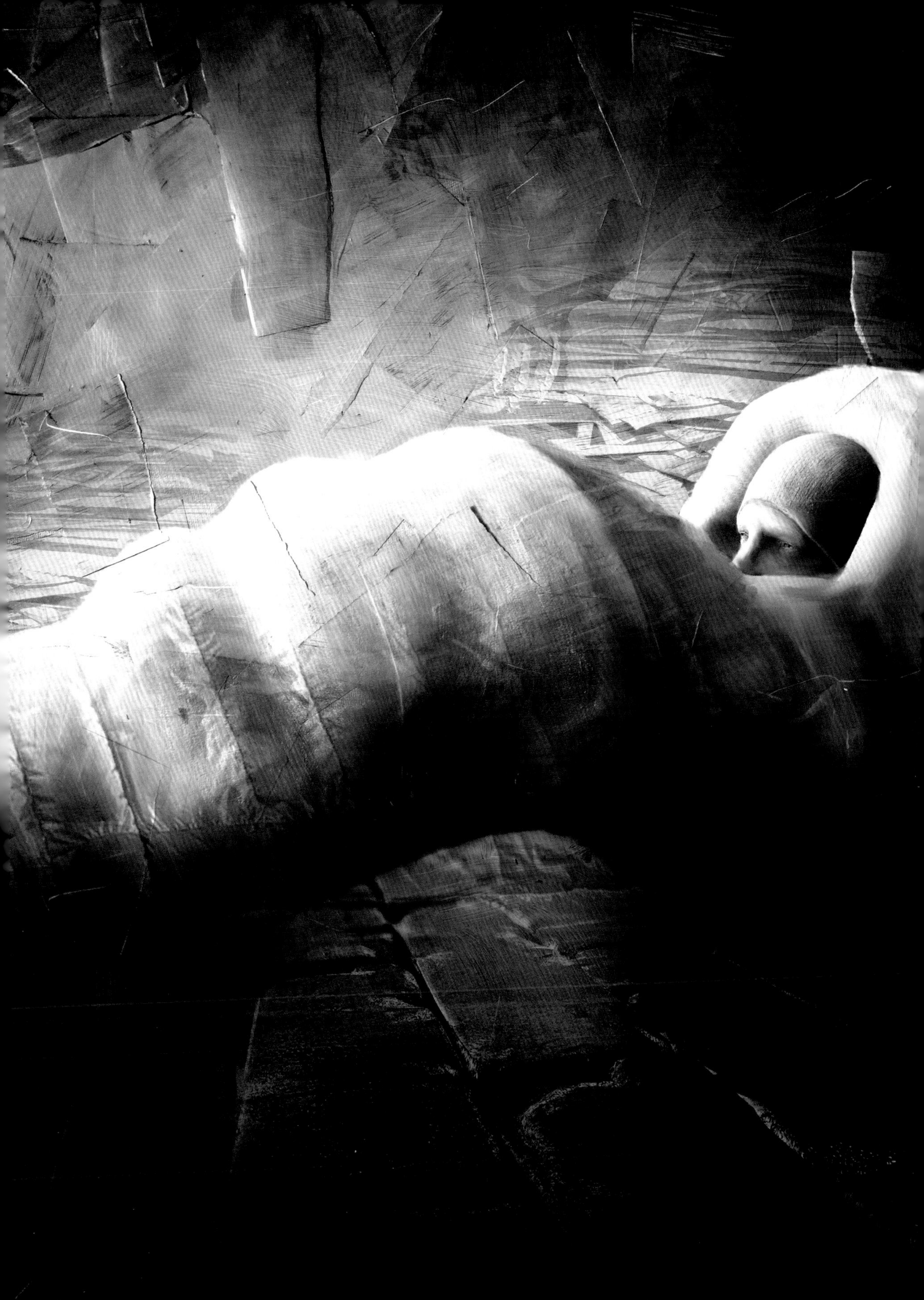

The homeless line the streets, insulating themselves with unsold fashion magazines.
Adverts glamourising emaciated models litter the gutters and pavements.

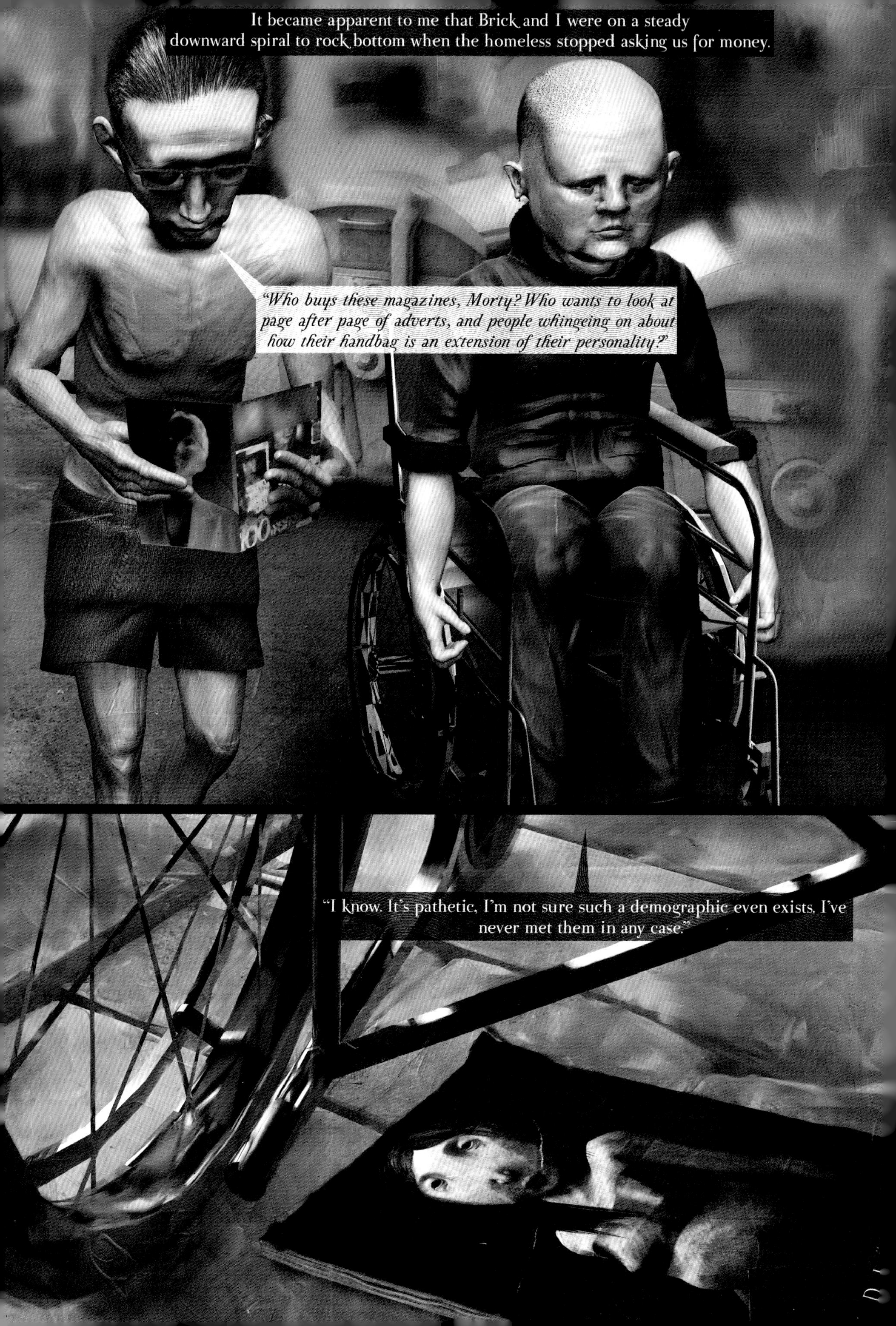
It became apparent to me that Brick and I were on a steady downward spiral to rock bottom when the homeless stopped asking us for money.
"Who buys these magazines, Morty? Who wants to look at page after page of adverts, and people whingeing on about how their handbag is an extension of their personality?"
"I know. It's pathetic, I'm not sure such a demographic even exists. I've never met them in any case."

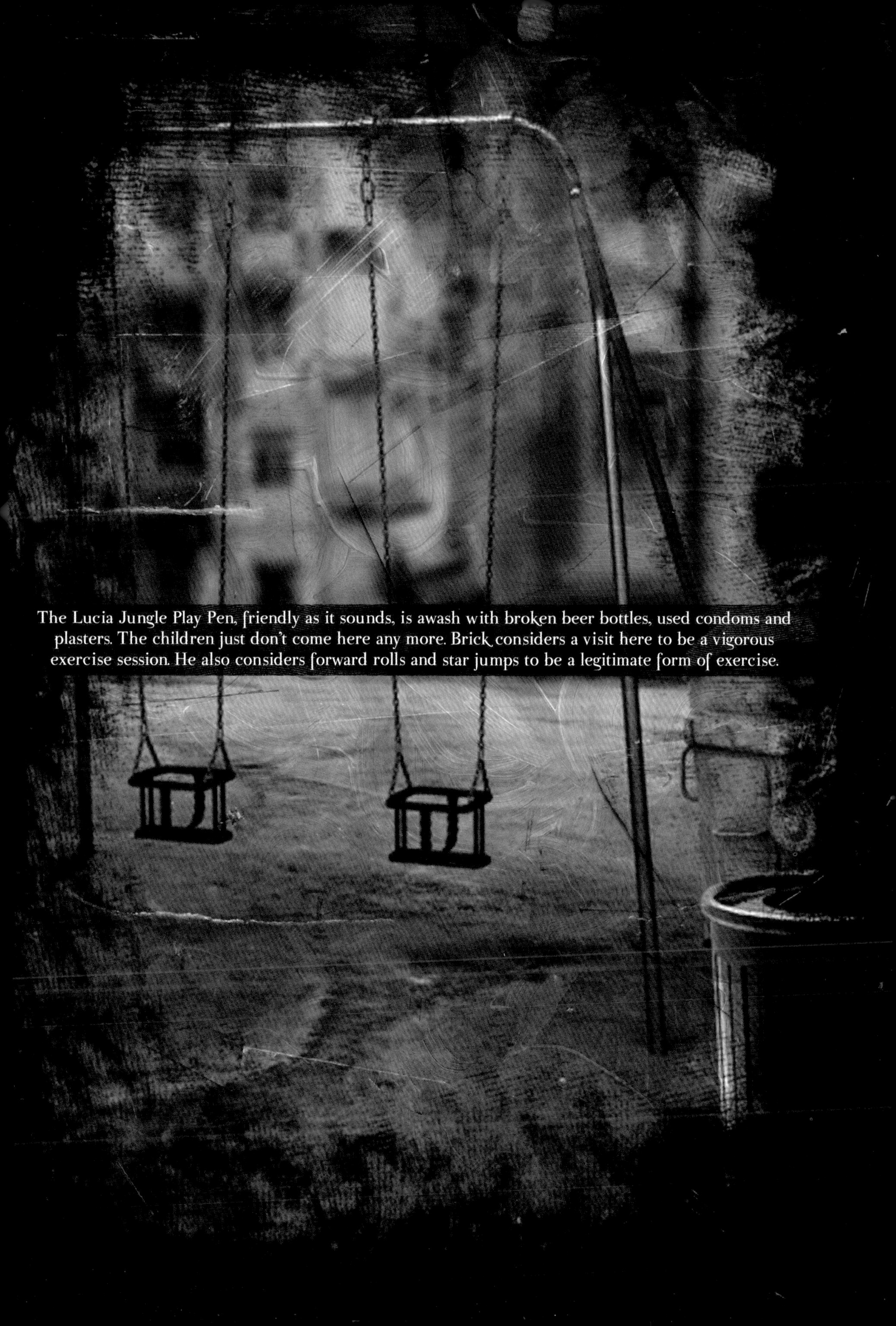

The Lucia Jungle Play Pen, friendly as it sounds, is awash with broken beer bottles, used condoms and plasters. The children just don't come here any more. Brick considers a visit here to be a vigorous exercise session. He also considers forward rolls and star jumps to be a legitimate form of exercise.

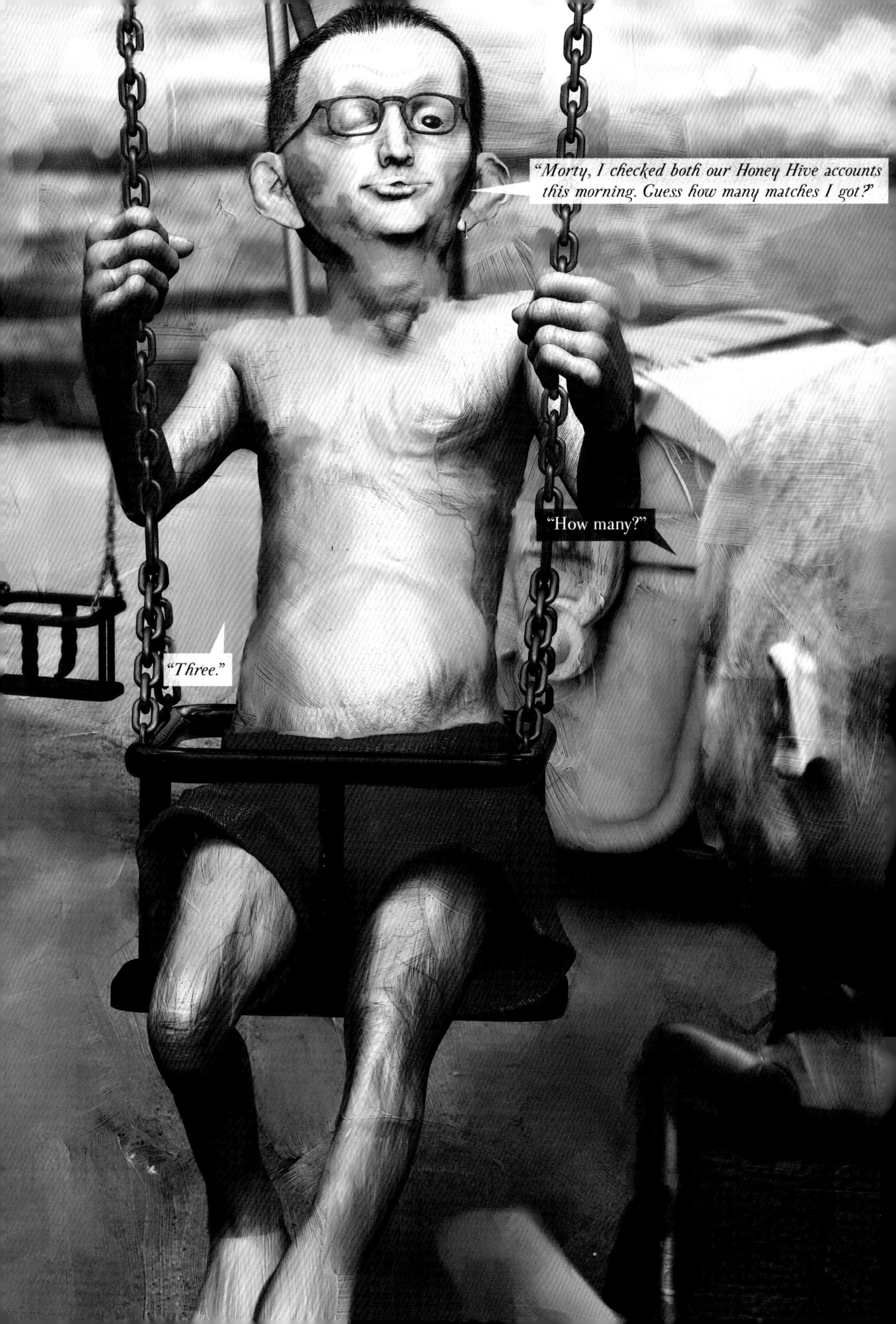
"Morty, I checked both our Honey Hive accounts this morning. Guess how many matches I got?"
"How many?"
"Three."

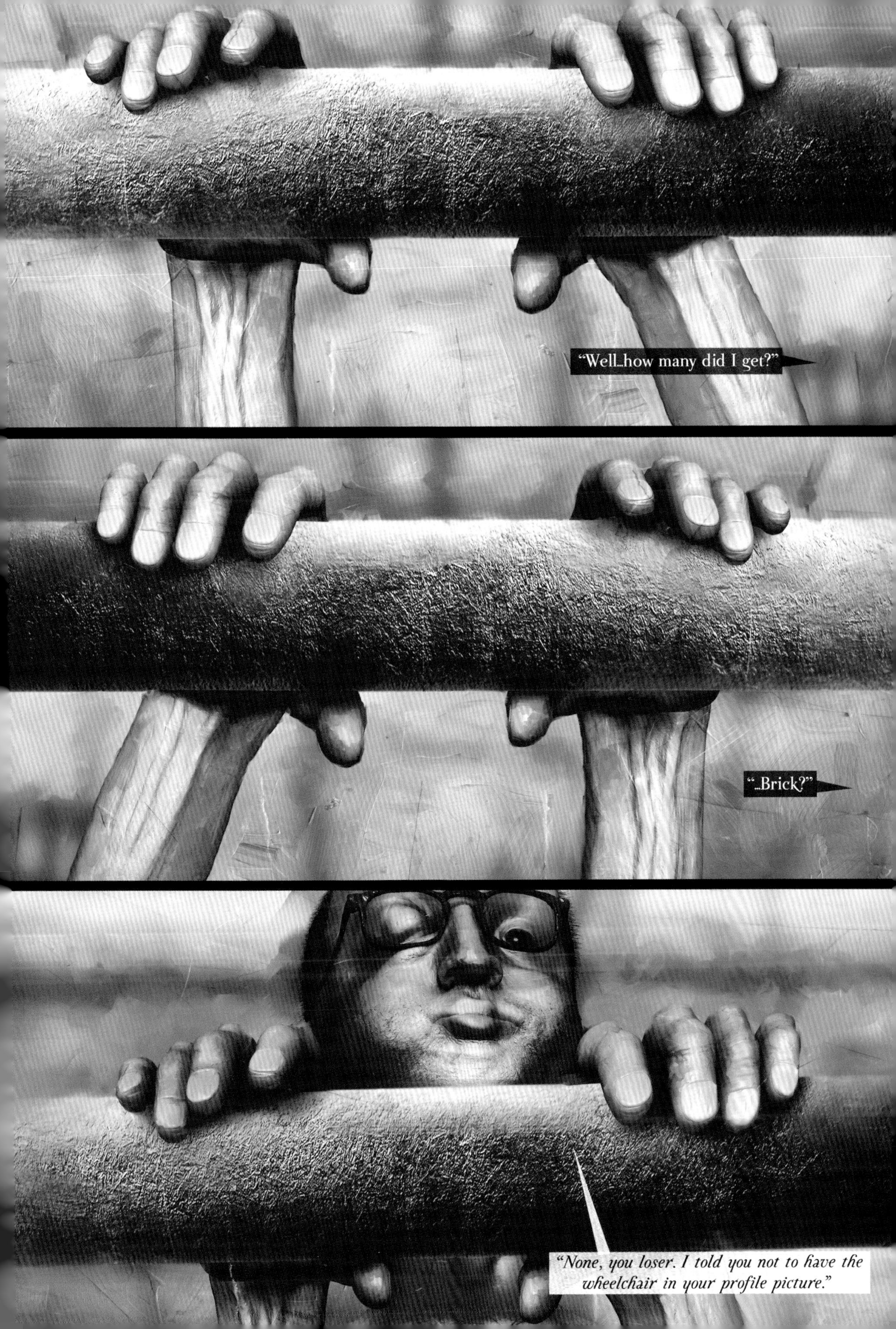
"Well..how many did I get?"
"...Brick?"
"None, you loser. I told you not to have the wheelchair in your profile picture."

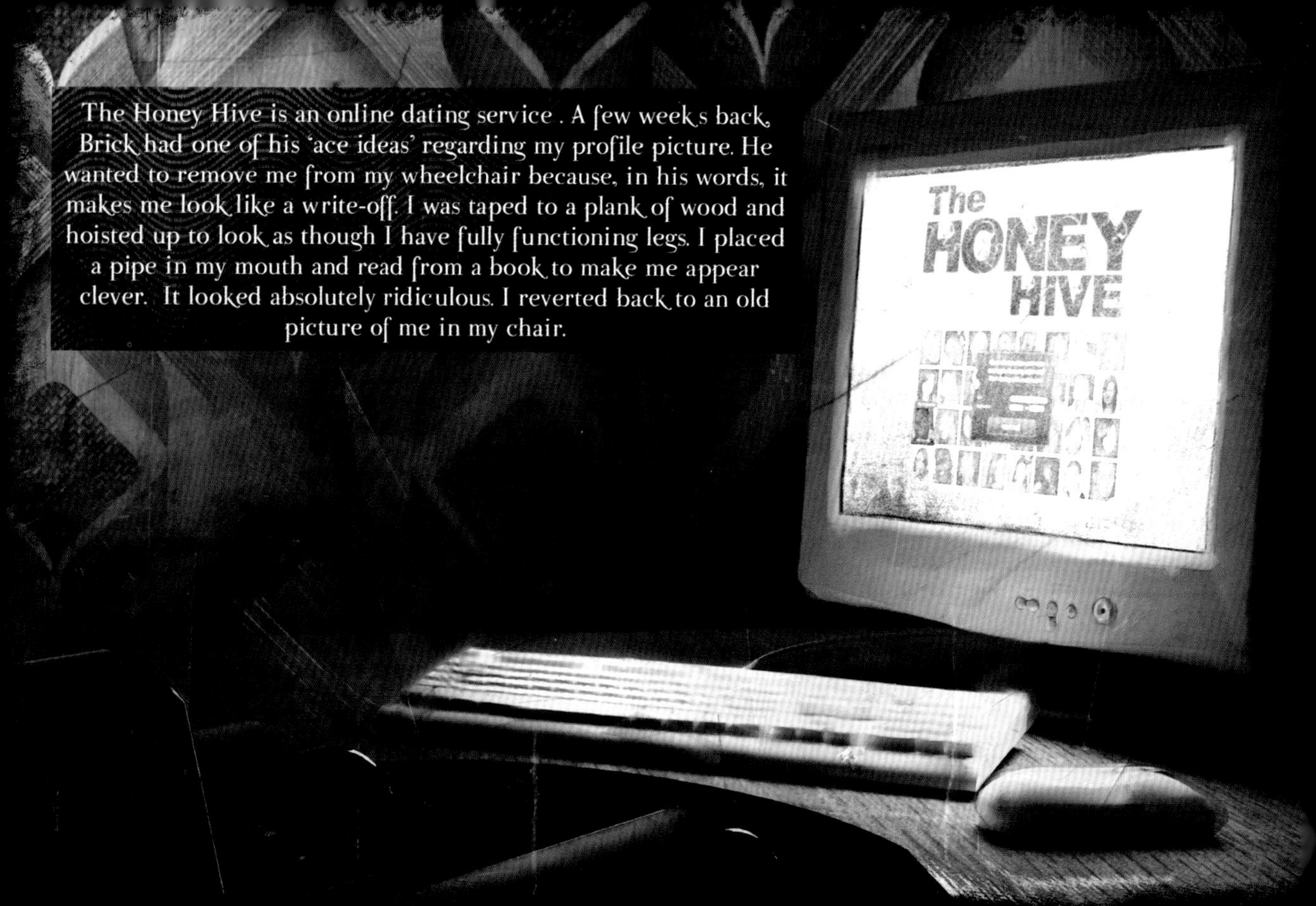
The Honey Hive is an online dating service . A few weeks back, Brick had one of his 'ace ideas' regarding my profile picture. He wanted to remove me from my wheelchair because, in his words, it makes me look like a write-off. I was taped to a plank of wood and hoisted up to look as though I have fully functioning legs. I placed a pipe in my mouth and read from a book to make me appear clever. It looked absolutely ridiculous. I reverted back to an old picture of me in my chair.
The HONEY HIVE

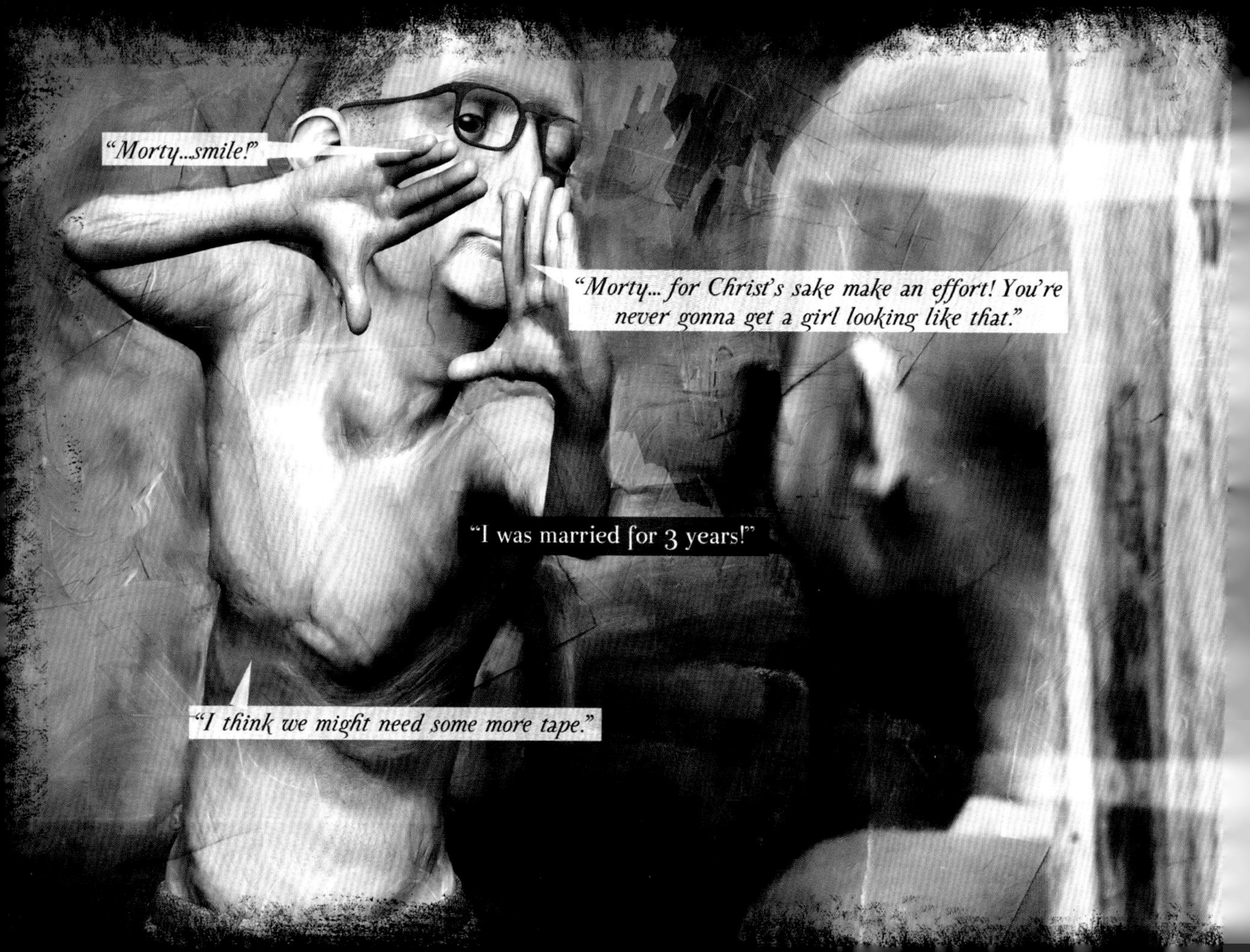
"Morty...smile!"
"Morty... for Christ's sake make an effort! You're never gonna get a girl looking like that."
"I was married for 3 years!"
"I think we might need some more tape."

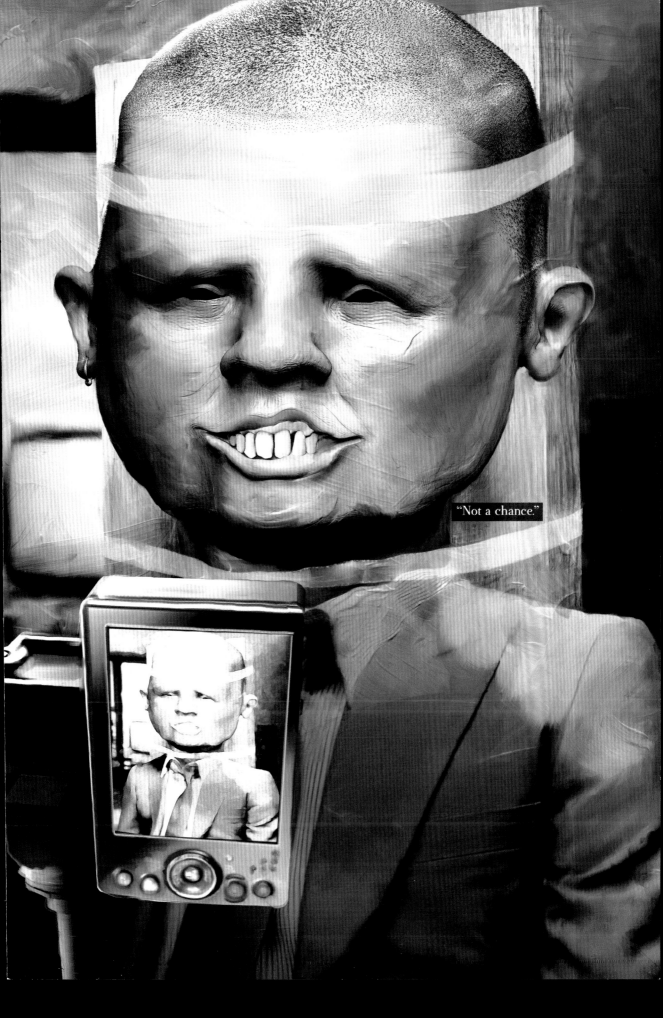

"Not a chance."

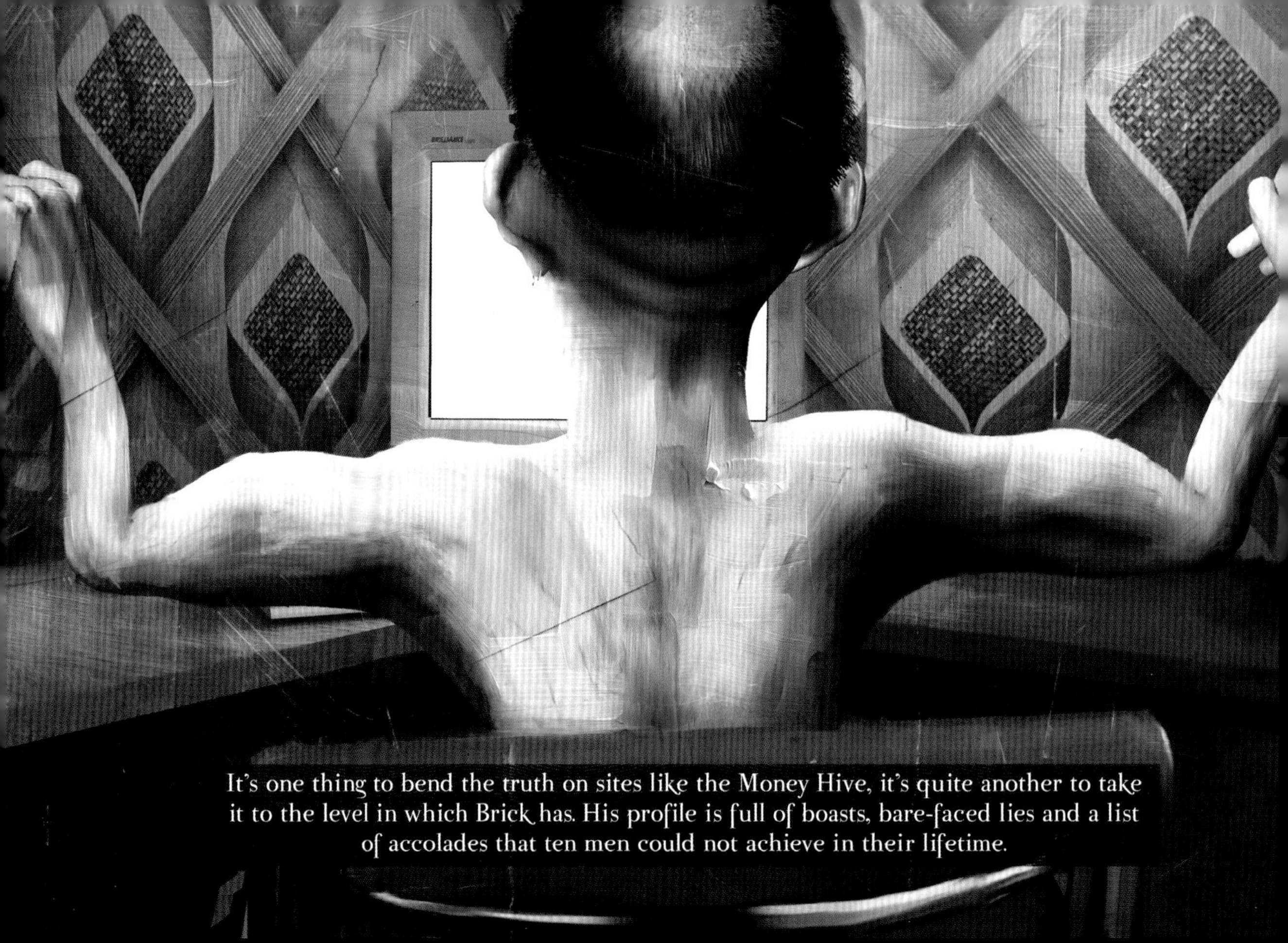

It's one thing to bend the truth on sites like the Money Hive, it's quite another to take it to the level in which Brick has. His profile is full of boasts, bare-faced lies and a list of accolades that ten men could not achieve in their lifetime.

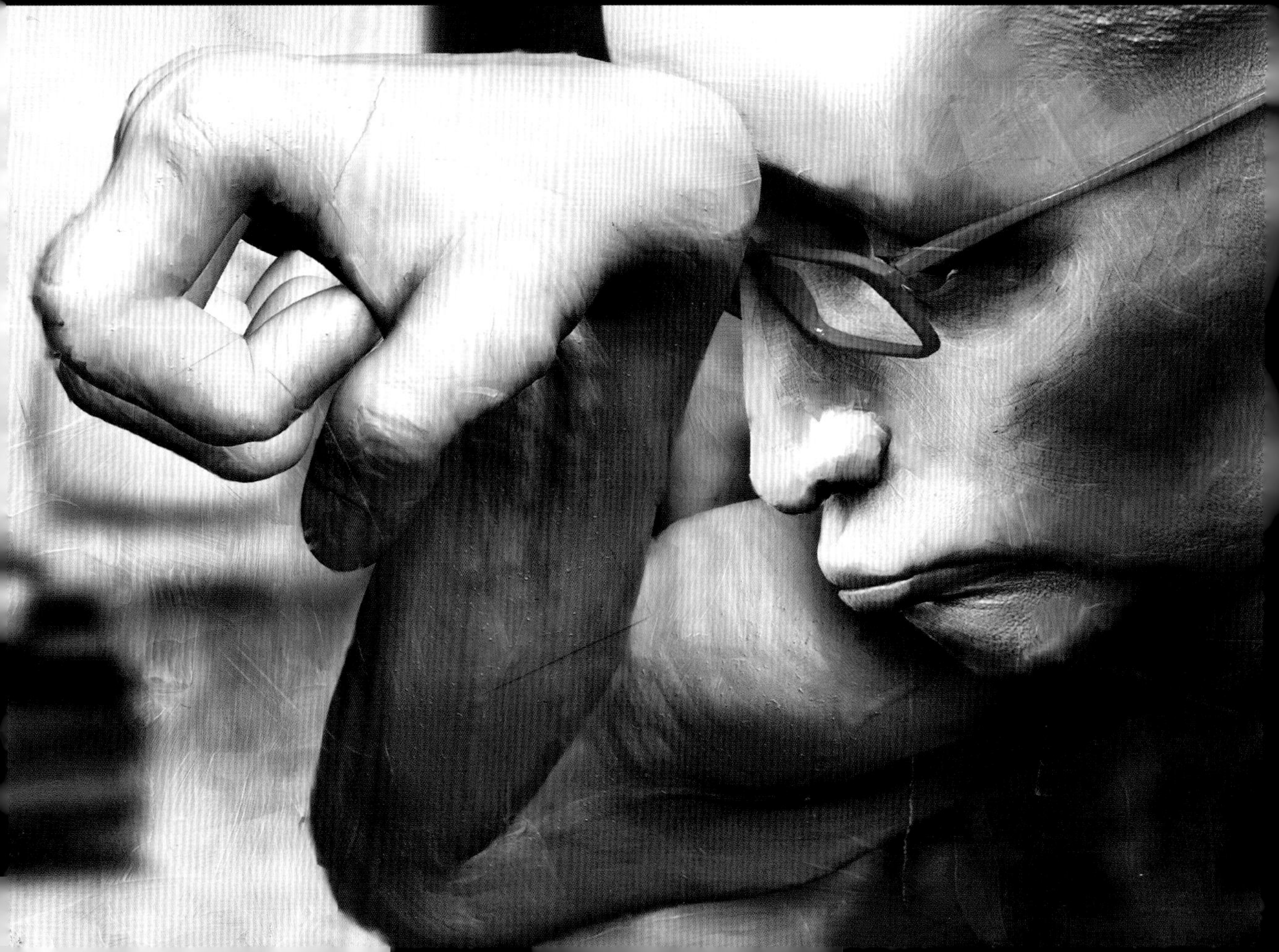

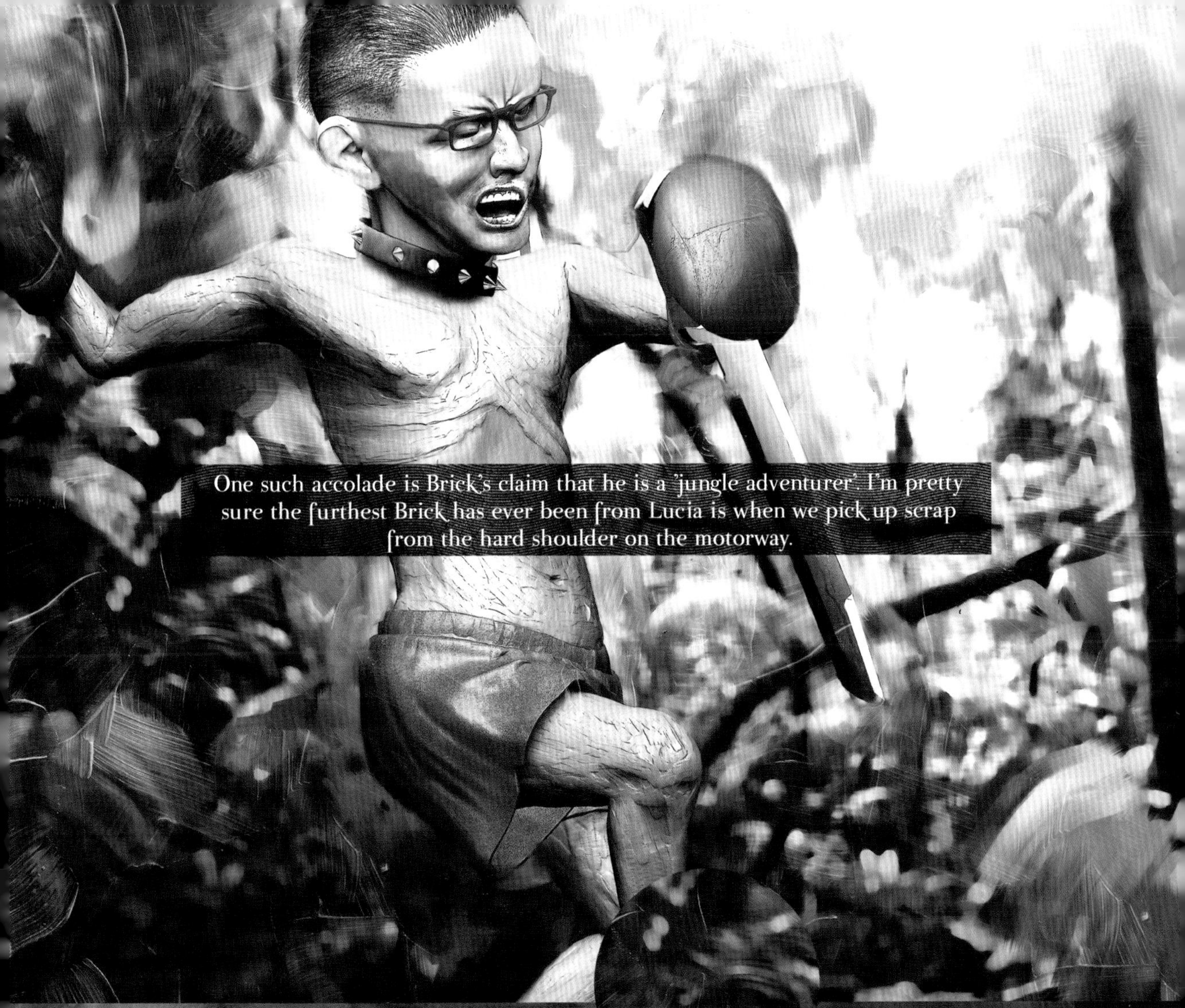
One such accolade is Brick's claim that he is a 'jungle adventurer'. I'm pretty sure the furthest Brick has ever been from Lucia is when we pick up scrap from the hard shoulder on the motorway.

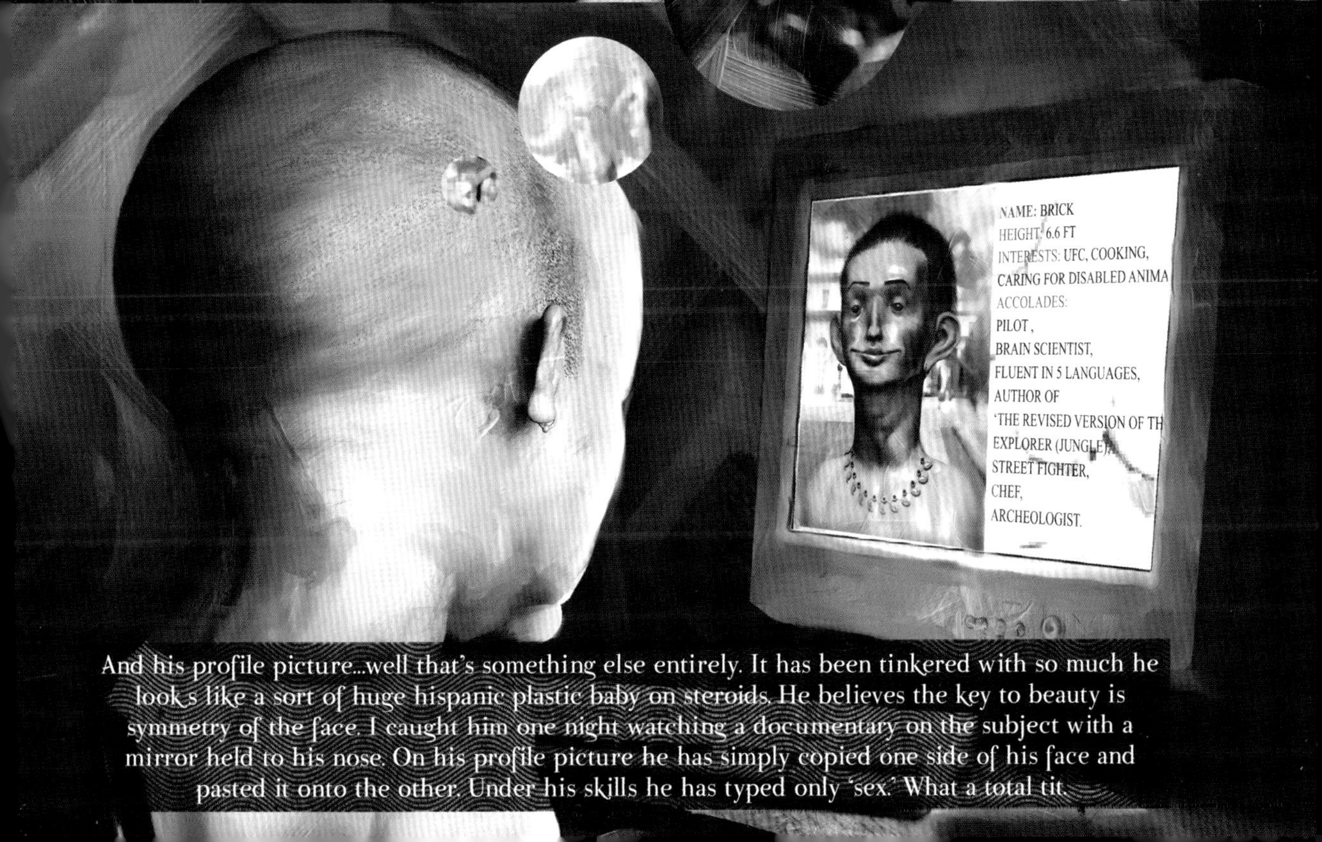
NAME: BRICK
HEIGHT: 6.6 FT
INTERESTS: UFC, COOKING,
CARING FOR DISABLED ANIMA
ACCOLADES:
PILOT ,
BRAIN SCIENTIST,
FLUENT IN 5 LANGUAGES,
AUTHOR OF
'THE REVISED VERSION OF TH
EXPLORER (JUNGLE)'
STREET FIGHTER,
CHEF,
ARCHEOLOGIST.
And his profile picture...well that's something else entirely. It has been tinkered with so much he looks like a sort of huge hispanic plastic baby on steroids. He believes the key to beauty is symmetry of the face. I caught him one night watching a documentary on the subject with a mirror held to his nose. On his profile picture he has simply copied one side of his face and pasted it onto the other. Under his skills he has typed only 'sex.' What a total tit.

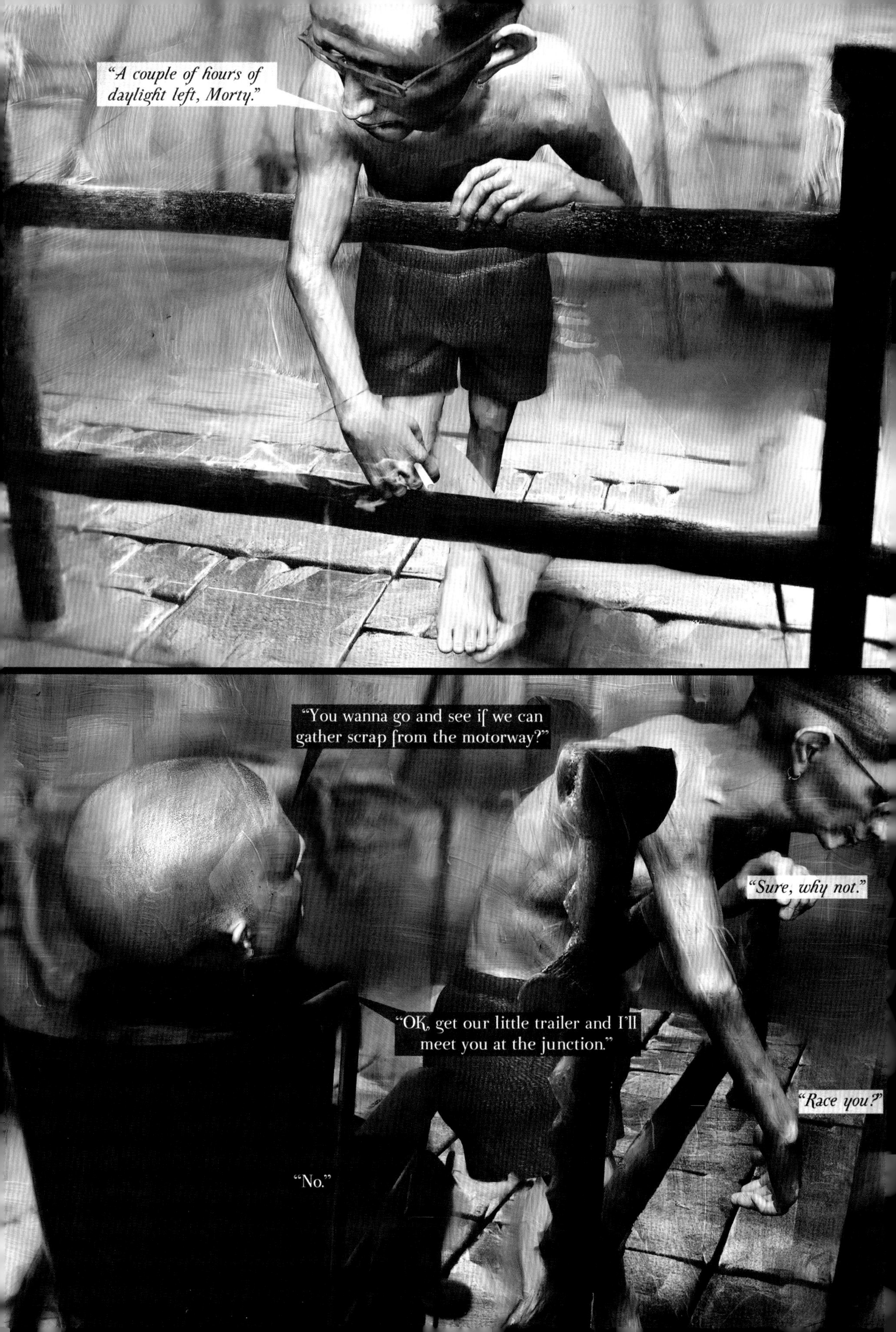
"A couple of hours of daylight left, Morty."
"You wanna go and see if we can gather scrap from the motorway?"
"Sure, why not."
"OK, get our little trailer and I'll meet you at the junction."
"Race you?"
"No."

Funding Brick's VHS habit is not cheap. We have an additional revenue stream: collecting scrap metal from the motorway hard shoulder. It is highly dangerous, but you don't get a collection of tapes as impressive as ours, and the latest video player with all the new digital read-outs, by not taking risks.

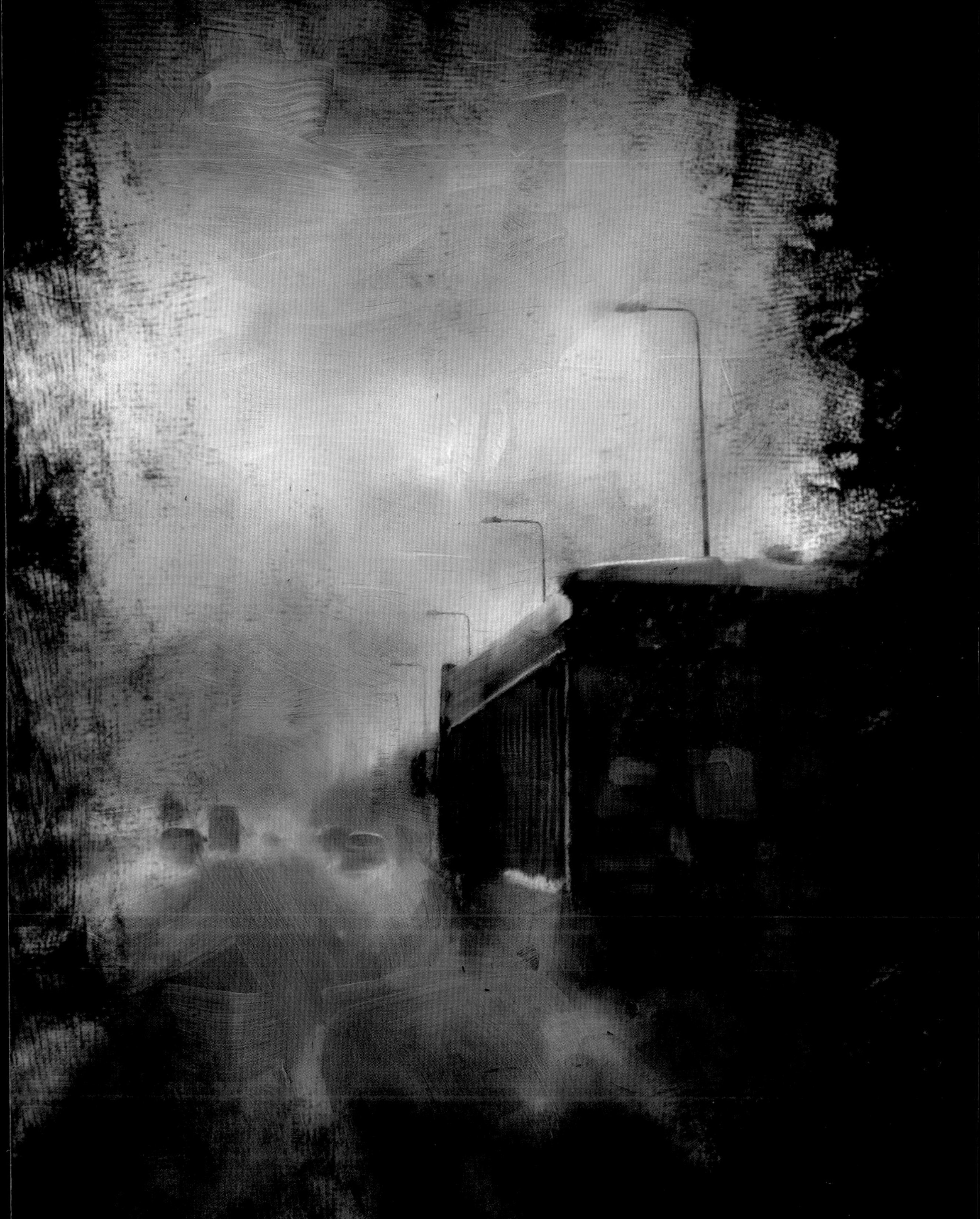

The motorway is flooded with an inch of stagnant water that never seems to disappear, even in the summer months. Tyres plough through the water kicking up a fine spray. Headlights shine through it creating a rainbow. This stretch of road is littered with pots filled with scrap silver.

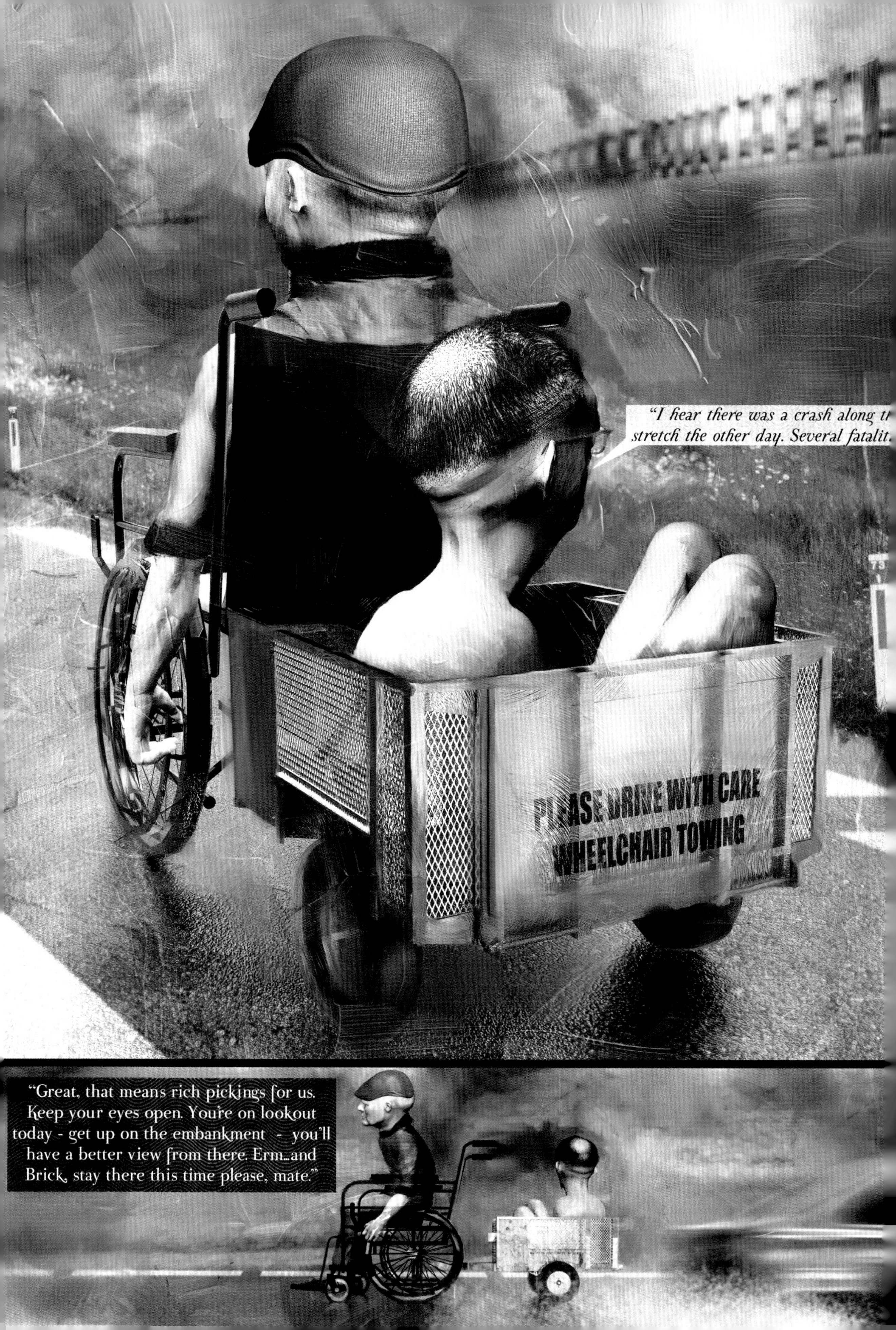

“I hear there was a crash along t
stretch the other day. Several fatalit
PLEASE DRIVE WITH CARE
WHEELCHAIR TOWING
“Great, that means rich pickings for us. Keep your eyes open. You're on lookout today - get up on the embankment - you'll have a better view from there. Erm...and Brick, stay there this time please, mate.”

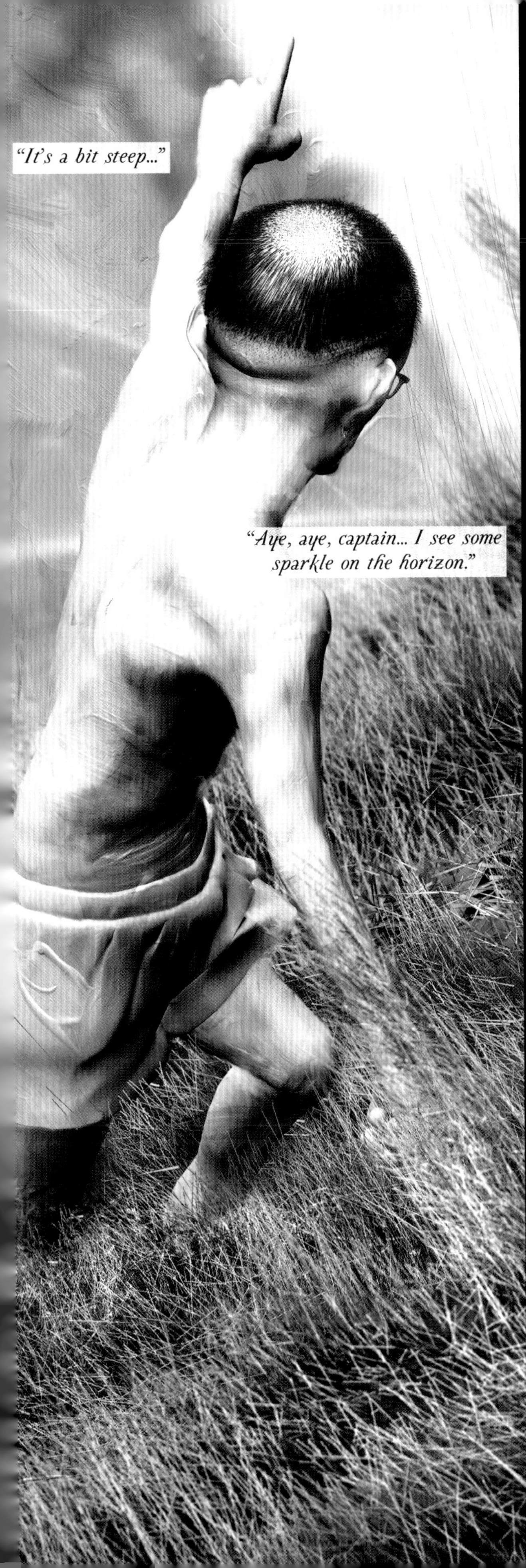
"It's a bit steep..."
"Aye, aye, captain... I see some sparkle on the horizon."

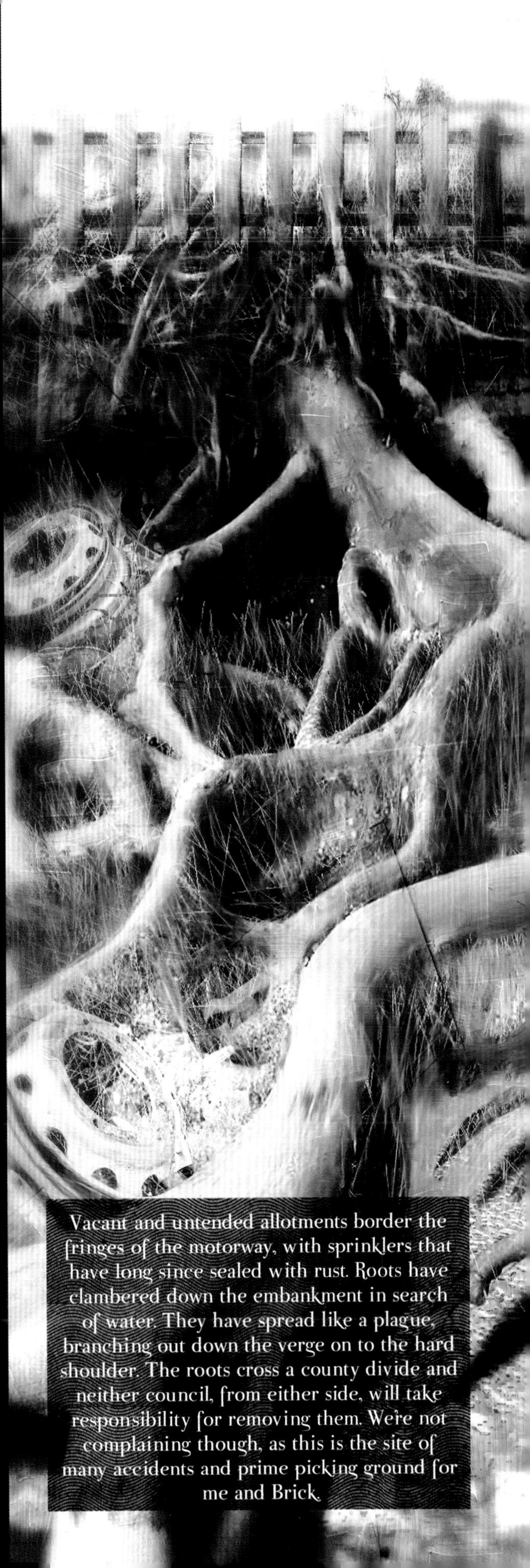
Vacant and untended allotments border the fringes of the motorway, with sprinklers that have long since sealed with rust. Roots have clambered down the embankment in search of water. They have spread like a plague, branching out down the verge on to the hard shoulder. The roots cross a county divide and neither council, from either side, will take responsibility for removing them. We're not complaining though, as this is the site of many accidents and prime picking ground for me and Brick.

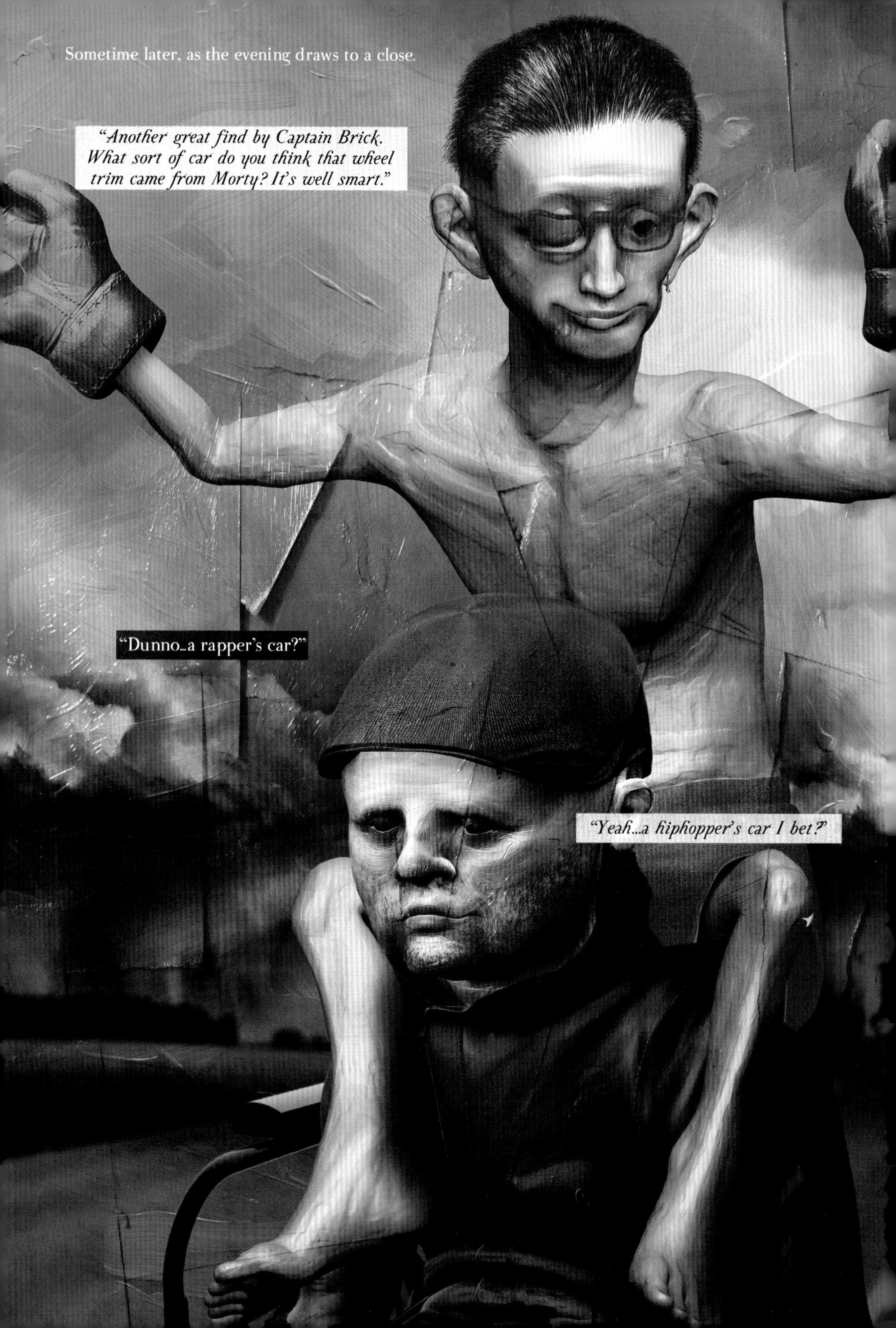
Sometime later, as the evening draws to a close.
"Another great find by Captain Brick. What sort of car do you think that wheel trim came from Morty? It's well smart."
"Dunno...a rapper's car?"
"Yeah...a hiphopper's car I bet?"

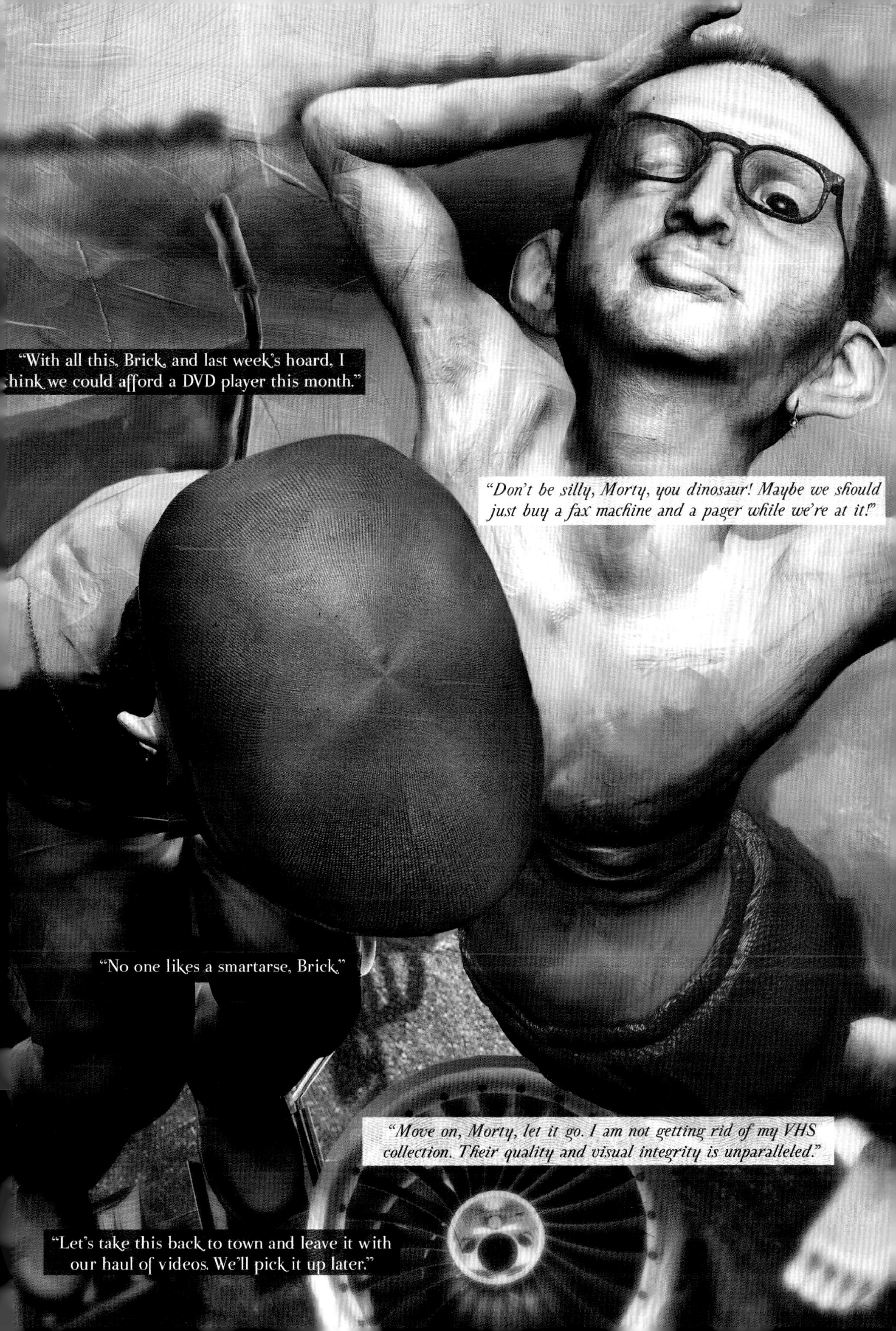
"With all this, Brick, and last week's hoard, I hink we could afford a DVD player this month."
"Don't be silly, Morty, you dinosaur! Maybe we should just buy a fax machine and a pager while we're at it!"
"No one likes a smartarse, Brick."
"Move on, Morty, let it go. I am not getting rid of my VHS collection. Their quality and visual integrity is unparalleled."
"Let's take this back to town and leave it with our haul of videos. We'll pick it up later."

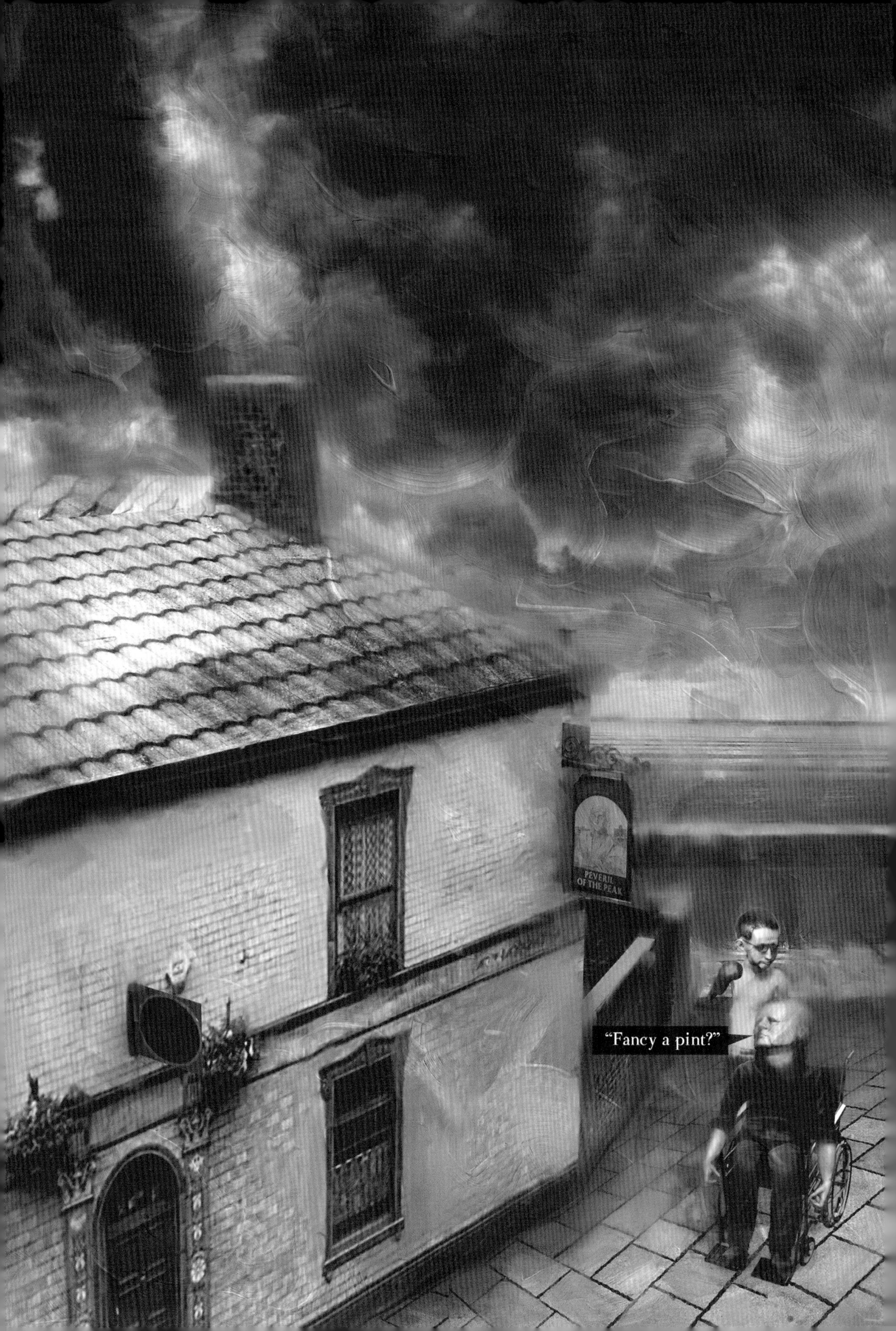
PEVERIL OF THE PEAK
"Fancy a pint?"

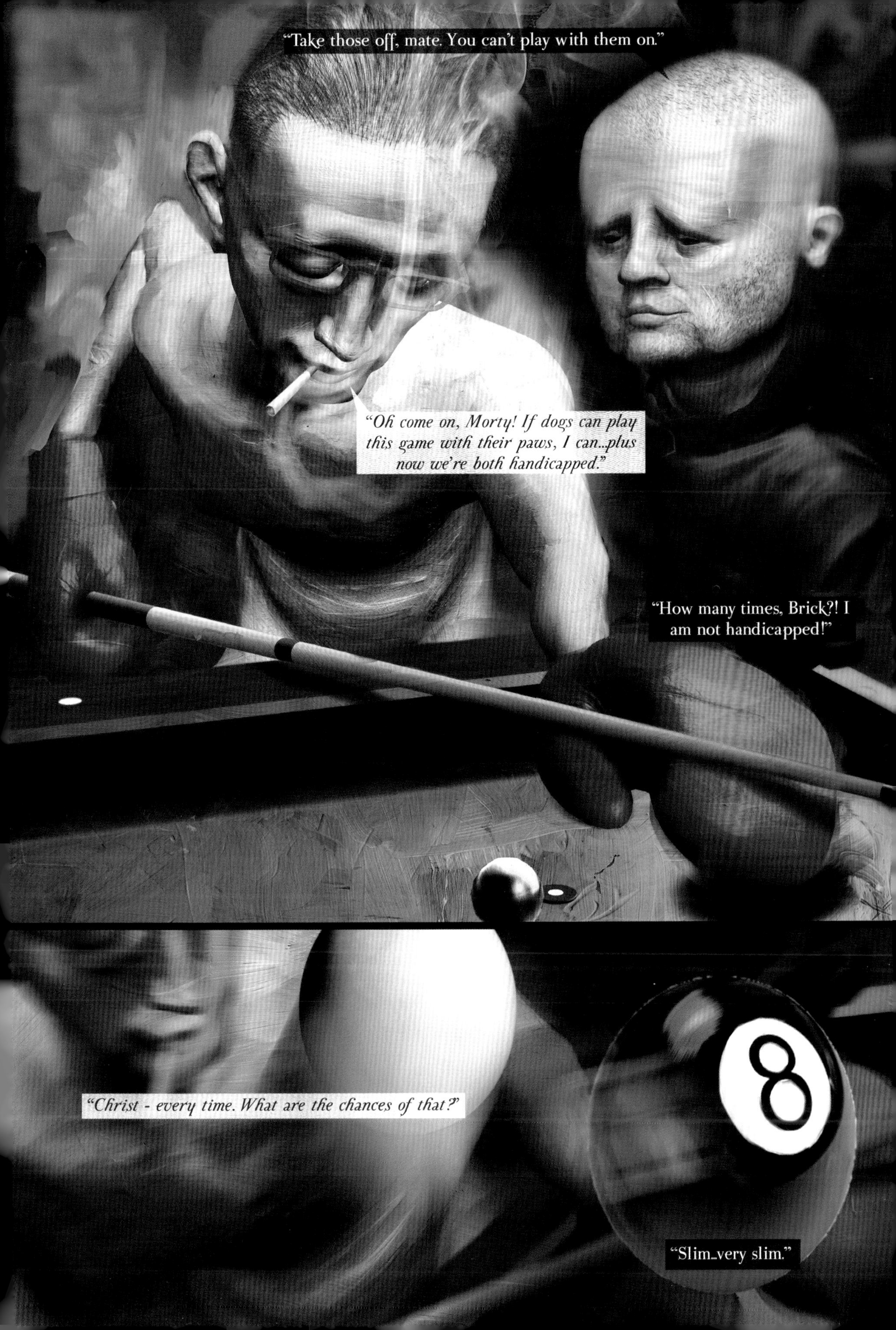
"Take those off, mate. You can't play with them on."
"Oh come on, Morty! If dogs can play this game with their paws, I can...plus now we're both handicapped."
"How many times, Brick?! I am not handicapped!"
"Christ - every time. What are the chances of that?"
8
"Slim...very slim."

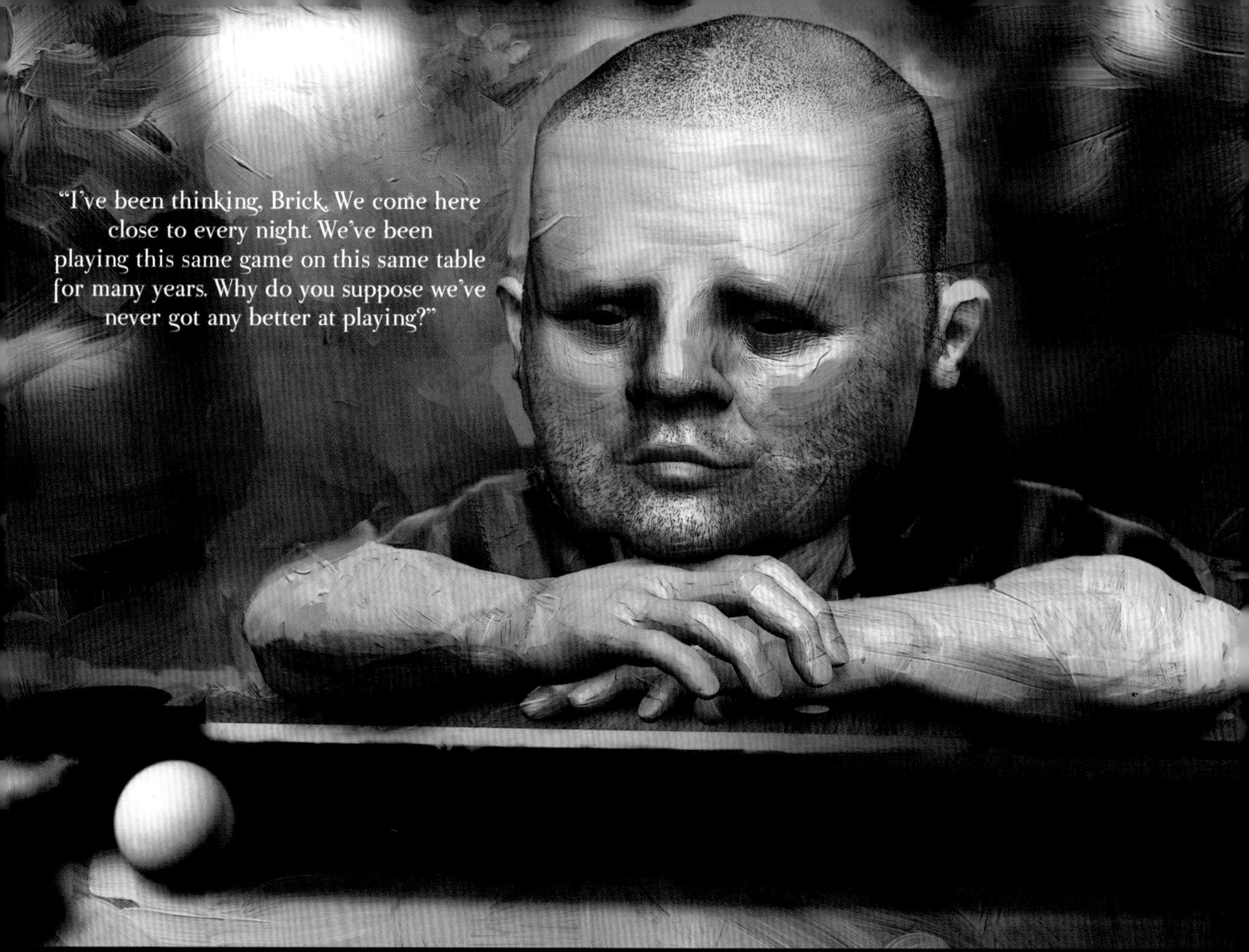
"I've been thinking, Brick. We come here close to every night. We've been playing this same game on this same table for many years. Why do you suppose we've never got any better at playing?"

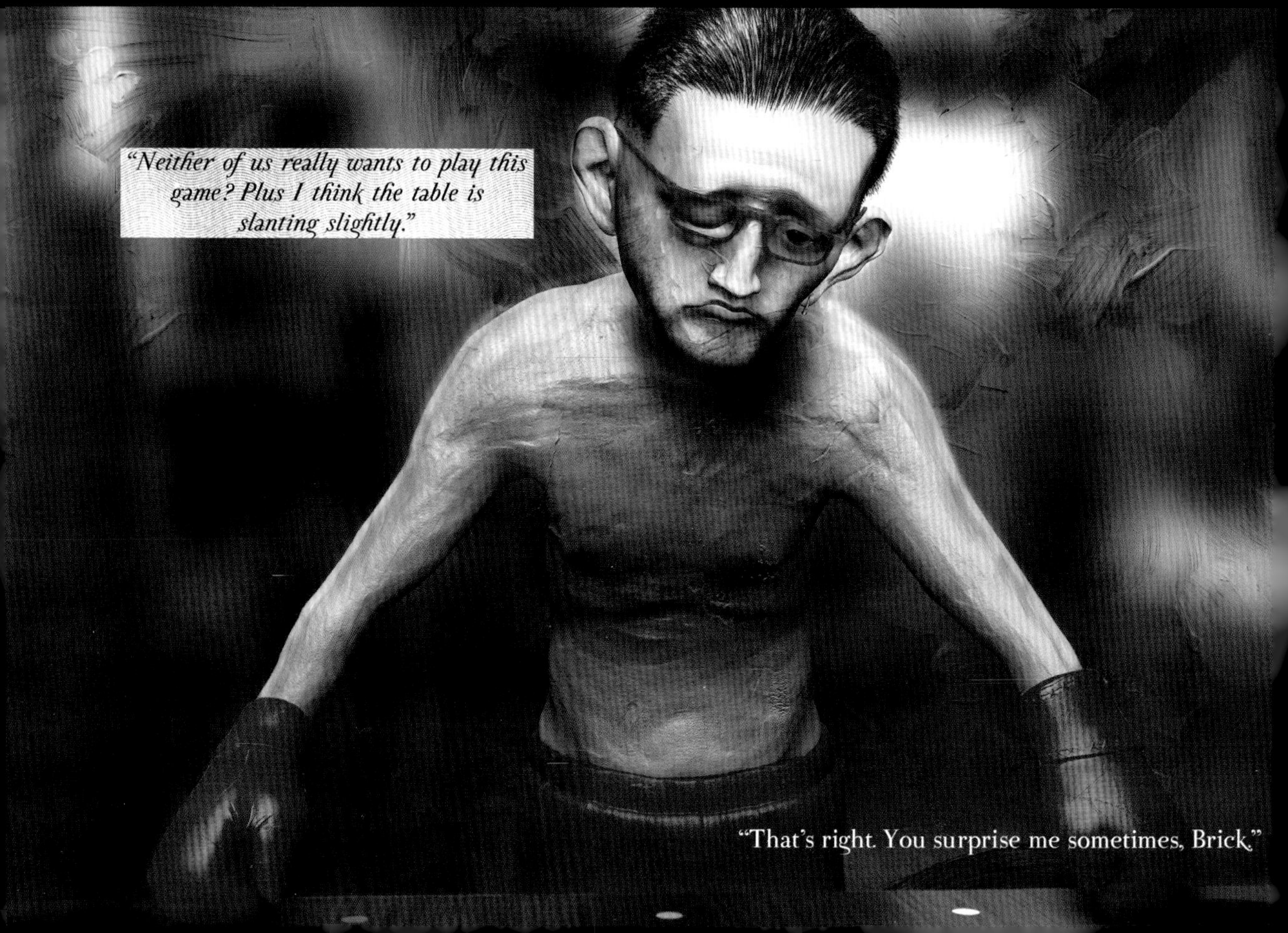
"Neither of us really wants to play this game? Plus I think the table is slanting slightly."
"That's right. You surprise me sometimes, Brick."

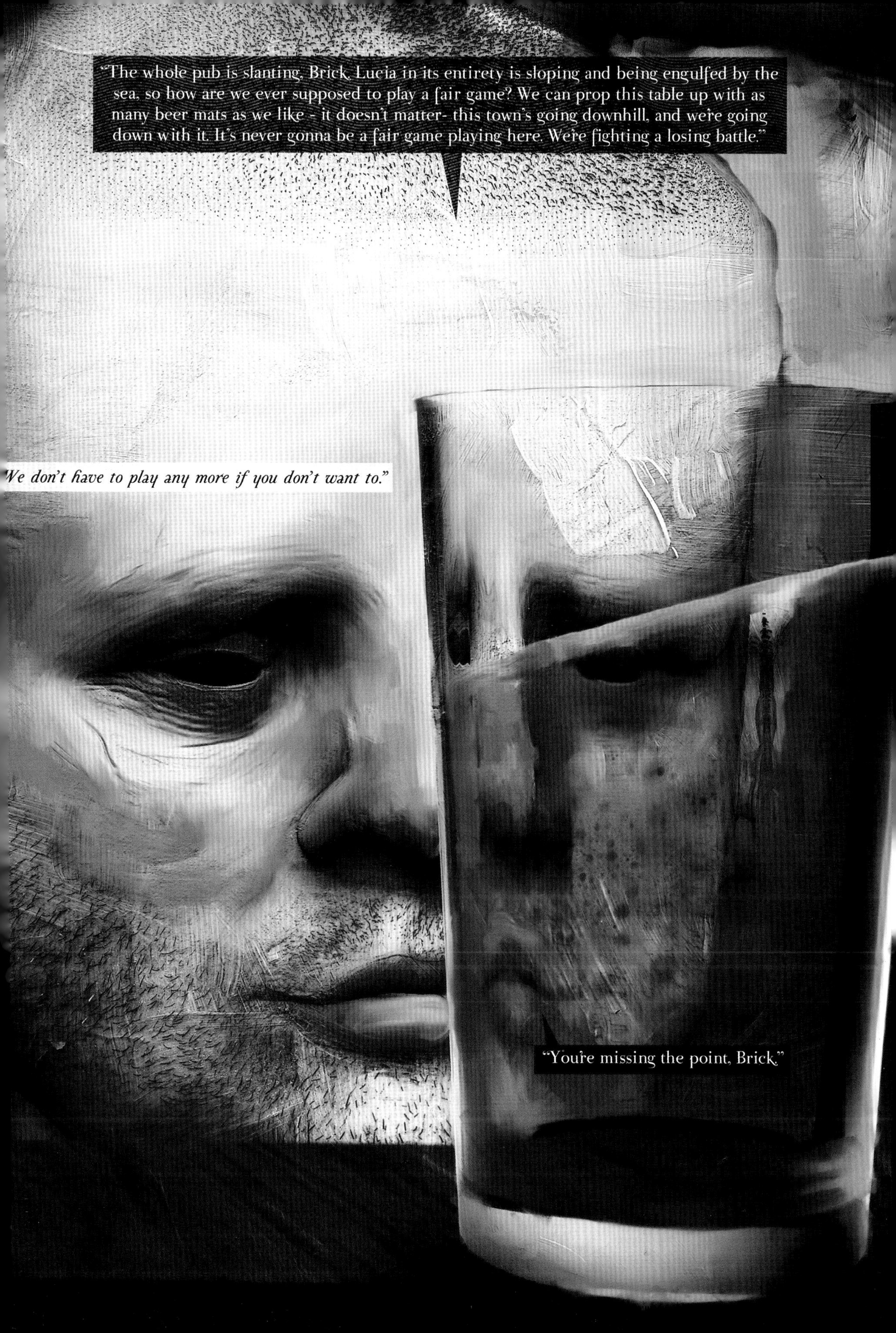
"The whole pub is slanting, Brick. Lucia in its entirety is sloping and being engulfed by the sea, so how are we ever supposed to play a fair game? We can prop this table up with as many beer mats as we like - it doesn't matter- this town's going downhill, and we're going down with it. It's never gonna be a fair game playing here. We're fighting a losing battle."
Ve don't have to play any more if you don't want to."
"You're missing the point, Brick."

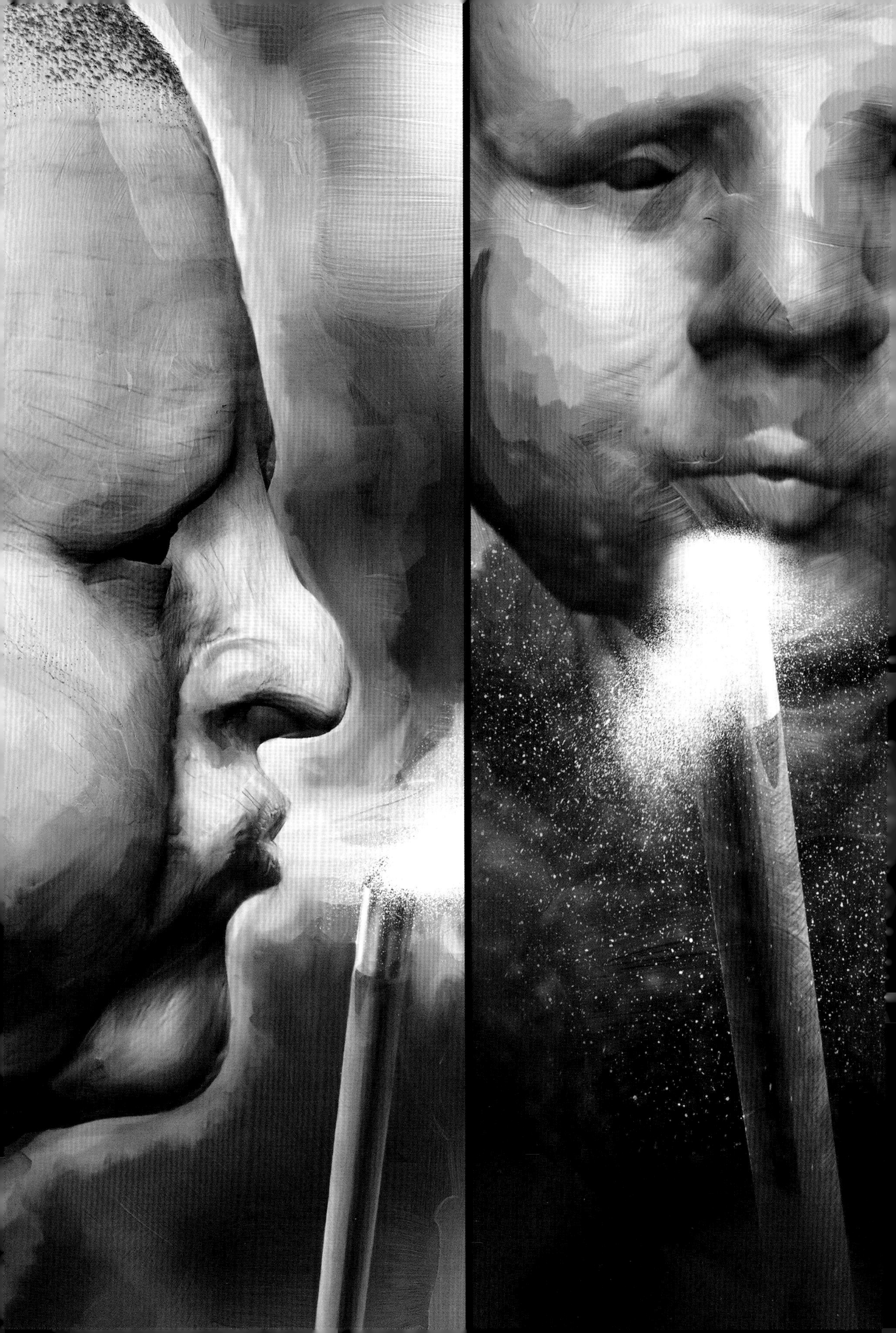

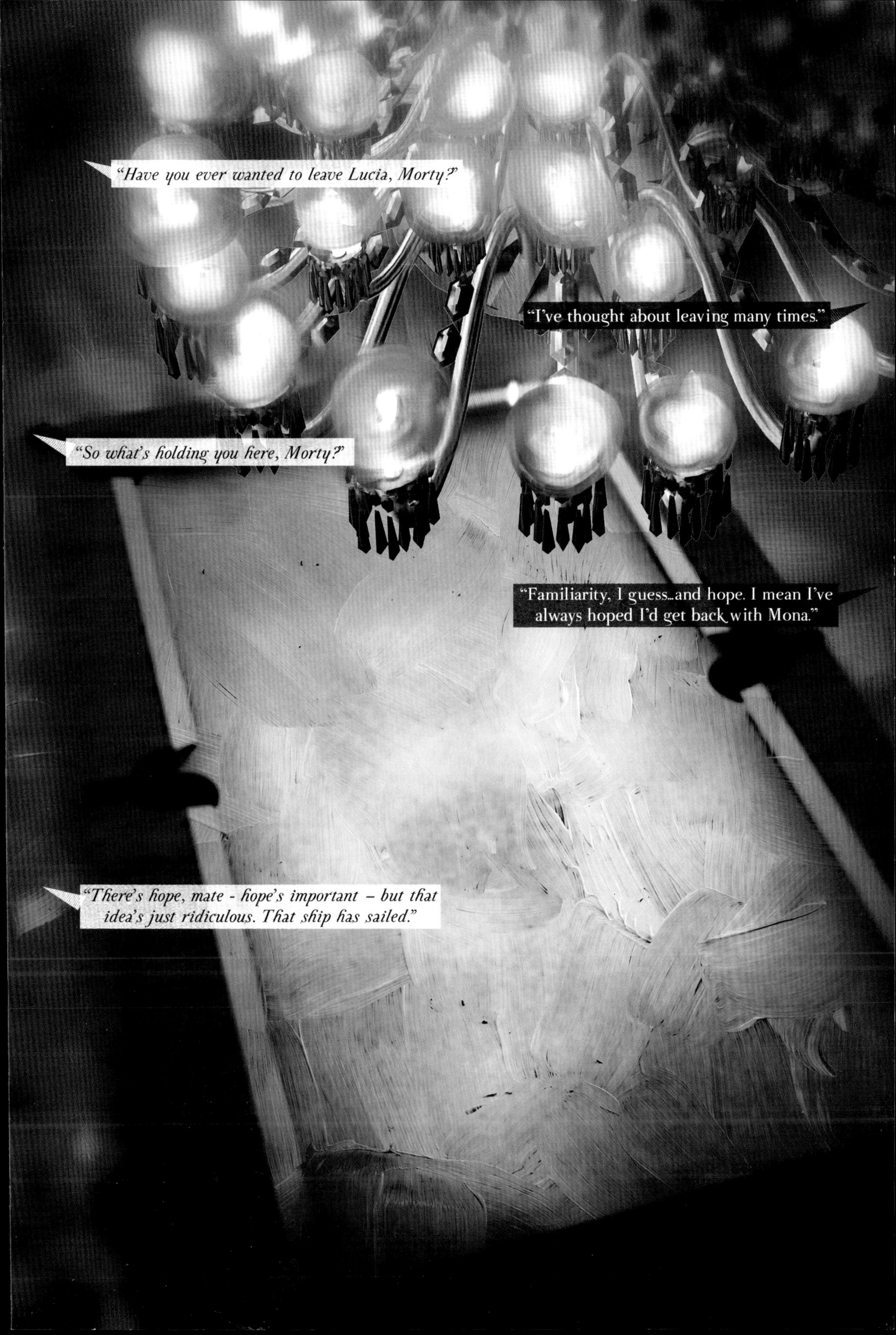
"Have you ever wanted to leave Lucia, Morty?"
"I've thought about leaving many times."
"So what's holding you here, Morty?"
"Familiarity, I guess...and hope. I mean I've always hoped I'd get back with Mona."
"There's hope, mate - hope's important – but that idea's just ridiculous. That ship has sailed."

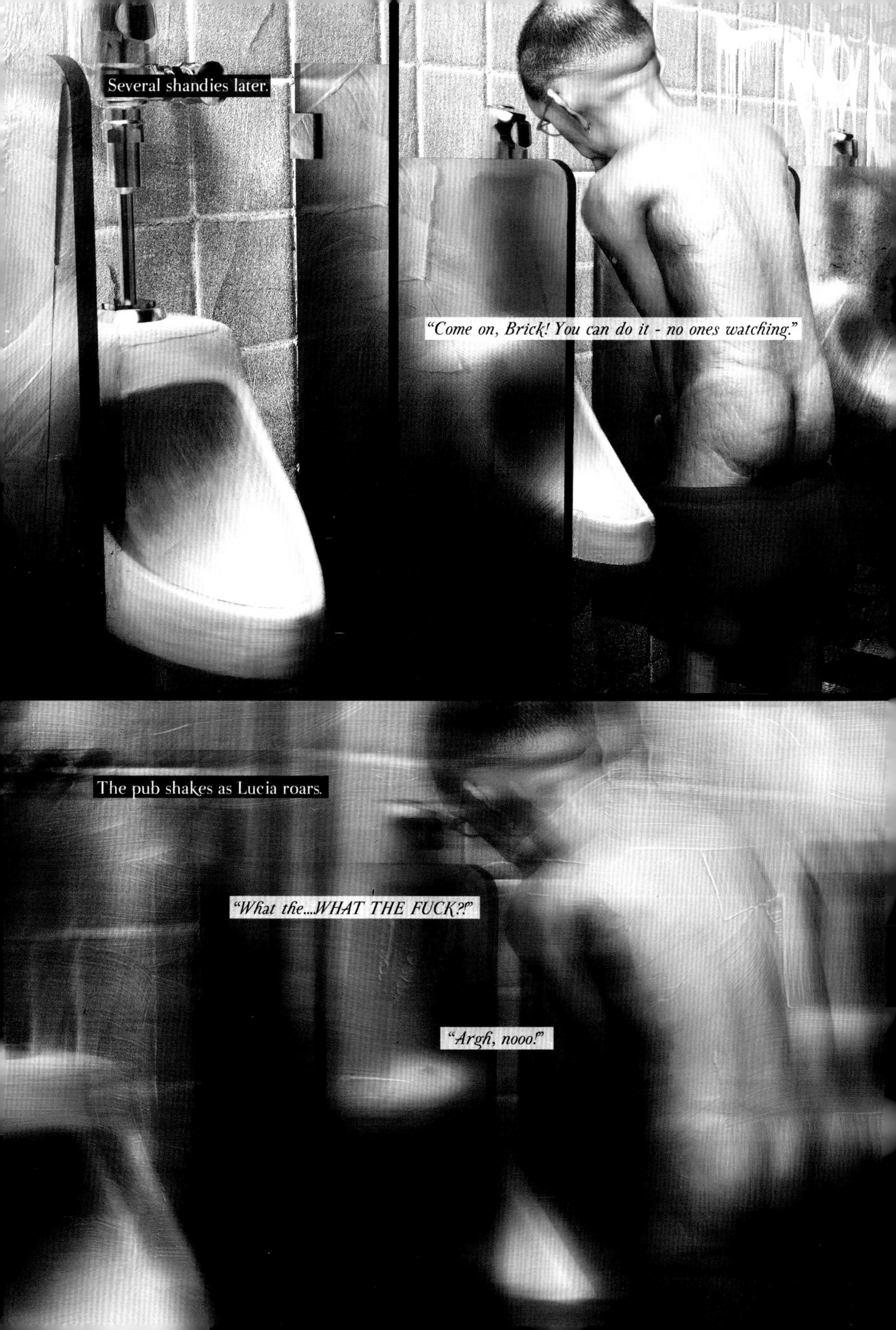
Several shandies later.
"Come on, Brick! You can do it - no ones watching."
The pub shakes as Lucia roars.
"What the...WHAT THE FUCK?!"
"Argh, nooo!"

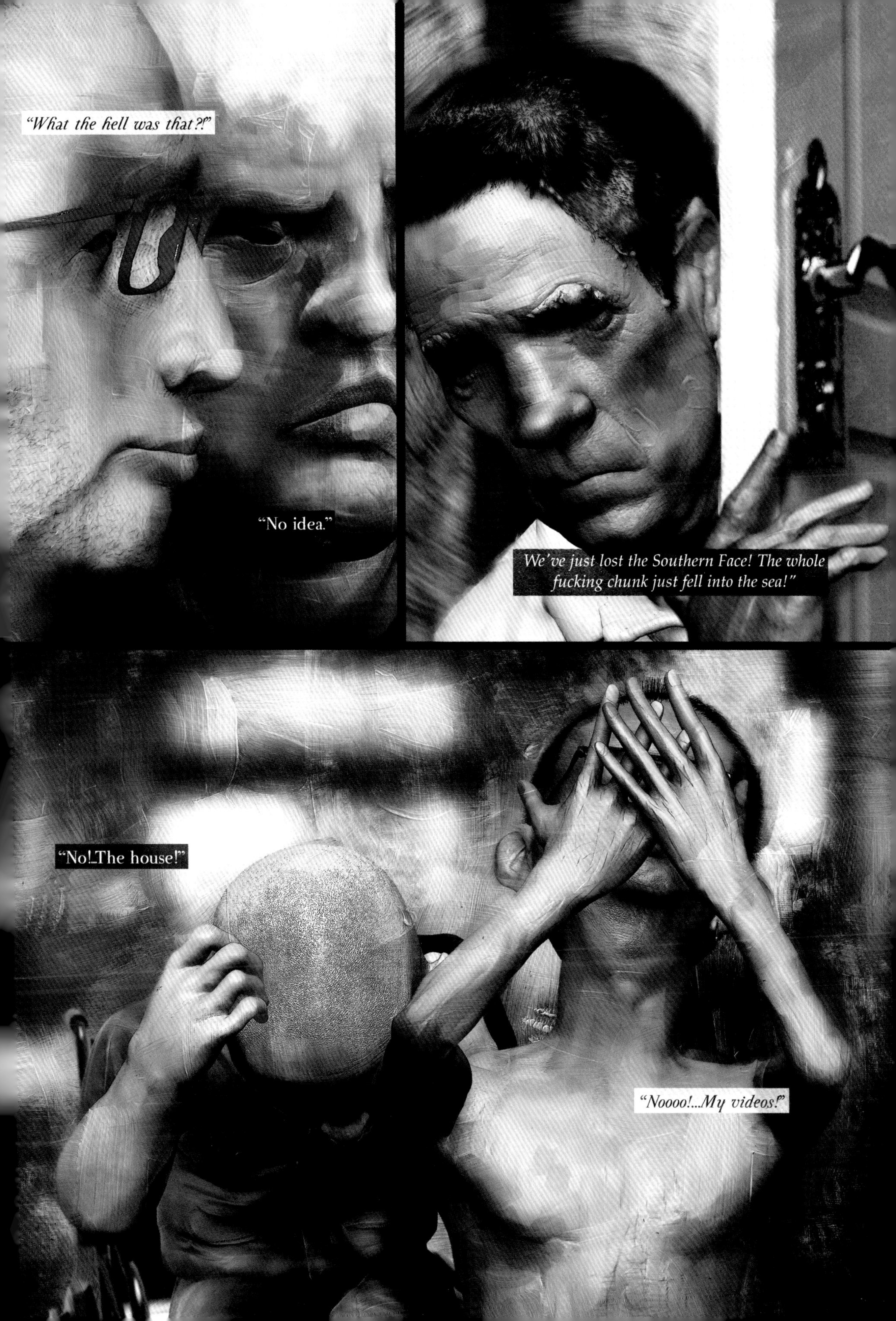
"What the hell was that?!"
"No idea."
We've just lost the Southern Face! The whole fucking chunk just fell into the sea!"
"No!..The house!"
"Noooo!...My videos!"

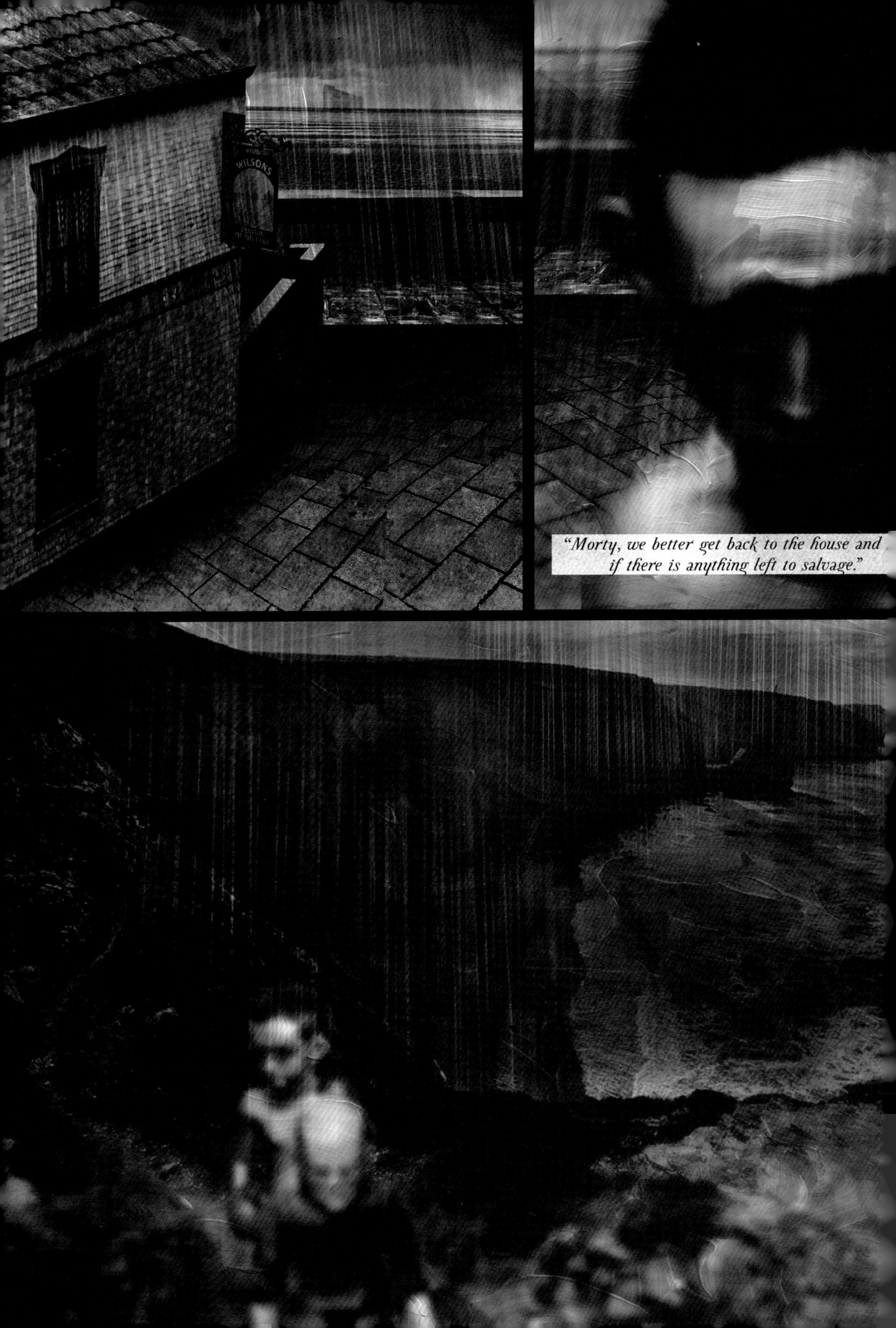
WILSONS
"Morty, we better get back to the house and
if there is anything left to salvage."

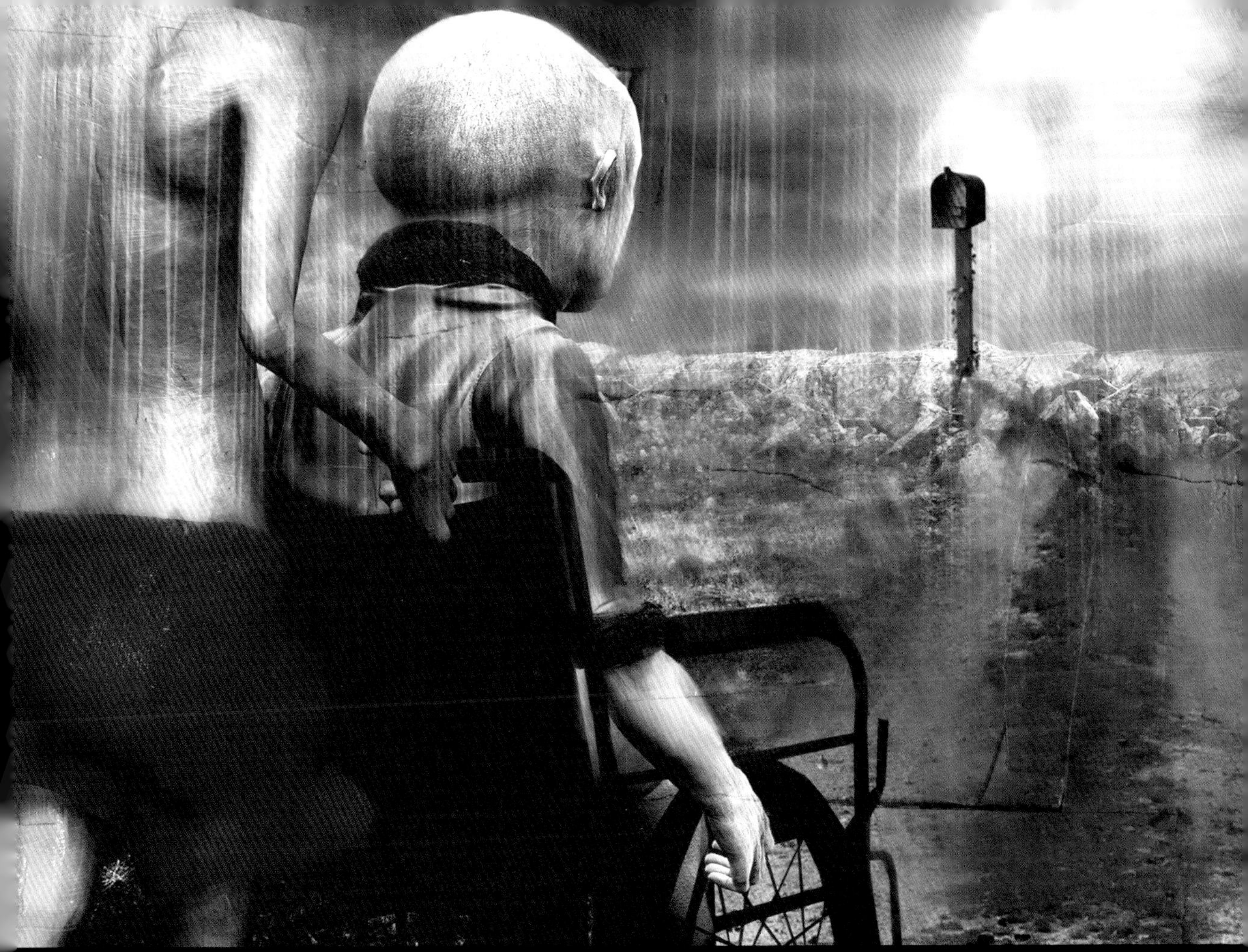

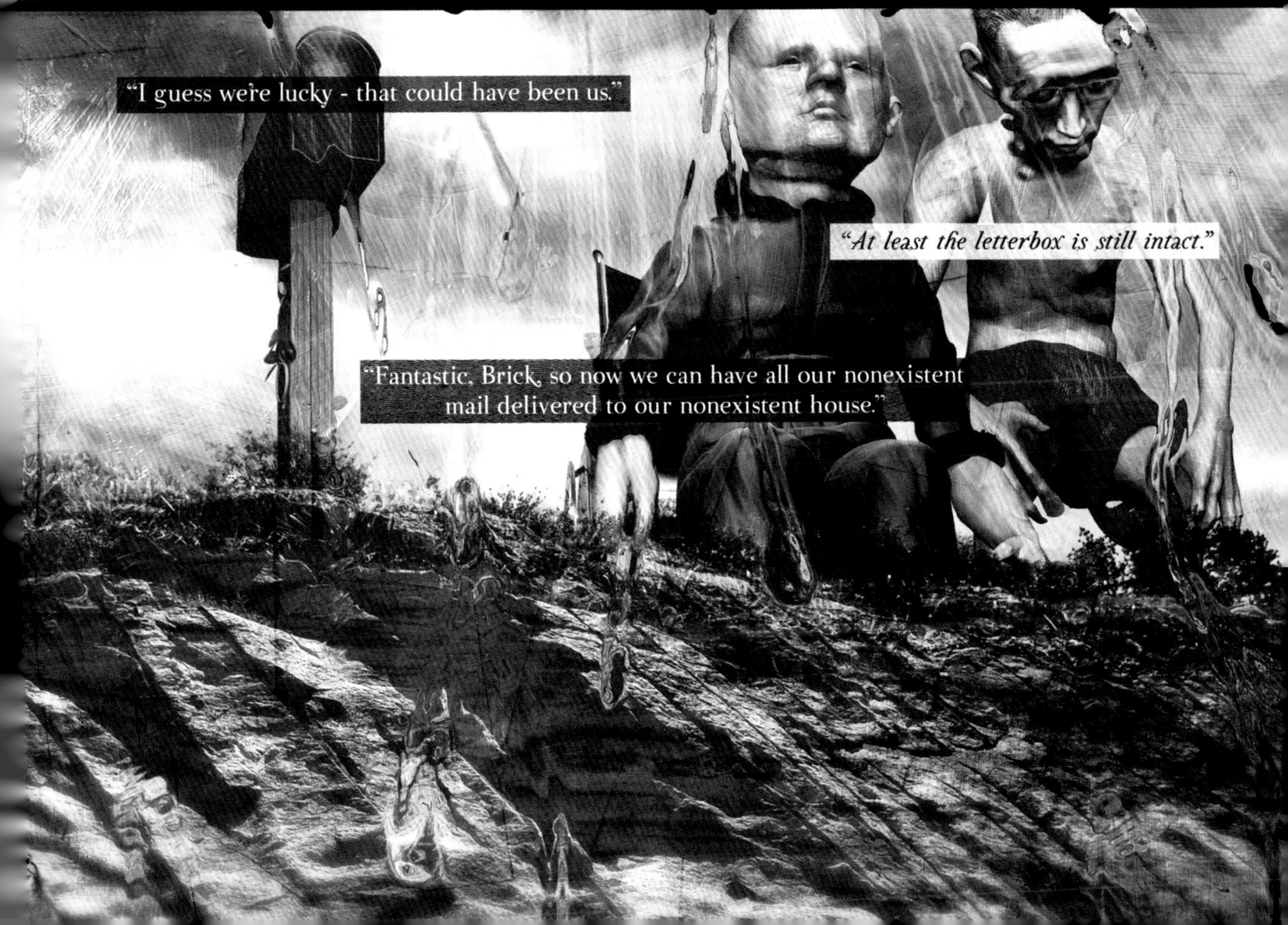
"I guess we're lucky - that could have been us."
"At least the letterbox is still intact."
"Fantastic, Brick, so now we can have all our nonexistent mail delivered to our nonexistent house."

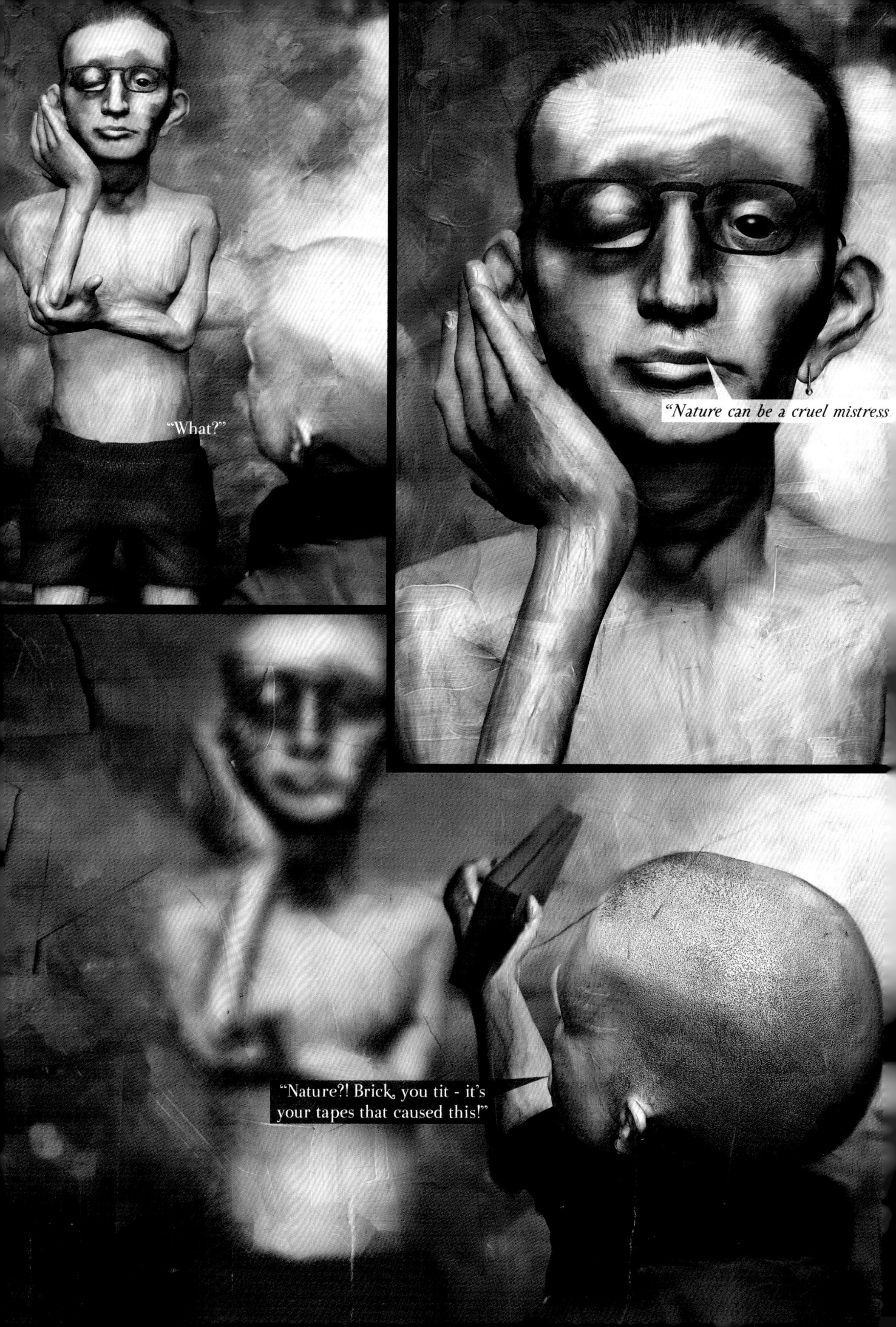
"What?"
"Nature can be a cruel mistress
"Nature?! Brick, you tit - it's
your tapes that caused this!"

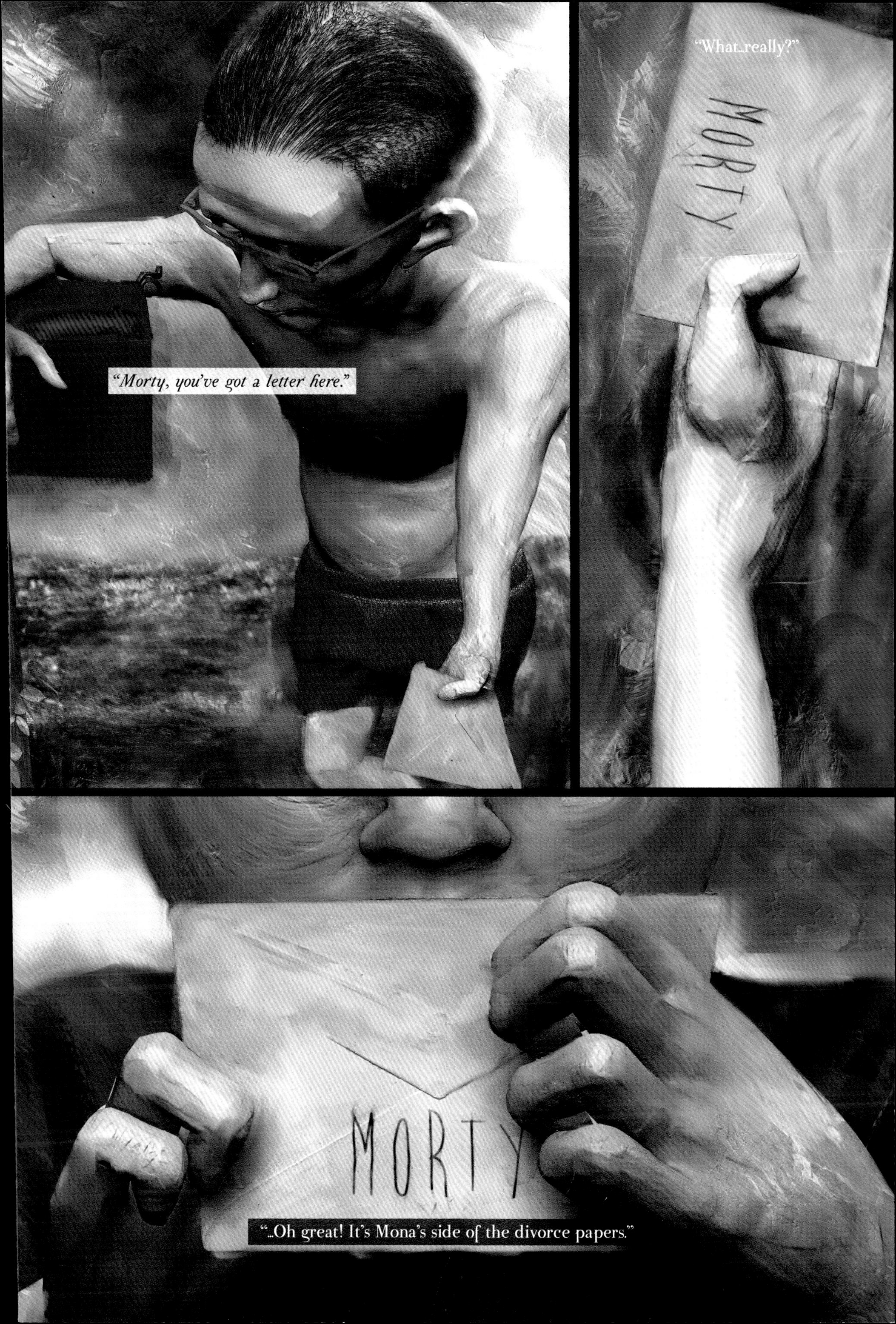

"Morty, you've got a letter here."
"What...really?"
MORTY
MORTY
"...Oh great! It's Mona's side of the divorce papers."

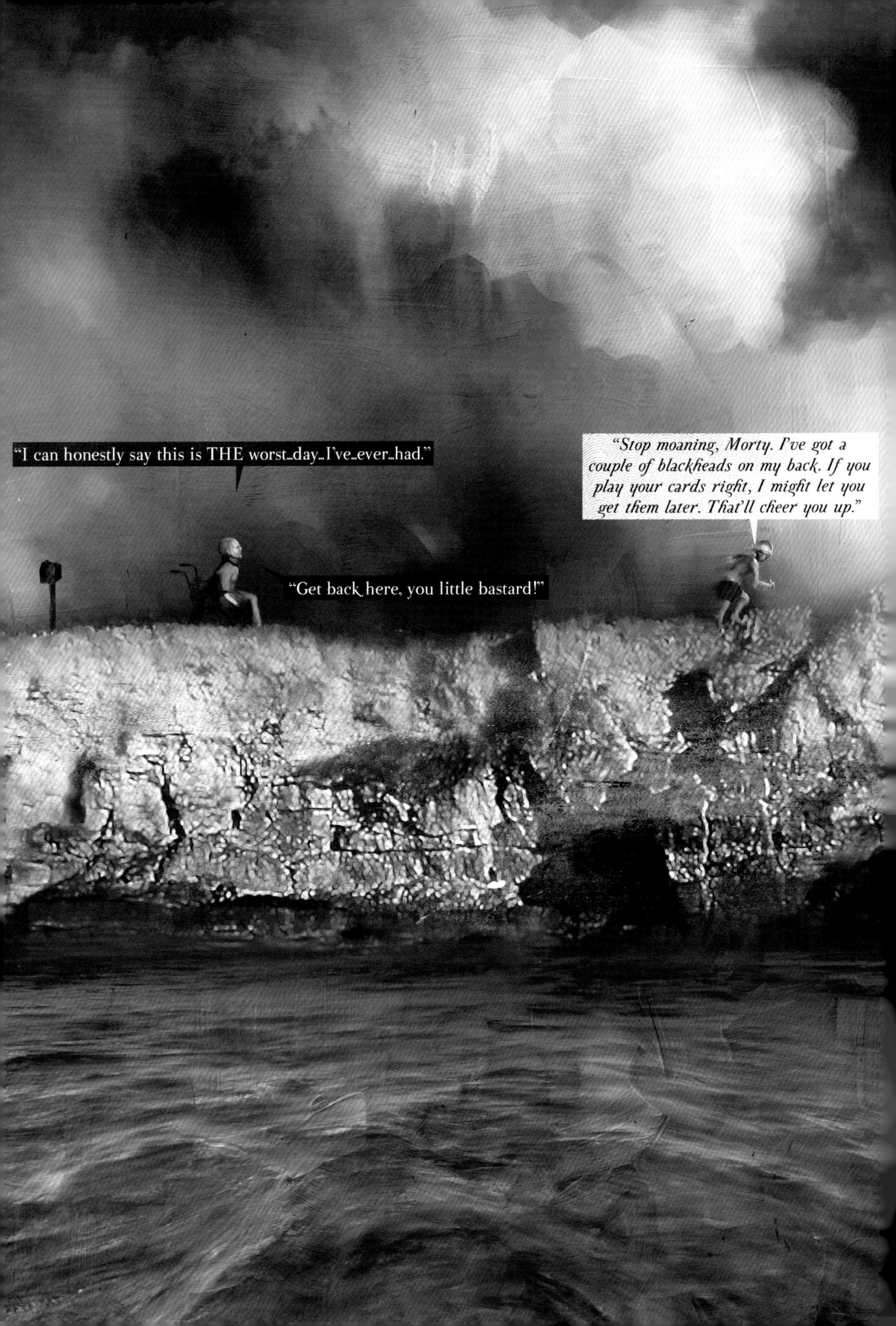
"I can honestly say this is THE worst..day..I've..ever..had."
"Get back here, you little bastard!"
"Stop moaning, Morty. I've got a couple of blackheads on my back. If you play your cards right, I might let you get them later. That'll cheer you up."

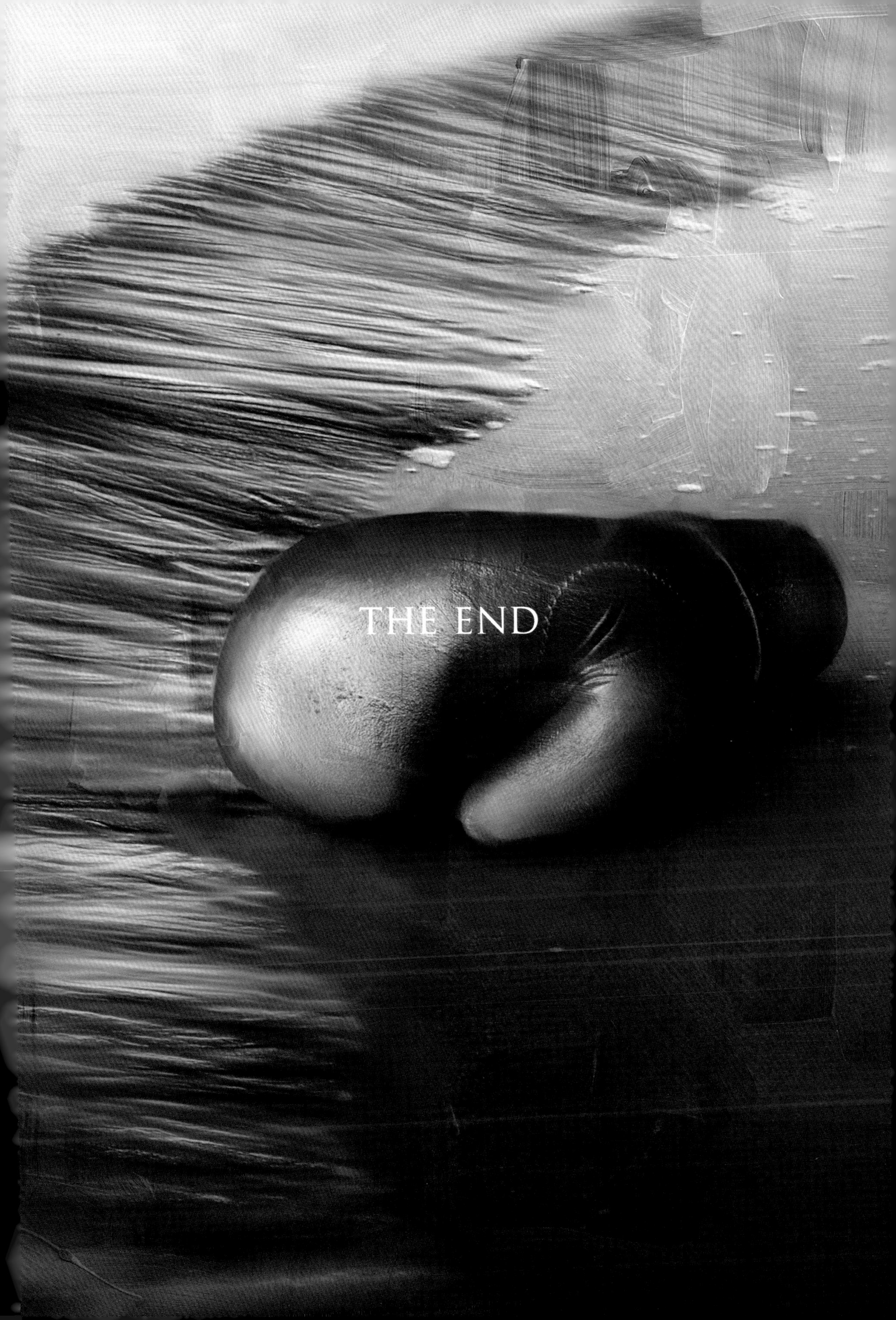
THE END

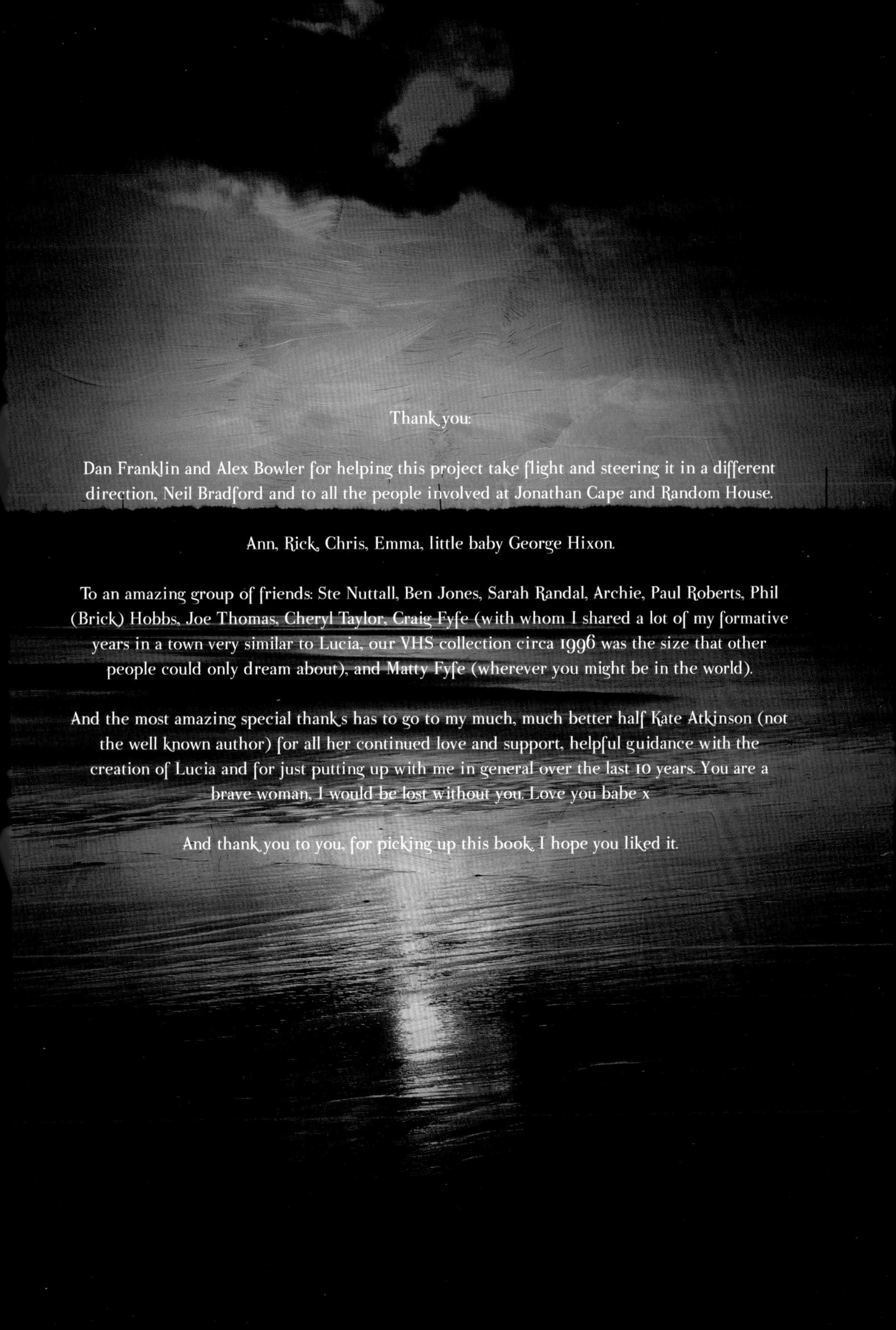

Thank you:

Dan Franklin and Alex Bowler for helping this project take flight and steering it in a different direction, Neil Bradford and to all the people involved at Jonathan Cape and Random House.

Ann, Rick, Chris, Emma, little baby George Hixon.

To an amazing group of friends: Ste Nuttall, Ben Jones, Sarah Randal, Archie, Paul Roberts, Phil (Brick) Hobbs, Joe Thomas, Cheryl Taylor, Craig Fyfe (with whom I shared a lot of my formative years in a town very similar to Lucia, our VHS collection circa 1996 was the size that other people could only dream about), and Matty Fyfe (wherever you might be in the world).

And the most amazing special thanks has to go to my much, much better half Kate Atkinson (not the well known author) for all her continued love and support, helpful guidance with the creation of Lucia and for just putting up with me in general over the last 10 years. You are a brave woman, I would be lost without you. Love you babe x

And thank you to you, for picking up this book. I hope you liked it.

Published by Jonathan Cape 2015

2 4 6 8 10 9 7 5 3 1

First published in Great Britain in 2013 by
Jonathan Cape
Random House, 20 Vauxhall Bridge Road,
London SW1V 2SA

www.vintage-books.co.uk

Addresses for companies within The Random House Group Limited can be found at:
www.randomhouse.co.uk/offices.htm

The Random House Group Limited Reg. No. 954009

A CIP catalogue record for this book is available from the British Library

ISBN 9780224099301

The Random House Group Limited supports The Forest Stewardship Council® (FSC®), the leading international forest-certification organisation. Our books carrying the FSC label are printed on FSC®-certified paper. FSC is the only forest-certification scheme supported by the leading environmental organisations, including Greenpeace. Our paper procurement policy can be found at www.randomhouse.co.uk/environment

MIX
Paper from responsible sources
FSC www.fsc.org FSC® C008047

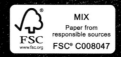

Printed and bound in China by C&C Offset Printing Co., Ltd

Andy Hixon lives and works in Sheffield although can frequently be seen bar-hopping in Manchester.

His work can be seen at www.andyhixon.com, andyhixon.blogspot.com

Or ranting/venting on www.twitter.com/andyhixon

andyhixon@googlemail.com

The Tale of Brin and Bent and Minno Marylebone is also available via Jonathan Cape.

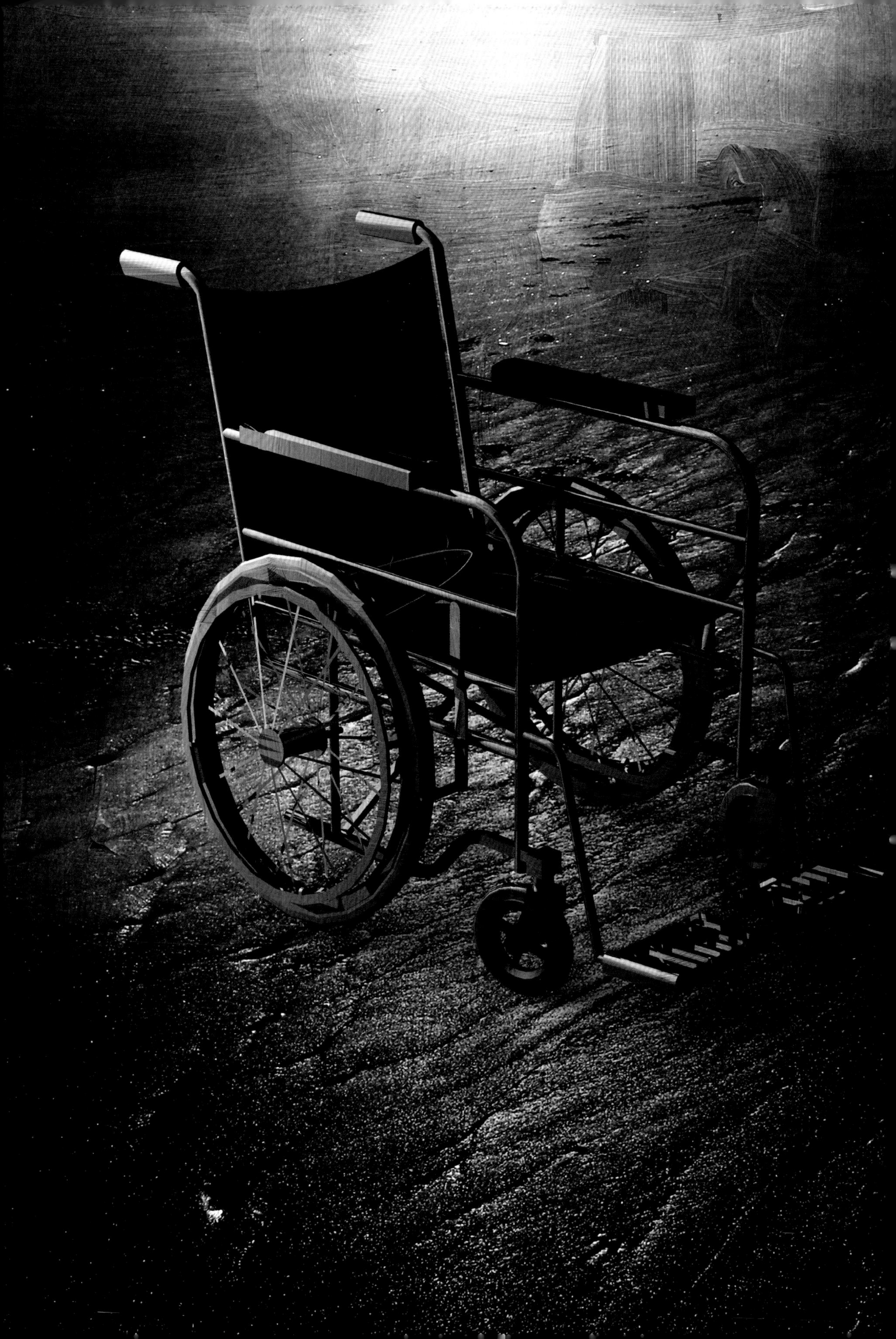